Diving Into the Past

Bell found on the bottom of the sea near the island of Giglio

Diving Into the Past

ARCHAEOLOGY UNDER WATER

By Hanns-Wolf Rackl   *Translated by Ronald J. Floyd*

CHARLES SCRIBNER'S SONS   NEW YORK

Jacket: Color photograph by S. Köster
       Black and white by Freddy Knorr

The author expresses his thanks to Mr. Gerhard Kapitän for his valuable assistance, especially for reviewing the manuscript.

Contents

Introduction

"Whoever wishes to understand his own time must view it from a distance. How far should that distance be? Very simply—just far enough for him to be unable to distinguish Cleopatra's nose." These words of the Spanish philosopher Ortega y Gasset, with which C. W. Ceram prefaced his work on archaeology, *Gods, Graves, and Scholars*, might also serve as a byword to this book.

Only when we have understood the past can we understand our relationship to the present. It is for this reason that generations of scholars dedicate their lives to archaeology, a branch of science that is like an exciting treasure hunt. However, the real treasures that archaeologists wrest from the earth are not gold and silver, but information about man. Relics reveal to us the empires and cultures of the past, the thought and feeling of ancient peoples.

This is equally true of archaeology under water, an offspring of archaeology. Inspired by the example of the excavator with his shovel, courageous men penetrate into the "silent world" of the oceans, rivers, and lakes, battle their way farther and farther into the deep, and retrieve from it the secrets of sunken ships and cities. Their findings are of great significance to all aspects of ancient history, for ancient cultures were located between seas and the major portion of ancient trade was carried on across the water. Men took with them across the sea their culture, art, philosophy, and religion —including Christianity. However much the proud *polis* of Athens may have looked down on Piraeus, the magnificent city-state of the fifth century B.C. was dependent on its seaport. And the splendid Rome of the Caesars would have been ravaged by hunger in a matter of weeks had the grain imports from overseas been interrupted. The sea can reveal to us much about the past that we could not know otherwise.

The story of underwater archaeology is not just one of sober planning and scientific institutes. Fishermen on treasure hunts, adventurers, dreamers, and daring amateur divers have played a part, along with scholars and a certain amount of lucky coincidence, in determining its history. It is only fitting, then, that they should also be included in our story of a young, adventurous science.

H.-W. R.

Diving Into the Past

I

Gods From the Depths
of the Sea

In 1907, Alfred Merlin, the French scholar, stopped in amazement on his way through the Arabian bazaar in Tunis and stared at some small figurines that an old shopkeeper had displayed among copper vases, camel saddles, and other wares.

The scholar stepped closer; the encrusted and partly broken bronze figurines were rare works of Greek art. A skillful restorer would be able, in a few days' time, to remove the dirt, repair the broken places, and return the small statuettes to their original beauty.

Merlin was sure that they were Hellenistic from the period around 200 B.C., even though he could not explain how the figures had managed to land in Ibrahim's shop. He knew, for example, that the Louvre in Paris possessed similar figurines. The officials at the Louvre watched these small statues more closely than gold, for bronze works of art by ancient masters are valuable and irreplaceable. Only a few of them have survived the millennia. Instead of sculptures by Greek artists, archaeologists usually find only poor marble copies from later centuries.

The old shopkeeper must have eyed the stranger with mistrust. He had already had a stall at the bazaar in Tunis for more than a quarter of a century when the French occupied the country in

1881. Since then he had learned from a distance to distinguish the French colonial officials from the wealthy tourists who in recent years visited the bazaar in ever-increasing numbers, searching for souvenirs—it was for the tourists that he displayed the figurines. He felt a bit uneasy with colonial officials, for the Bey of Tunis had, upon the advice of the French, established a law requiring that all discoveries of ancient works of art be reported to the officials.

Actually, the bronze figurines had not been found on Tunisian soil and had a unique history. But even so, the shopkeeper may not have been too sure of his situation. He must have been angry that he hadn't noticed the stranger sooner—probably a French official —for it was already too late to cover the little statues quickly and inconspicuously with a colored cloth. So the old man continued to puff on his long hashish pipe and look indifferent.

The shopkeeper was right: the stranger was not a tourist but the director of the Tunisian National Museum and head of Tunisian Archaeological Research. The old dealer was forced to tell him the story of the statues. He explained that he had bought them from Greek sponge divers, who had found the figurines in the waters off Mahdia, on diving operations during the sponge harvest. That was all the shopkeeper knew.

The appearance of the statues assured Merlin that the old shopkeeper was not just spinning a tale, because they were encrusted with limestone and other sea deposits.

The scholar acquired the art pieces for the Tunis museum and decided to follow up the story immediately.

It was possible that there were more treasures buried in the sea by Mahdia. In the early twentieth century Mahdia was a small, insignificant town, but it had a history going back thousands of years. The Carthaginians, who had waged bitter wars with Rome— the three Punic wars, 264–146 B.C.—had carved Mahdia's small harbor from the rocky cliffs. Later, the farming and fishing village had been a thriving Roman provincial city. Pirates had ruled in Mahdia after the Romans, and in the eleventh century a vassal of the Norman king of Sicily, Roger II, had established himself there.

Perhaps a Punic or Roman ship or a pirate ship loaded with booty had sunk off Mahdia.

That very day Alfred Merlin and other officials rode on horseback through the burning heat across the northeast chain of the Atlas Mountains toward Mahdia. Merlin was in luck. The sponge harvest was not yet finished. The Greek diving boats were just being readied for a new work day as his horse raced through the narrow streets of the little town situated between Susa and Sfax. It didn't take him long to find the boat whose crew had discovered the works of art.

The Greeks were alarmed by the officials, who, covered with dust from the desert, boarded their small boat. None of the sponge divers would admit that he had brought the antique sculptures up from the bottom of the sea. The divers were afraid they might lose the right to dive in the waters off the Cape of Africa. These waters had provided their village with a livelihood for two thousand years. Every summer during those two thousand years their ancestors had come from Greece to this flat coast, where sponges abound on the muddy bottom.

Only when Merlin assured the Greeks they would not be prosecuted and suggested that they might even be well paid for helping him find more works of art did they tell him about their discovery.

One of the divers reported, after returning from a descent, that he had seen cannon barrels half-buried in mud on his dive. His tale had caused great excitement on board, for in this area there was an old legend that a large, sunken city lay at the bottom of the sea off Mahdia's shore. In the middle of the city there was supposed to be a wide plaza with marble columns and a huge mounted statue.

The captain of the sponge boat had immediately sent a second man down. The diver had remained below a long time and then surfaced with the ancient bronze figurines in his arms. The "cannon barrels" were actually marble columns covered with mud. Around the columns the divers had found statues of bronze, fragments of statues, and pieces of pottery strewn in the mud and

Bavaria Verlag

*Sponge divers from the Aegean coast sail each spring
to the sponge beds, as they did in Homer's time.*

sand. There was nothing else down there, they said, and they had salvaged all the works of art they had seen lying around. One of the Greeks estimated the length of the rows of columns at about ninety feet and the width at less than thirty.

Merlin calculated feverishly. He realized that he was on the track of a great discovery. The dimensions of the rows of columns could mean the cargo of a ship. Perhaps other works of art lay buried in the mud below. But to find them he would need a well-equipped expedition.

Alfred Merlin rode back to Tunis and wrote detailed reports to the governments in Tunis and Paris and to scientific organizations, for organizing an expedition is not easy—he would need ships, a crane, and, above all, money with which to pay the crews and divers. But in a matter of only a few days a small expedition fleet began to gather in the rock-bound harbor of Mahdia. The French Navy had lent the scholars the harbor tug *Cyclope*, which was equipped with a crane, and the Harbor Bureau in Tunis had ordered the steamer *Eugène Resal* to Mahdia.

On their sleek sailboats the Greek sponge divers prepared for the descent. The diving suits and air pumps were checked out while the boats sailed slowly out into the Gulf of Gabes and the two steamboats pounded along behind them.

A fresh wind came up, Mahdia disappeared behind a landspit, and soon the coast of Africa was only a thin line to the southwest. After an hour, the Greeks dropped anchor. The captain told Alfred Merlin that they were over the spot.

The first of the divers disappeared below the surface. After only a few minutes the signal line jerked. The diver emerged from the waves empty-handed and said there were no columns down there. The captain looked disappointed. He had made only a rough notation of the location, and all he knew was that it lay even with a small fortress on the distant shore.

Alfred Merlin was furious. He had stirred up all the ministries and bureaus in France and Tunisia in order to make this expedition possible. And now the Greek didn't remember where his men had sighted the wreck!

A sponge diver is lowered into the deep.

It was very frustrating. The chances of finding the wreck were slim, for in the early twentieth century there were no frogmen and underwater vehicles. The divers descended into an unfriendly world in which they pushed forward against the currents with the aid of clumsy leaden shoes on their feet. In the depth at which they had found the marble columns, a diver had to be relieved after a mere half hour. During this short time he was able to inspect only a tiny area, for under water, vision is greatly impaired.

But Alfred Merlin did not give up. For eight days, one diver after the other was sent to the bottom of the sea. Always the men came back shaking their heads. The scholar sat bitterly in the cabin of one of the Greek sailboats—until finally, on the eighth day, his perseverance paid off. The columns had been found again, and the underwater excavation could begin.

But the Greeks had been right when they told Merlin that there were no more art treasures. Only marble capitals lay strewn around the columns.

Merlin had the Greeks prepare him a sketch showing the positions of the columns on the sea floor. On board the *Cyclope*, he sat bent over it for a long time.

The major portion of the columns arranged in a manner that resembled the outline of a large, heavy ship. Doubtless they lay now

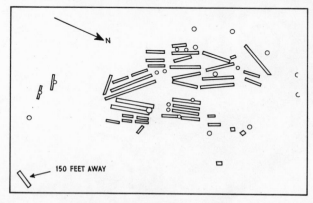

Position of marble columns on the sea floor: wreck off Mahdia

just as they once had lain while fastened to the deck of the sailing freighter. Surrounding the wreck there were only smaller pieces of marble. The ship had apparently sunk to the bottom without tipping over. Had the ancient seafarers perhaps stowed more works of art in the belly of the ship, under the columns?

The scholar decided to ask the sponge divers to penetrate into the interior of the ship.

Now began the murderous battle against the tricky depths of the sea. With bare hands, the Greeks worked their way between the columns and through the mud, for under water one cannot swing a

An Ionic marble capital from the wreck off Mahdia

Les Requins Associés

shovel. But the thick mud, which had settled over thousands of years, rose, swirled through the water, and darkened it to a black fog. The divers could hardly see their hands before their faces, and they were repeatedly swept away by currents. Meanwhile the Greek signal men sat at the pumps and made certain that no kinks got into the airhoses on which the lives of the men on the bottom depended. Although man is accustomed to an air pressure of one atmosphere, at a depth of twenty fathoms an additional four atmospheres of water pressure weigh on his body and would crush his chest if he didn't have air constantly pumped into his lungs from the pumps on board the diving ships.

Then the divers came upon great wooden planks. They drew their knives and bored into the splintering beams. The wood had become soft in the course of the centuries and soon gave way. But the columns still lay too close together; the men could not squeeze between them. Sometimes on their knees, and at times on their bellies, they undermined the columns with bare hands and sharp knives. Tackle from the ships was then shoved through the shafts, drawn around the columns, and knotted. The tug *Cyclope* lifted several of the larger ones with its crane and carried them into the open sea.

The Greeks dug their way deeper and deeper into the mud and sand. But as much as the divers and archaeologist cursed the mud, they were also thankful for it. For the mud had protected works of art of timeless beauty from stone borers just as the desert sands of Egypt had preserved the culture of the pharaoh period from destruction. The sponge divers found decorative mixing bowls of marble in which thick syrupy wines once were mixed with water, huge candelabra, artistic ledgings with reliefs and countless busts, and statues in marble and bronze. Only in some places had the marble been eaten down to a distorted image by stone borers, bivalves that in time can penetrate even the hardest stone. But most of the works of art had retained their silky white purity and noble form while buried under the sand and mud. Sailors scrubbed them down on board, and the marble shed its layer of dirt until it looked as if it had just left the workshop of some ancient sculptor.

Every summer for six years the small salvage fleet sailed out from Mahdia past Cape Africa and on to the sunken ship. Often the water got rough after only a half hour of diving. The Sea of Syrten is stormy and unpredictable, and the small boats, rigged with a single sail and twenty oars, fought their way home to the rocky harbor of Mahdia with difficulty.

Storms ripped out the marker buoys with which the expedition had marked the location of the wreck, and the tedious search began anew. But all these efforts were rewarded. The divers fished more and more new finds out of the sea—sculptures of animal heads and countless pottery fragments.

A whole gallery of ancient gods in marble and bronze images was brought up. The men found the god of wine Dionysus, and not far from him his companions—satyrs; maenads; Aphrodite, the goddess of beauty; the goddess of the hunt and moon Artemis; Athena, daughter of Zeus; the messenger of the gods Hermes; and the god of the art of healing, Aesculapius, with his daughter Hygeia. One bronze statue bore a meaningful signature: scratched in the metal was: "the work of Boëthus of Chalcidon." Boëthus of Chalcidon was one of the most significant masters of the Hellenistic period.

Some of the bronze statues were in pieces. Deep in the hold of the ship the divers found bronze legs and wings, which were almost life size. After examining them, Merlin and his assistants waited eagerly to see whether the divers would recover the rest of the figure. They sent more and more fragments up with the hoist, and finally the torso, crushed by the weight of the heavy marble. Merlin knew that the restorers at the museum would be able to free the fragments of sea growth, piece them together, and thereby bring the work of art back to its original form. And in fact they did reconstruct out of fragments a god who seems to have just descended from the heavens and who, his wings still quivering, is stringing his bow—a copy of a fourth century B.C. work by Praxiteles or Lysippus, both among the greatest Greek sculptors.

Sometimes, however, terror struck the ships of the expedition. Divers would come up with their limbs horribly twisted, groaning in excruciating pain. They had fallen victim to the bends. This

Winged Eros of Mahdia

Gerhard Kapitän

malady appeared among the Greeks like a ghost, claiming the men more and more as their work kept them longer in the deep. At the beginning of the twentieth century, the cause of this affliction was not known, and it could neither be prevented nor cured. Some of the divers were affected by it for the rest of their lives and could never return to the bottom of the sea.

While the Greeks were bringing up further treasures from the Sea of Syrten, Alfred Merlin and other scholars deduced the story of the ill-fated sunken vessel; the findings made it an open book. Among the recovered items Merlin had immediately noticed a small clay lamp—a plain oil lamp, from which a partly burned wick still protruded. The shape had been common at the end of the second century B.C. After the turn of the first century, however, this type of lamp was no longer produced. This gave Merlin the first clue. He and other scholars determined that some of the gods' images showed markings typical of Athens. Had the ship therefore loaded its cargo at Athens?

Soon the divers brought further proof to the surface, steles—large stone slabs—with inscriptions indicating Pireaus, the harbor of Athens. In the year 86 B.C. Lucius Cornelius Sulla, Roman general and later dictator of Rome, had defeated Mithradates, king of Pontus on the Black Sea and a threat to the Roman Empire, put down the revolutionary Greeks, and caused Athens to be plundered. It was possible that the wreck by Mahdia was one of Sulla's ships which he had loaded with loot and sent to Rome. This explanation would account for the freighter's mixed load. There was an entire marble villa, including columns, capitals, and ledging, on board, along with beautiful furniture, vases and candelabra, often only partly finished, rough-hewn chunks of marble, and priceless works of art.

Maybe the wreck off Mahdia had even carried Sulla's personal war loot, for Alfred Merlin's divers found a group of small, grotesque bronze statuettes—dwarflike musicians, dancers, and actors—images of the entertainers who performed before guests at feasts in the Hellenistic period of Greece. We know from ancient writers that Sulla had a particular fancy for these entertainers. These little figurines might have been destined for his own villa. While his family in Rome awaited the arrival of the treasures, the ship was caught in the ferocious *grecale*—a northeasterly storm, notorious in the Mediterrenean Sea. This storm must have driven the ship five hundred miles off course onto the northern coast of Africa, where it was wrecked.

The ship had sunk with all aboard. In the hold of the ship the sponge divers found bones of rabbits, sheep, pigs, and remains of human skeletons.

When the excavations on the sea floor off Mahdia were finished in 1913, the El Alaoui (Bardo) Museum in Tunis could hardly hold all the recovered works of art.

Soon, however, some scholars began to doubt whether the ship had carried a part of Sulla's war spoils, for many of the sculptures were copies of originals in marble and bronze. Archaeologists detected evidence in them of the "pointilistic" method, a wide-

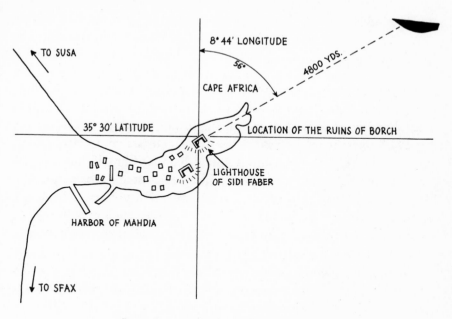

Location of the wreck off Mahdia

spread ancient copying technique. Some concluded that the ship was carrying merchant freight for the art market in Rome. Many ancient writings testify to the enthusiastic admiration of the wealthy senators and warriors of the Roman republic for the art works of Greece. Consequently, Alfred Merlin suspected that "the producers of such copies, contrary to previous assumption, had not emigrated to Italy, but had remained in Greece or in Athens itself, and that from then until the last century of the Roman republic thousands of shiploads of statues, columns, richly decorated furniture, and selected jewelery were exported to Italy."

If Merlin's conclusions were correct, then many such cargoes might have sunk to the bottom of the sea.

Already there were scholars who sensed that the ocean held greater buried treasures. The sunken cargo by Mahdia was, in fact, not the first treasure to be recovered from the ocean. In the autumn of 1900, a similar adventure had befallen some Greek sponge divers in the Aegean Sea. . . .

A Bronze Arm

Lightning flashed across the cloudy sky in the autumn of 1900; a fierce northern storm was whipping the Aegean. Two small sailing ships struggled eastward through the choppy waves. Foam sprayed over their bowsprits, and their masts and yards were bowed by the groaning wind. Captain Kondos himself stood at the helm of the *Euterpe*, while his men hung exhausted in the sheets and tried to keep the ship on course in spite of the storm. Between glances at the compass, the captain cast a concerned eye on the already partially rotted ship *Kalliope* which pounded through the waves alongside the *Euterpe*.

Again and again storm and rain had interrupted the work of his divers along the Tunisian coast. The sponge harvest was still small, and the days were already beginning to get shorter. But the courageous *sphoungarades*, as the sponge divers were called, had not given up, and were working on through the beginning of the autumn storms, for the sponges meant food for their home island, Syme. To find them they now had to sail their small boats in the dangerous weather across the Mediterranean to the distant Sporades Islands.

Captain Kondos had intended to follow the route from Elephonisou between the island of Cythera and Cape Malea. But no one knew where they were now. Suddenly a black silhouette loomed up between sea and clouds.

Kondos yelled through the storm to his men at the wheel, and they put their last effort into the sheets. The helmsman on the *Kalliope* must have sighted the land also—the boat followed at the same speed. Kondos knew the ridge that had loomed up ahead of them. It was the Glyphadia foothills of the island Anticythera, or Stus Ljus, according to its inhabitants.

Anticythera is a desolate, uninhabited spot except for the tiny fishing port of Potamos in a protected bay. But Kondos didn't like the port or its taverns. He led his ships to the south, around the foothills, and dropped anchor where the rugged cliffs shielded them from the wind. Here, only sixty feet from land, ships and crews were safe from the storm.

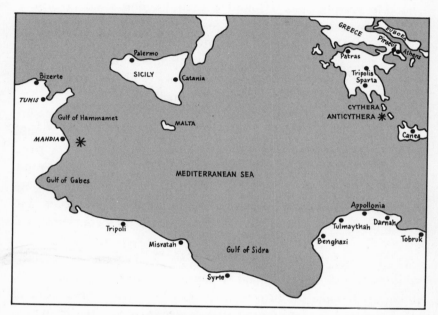

Mahdia and Anticythera

The anchorage was desolate. Only a single goatherd lived on the desert plateau with his animals. But the water looked as if it harbored good sponge grounds, so Captain Kondos decided to have a look.

As the storm died away, Elias Stadiatis, one of Kondos' divers, climbed into his rubber suit and his heavy helmet was screwed into place. The air pump squeaked, and Stadiatis jumped into the water and sank.

Stadiatis soon realized that it was too deep for a sponge diver. He reached bottom at eight fathoms, surrounded by a blue-green twilight. Gradually his eyes adjusted to the darkness. Suddenly he

15

jerked back. In front of him a monumental horse's head loomed out of the darkness. Then he noticed that he was surrounded by figures. Some of them were in mud up to their hips. He stared at them in amazement. Black arms and legs extended from the mud and rocks. Elias Stadiatis moved slowly forward toward a black hand. He grasped it and found himself holding a whole arm.

The sponge diver jerked the signal line four times, the signal to pull him up. With the more than life-size arm, he rose to the surface. Captain Kondos inspected the arm and saw that it was made of bronze. But he didn't completely believe Stadiatis' story. In the confusion of the deep, men often see unusual things.

To confirm his doubts, he asked for his diving suit and a measuring tape and descended into the water. There, Kondos also found bronze and marble statues, pieces of gear and remains of a large ship, all in a heap a hundred and fifty feet long. The wreck must have been an ancient one, for Kondos knew that scholars and archaeologists were excavating similar statues all over Greece. He stowed the bronze arm in the cabin and set sail on a course toward Syme.

The story of the ancient treasure ship spread on the sponge fishers' home island while Captain Kondos consulted the island elders. At the conference the bronze arm was passed from hand to hand and admired. A merchant told of Paris, London, and Berlin, where people were crazy about such ancient figures. He guessed one could easily sell a few bronze sculptures for a half million gold drachmas. The fishermen's eyes shone as they calculated that together with the small earnings of their vineyards, their olive groves, and their fishing, the entire population of Syme could live on that sum for years. The sponge fishermen would no longer need to go out on the stormy sea and dive into the depths, where every year men were lost and survivors were often crippled for life. They inquired of Kondos what they would need in the way of boats, divers, and gear to raise the treasure, and began immediately to make plans. But an old fisherman called Ikonomu raised an objection.

This fisherman enjoyed great respect, for his son was a scholar and famous man in distant Athens—a university professor of archaeology. Ikonomu was thinking of him now. He explained that one could not treat ancient works of art as ordinary items of trade. The scholars in Athens, who were dedicating their lives to the study of ancient times, had a certain right to see and study recovered objects.

These works of art—witnesses to a great and famous past—were the possession of the entire Greek people. All should be permitted to admire them—the peasants and goatherders of Attica as well as the king and his ministers. They should not be taken from the Greeks and sold to foreign lands; it was illegal.

The Symiots were embarrassed. They thought awhile and then had to admit that Ikonomu was right.

Fortunately, Ikonomu was able to console them, because he knew that the royal government gave generous rewards to the finders of ancient works of art. He guessed they would surely get tens of thousands of drachmas for the ship's freight Captain Kondos had described. He advised the council of Syme to send a delegation from the island with the bronze arm to Ikonomu's son in Athens. And so it was decided.

Captain Demetrius Kondos and the diver Elias Stadiatis donned their best suits and shoes, packed the bronze arm carefully in an old suitcase, and traveled to Athens.

They could hardly have picked a better time to arrive in Athens. Since the days of Roman Conquest more and more art treasures had been carried out of the country. What the Roman occupation, tribal migrations, Byzantine and Turkish rule had overlooked, the English, French, and Germans had carried off to their museums. Now, however, around 1900, the first significant Greek archaeologists were beginning to appear. They gathered and organized what was still left in the country and waited for the opportunity to conduct a large-scale excavation.

The archaeologist Ikonomu received the seamen from his home of Syme and took them to the Greek Minister of Culture the same day. Minister Valerios Stais was somewhat suspicious. To be sure, the arm was doubtless genuine and came from a very old and valuable work of art, but weren't the seamen just spinning a sailor's yarn, making a whole ship's cargo out of a single statue, which in ancient times had accidentally fallen into the sea? On the other hand, no archaelogist had ever found a sunken ship full of Greek art treasures. And who knew what one might find in the wreck! Stais thought of the many works of art of the greatest masters of ancient Greece, which were known only through descriptions. He asked Kondos what kind of technical assistance he needed.

The captain demanded a large ship with hoists, strong tackle, and chains. He had estimated the weight of the stone pieces in the cargo; it was tremendous. These weights would pull his own ships under.

Stais immediately sent a messenger to the Ministry of Marine Affairs and promised the men a special reward in addition to the ordinary one if they did indeed bring valuable works of art out of the deep.

By November 24, the Greek Navy supply ship *Mykale* was steaming out toward Anticythera with both of Captain Kondos' small boats in tow. On the decks of the sponge boats stood six Symiot divers—the most courageous and toughest divers of the Greek islands and coast. The place for the descent was quickly located. An unusual yellow vein of rock in the foothills of Glyphadia marked the spot.

A storm whipped around the rocks of the cape, changed direction suddenly, and threatened to smash the boats anchored by the cliffs against the reef. The *Mykale* was unable to help the fishing boats. She drew too much water for this coastal stretch, for the sea floor climbed sharply from the location of the sunken ship.

In spite of this, the divers insisted on going down. The first one jumped into the water. Captain Kondos watched the yellow air hose uneasily, for the movement of the ship in the storm threatened constantly to snap it in two. He watched the clock. Four minutes. The diver must have reached bottom. Five minutes more. . . . He began to get anxious. Why was there no signal? Suddenly the signal bell sounded. Surface! Another three and a half minutes crept by. Then the shiny copper helmet of the diver broke the surface. He was holding a large, light-gray object.

The archaeologist Ikonomu, who was leading the expedition, almost tore it out of the diver's hands. Hastily he wiped off the mud. It was a bronze statue of a bearded man with a wise, gentle gaze—that of a philosopher. Encased in mud and slime, it had withstood millennia on the sea floor unharmed.

The philosopher of Anticythera

The next divers descended into the depths, and none of them came back empty-handed. Containers of clay and bronze, a sword, and then fragments of marble statues were brought to the surface. But the marble, once white, had taken on the color of rock ceaselessly whipped by the waves of the sea. The works of art were eroded by the water, eaten away and encrusted with salt and mussels.

The archaeologist and the sponge divers were bitterly disappointed. While Ikonomu steamed back to Piraeus on the *Mykale*, which was unsuited for this kind of research, the sponge fishermen sought protection in the harbor of Avlaemon on the neighboring island of Cythera. But the Symiots did not want to give up so easily. They requested a smaller auxiliary ship. The Minister of

Culture Stais sent them the steamer *Syros* along with Vyzaninos, the supervisory official over all ancient Greek art treasures.

The hard, tedious work continued. But again only fragments were brought to the surface. Disappointed, Vyzaninos also returned to Athens. Only the secretary of the archaeological department of the ministry did not give up and stuck it out with the sponge divers, who worked bravely on.

Two five-minute periods were all a diver could work in a day, at that depth. At the site of the wreck, the bottom fell sharply from twenty-two fathoms to almost thirty fathoms. That exceeded the usual diving depth of the Symiots. The steep bottom offered no foothold. Again and again a man would lose his footing. Often two or three days would pass before a piece could be brought up.

But the courage and endurance of the divers paid off—they found some very promising fragments of a bronze statue. The secretary sent a dispatch to Athens immediately, and Stais again sent the *Syros,* which, in short time, was steering a course back toward the capital with the bronze pieces aboard. When the parts had been cleaned and fitted together, scholars throughout Europe became excited. The divers had recovered a great work of the fourth century B.C., a bronze statue of a god by the master Lysippus, the court sculptor of Alexander the Great.

Lysippus was the last of the great classic sculptors of Greece. According to Pliny, he is supposed to have created more than five hundred statues. Yet except for the one found near Anticythera, not one of his works has been preserved. Not even Roman copies survive. Like countless other precious works of the ancient Greeks, his sculptures were lost in wars and catastrophes, and especially in the wake of the migrations of peoples, or were destroyed later. In the Middle Ages, for example, people had little understanding of ancient art. It was considered "heathen." Bronze statues were melted down and recast into church bells, later cannons. Marble art works were crushed and thrown into ovens where they were converted to lime.

The old fisher Ikonomu was right, after all. Not only the scientists were exuberant about the bronze god from the sea. People from all over Greece streamed into Athens and stood respectfully before this witness to a great past.

The seamen and sponge divers of Syme were suddenly famous. The Minister of Culture Stais himself now rushed to Anticythera with the ships *Mykale, Syros,* and the *Aegialia.* The three vessels were supposed to aid the Symiots in the recovery of further large statues.

The exhausted divers had in the meantime withdrawn to Potamos on Anticythera and knew nothing of the excitement their find had caused. After Stais told them about it and encouraged them to dive again, they eagerly returned to work.

But the recovery activities became harder and harder. The major portion of the cargo lay under huge rocks. The Symiots were forced to undermine them and then feed giant cables through the shafts, so that the *Aegialia* might then raise the rock slightly. Farther out at sea the cables were severed, and the hunks of rock disappeared again in the sea. This was to cause the archaeologists great consternation, but not until a few days later, after it was too late.

On February 17th an especially large chunk of rock was to be disposed of in this way. The captain of the *Aegialia* commanded full speed ahead in the direction of open sea. But the cable broke. While the divers below were fixing it, Stais had a disconcerting thought. Was it possible that these huge blocks were giant statues, which the Symiots mistook for rocks in the dim light of the deep?

Despite the captain's protests, Stais ordered the block brought to the surface. The steam winch whirred. The ship leaned farther and farther. Then a monumental figure appeared on the surface: a Hercules of marble. It was so heavy that it had to be dragged in deep water to the *Mykale,* which then lifted it with its chain hoists.

Beneath the giant statues the divers dug up wooden pieces of the ship, remains of a luxurious bronze bed, glass and clay containers, and—human bones.

To the Greek divers that was a bad omen. After one of the

next descents, the courageous Kritikos could scarcely hide his pain any more. Soon lameness—a symptom of the bends—set in, and a short while later he was dead.

The Greeks gave him a burial at sea and calmly continued diving, until the sea claimed a second and a third victim. Two of the divers suffered cerebrospinal hemorrhage and were partially paralyzed. Furthermore, continued work below had become almost impossible. The Symiots now had to dig in hard ground. They collected the last findings and sailed to Athens. The royal government received them with great honors and paid the men a princely reward. The seamen were able to take 150,000 drachmas in gold back to Syme, and the Archaeological Society gave each diver an additional 500 drachmas out of its own treasury.

The Greek Minister of Education, Monferratos, tried in vain to hire diving specialists, although his call was sent throughout Europe. The divers demanded enormous sums which they knew from the start could not be paid by the Greek government, for no one wanted to venture so deep, where one man had met death and two more had become paralyzed. Today, a portion of the art treasure still rests on the sea floor off Anticythera. When the French underwater explorer Cousteau dived near Anticythera a few years ago, he determined that the treasure ship lay too deep even for frogmen, unless they wanted to work at constant risk to their lives.

The recovered art treasures, however, filled a whole gallery of the Athens National Museum. The most valuable of them, aside from the bronze statue of an athletic youth, are two statues from the age of Pericles, a group from which Stadiatis' bronze arm had come, and a bronze bed decorated with animals' heads. Among the many small finds were splendid glass vessels, an artistic golden earring, the dishes used by the crew, jugs for storing provisions, and lamps. The findings of the underwater expedition were richer than the most productive land excavation in Greece to date—with the exception of Mycenae.

Scholarly disputation soon began over the probable origin and fate of the ship and over the majestic life-size statue of the athletic youth, with jewels as eyes, in a plain, unassuming pose so seldom seen in Greek statues. Svoronos, the director of the Athens National Museum, noted that coins from Argos showed a young man in a similar pose. He holds a sword in his left hand; in his right he holds the head of Medusa. He is Perseus, a hero of Greek legend, who with the aid of the gods cut off the Gorgon's head, won the princess Andromeda for his bravery, and then ruled as king of Argos.

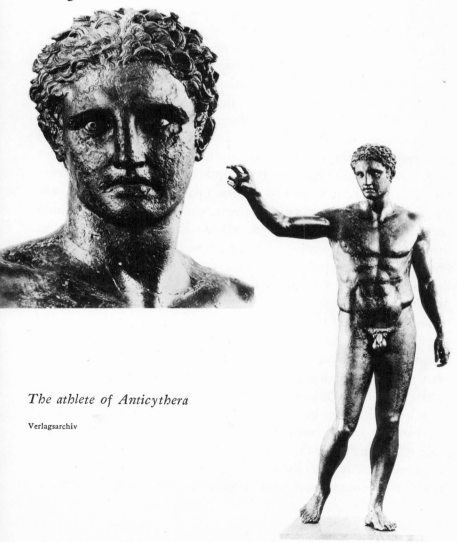

The athlete of Anticythera

Verlagsarchiv

Many scientists contradicted Svoronos' theory. They held that the god was Paris, Hermes, or Apollo. Since all were able to support their arguments with acceptable evidence, the nameless god was finally placed among the greatest works of art in the National Museum as the "Athlete of Anticythera."

The ship itself posed a seemingly insoluble problem to the scientists. Whereas excavations of ancient sites are usually referred to in writings of Greek or Roman poets, or written material is recovered in the digging which might give clues to the identity of the finds, no such evidence existed in this case. Had the Roman dictator Sulla also had this ship loaded with plundered treasures in Athens? Or was it a vessel belonging to pirate fleets, which even in ancient times attacked and looted large cities?

It took archaeologists decades to date the ship. The American researcher Gladys Davidson Weinberg at the American School in Athens fitted the clay fragments from the wreck together and then compared the forms with countless other vessels of ancient origin. Among findings from the islands of Rhodes and Kos, from the period between 80 and 50 B.C. she finally discovered some that showed similar features, thus proving that the ship had sunk around then, for each area—every little island—and each decade had in those times vessels unique in form. Probably the sailing ship was bound for Athens or Rome when it was caught in a rough storm between the eastern Mediterranean and its destination and driven off course.

Today we are almost certain that this happened in the year 80 B.C. We know this thanks to a mysterious instrument found in the wreck. The Greek archaeologist Minister of Culture Stais discovered it while examining chunks of bronze from the ship in the Athens National Museum, which had not been thrown away because it was felt that they might be fragments of statues. As the minister took the largest fragment in his hand, pieces of wood crumbled from it. In the dry air the wood had shrunk and became pithy. Stais scratched it away, revealing symbols of an ancient Greek inscription. A museum technician freed the piece from sea water residue, and the scientists who had been summoned stood astonished before a complicated mechanism with many small and large gears.

They could only see a small piece of the instrument and did not know what it had once been designed for. The sea water had severely corroded its bronze wheels and covered them with sediment as hard as stone. It is only recently that the museum restorers have been able at last to expose even a single part. They have deciphered a few words that are obviously instructions for the use of the instrument, which show that it was designed for astronomical calculations.

The scholars naturally wondered if it was a navigational device for observing the stars, but at first could find no satisfactory explanation. One thing they noticed immediately: it was an unusual instrument. Nothing comparable had ever been found, and no ancient writings made reference to such an instrument. Up until its discovery, it had been assumed that ancient men had been incapable of producing such a complicated instrument with such ingenious gears. The "Astrolabium," as the scientists called it, seemed rather to resemble the finest astronomical mechanisms of the late Renaissance. Yet its great age remains unquestioned.

The inscription specialist Dean Meritt established that the forms of the letters on the device were in use only in the first century B.C. The words themselves, and their astronomical meaning, support his contentions. The largest piece of the inscription is part of an astronomical calender which resembles the calendar of Geminos, a famous ancient astronomer who lived around 77 B.C. on Rhodes.

Again and again the technicians of the Athens National Museum attempted to wrest further secrets from the irregular chunk of bronze. A whole series of scholars occupied themselves with the device after additional pieces were exposed. But not until 1955, when the American researcher Derek J. de Solla Price attempted a solution to the problem, was any further light thrown on it. For several years de Solla Price occupied himself with studying microphotographs of the Astrolabium. In 1958, after this preparatory work, he turned to the object itself with the aid of the inscription specialist George Stamires. The two men deciphered further inscriptions, and found that—contrary to all previous assumptions—the bronze chunk still contained most of the mechanism. To be sure, some of the important parts still have not been identified. Nevertheless, the scientists have been able to explain its structure and purpose. An axle drove an incredibly ingenious system of gears, so that the ancient astronomer was able to take readings from three dials with hands. The largest, fully restored dial consists of a stationary scale with the signs of the zodiac. This dial lies directly over the main wheel of the mechanism and apparently showed the annual movement of the sun in the circle of animals of the zodiac. Key signs on the zodiac scale correspond to letters on the astronomical calendar from which the times of rising and setting and the constellations of the bright stars for the whole year were determined. The two smaller lower dials, which could not be entirely restored, gave the rising and setting times for the moon as well as the movements of the planets known to the Greeks, namely, Mercury, Venus, Mars, Jupiter, and Saturn.

The instrument from the wreck of Anticythera must have been an arithmetical counterpart to the geometric models of the solar system, which were known to Plato and Aristotle, and which were developed ultimately into the planetarium.

De Solla Price paid special attention to the positon of a movable ring on the front dial, and the result of his calculations was mystifying: the instrument had worked with the Egyptian calendar. This calendar counted 365 days per year, but had no leap year to make up the difference of six hours between the calendar year and the actual time that the earth circled the sun. For each year there was a certain corrective figure, which was noted by the relative position of the scales. De Solla Price calculated that the scales were 13½ degrees out of phase, the corrective value for the year 80 B.C. In that year the dial must have been used for the last time.

Eighty B.C. was the last time an ancient astronomer had the dial in his hand. Then it sank with the grounded ship off the rocky coast of Anticythera. The millennia have not moved its wheels one degree further.

Conquering the Silent World

The wrecks near Anticythera and Mahdia were not the first
archaeological discoveries from the sea bottom, but previously,
little attention was paid to the occasional statue recovered from
the sea. For example, in 1832, fishermen off the coast of the Tus-
cany, near Piombino, about forty-two miles south of Leghorn,

*A damaged tomb relief from Pompeii of the kind of ship wrecked off
Mahdia and Anticythera*

Fototeca Unione

found a bronze Apollo. Near the site of the find there once stood an ancient city, Populonium. The god, which today stands in the Salle des Bronces in the Louvre in Paris, got caught in a fisherman's net. Until a few years ago, when dredging activities at Piraeus uncovered a group of spectacular bronze statues, it was the only bronze original of the archaic period of Greek art (prior to 480 B.C.).

The Apollo of Piombino

Verlagsarchiv

Descriptions of a bronze torso and several portraits, discovered as early as the eighteenth century—two of them show Homer and Sophocles—include the remark "found in the sea." They were brought up from the waters of the Mediterranean near Livorno. In 1899, the "Zeus of Livadhostro" was recovered from the sea at the Gulf of Corinth.

Doubtless many statues taken from the sea have met with a sad end: fishermen have sold the damaged works of art, which specialists could have restored, to dealers in scrap metal who melted them down. The sites of discovery have not been noted. What treasures have been lost in this manner can only be guessed. Only in the last hundred years has word of archaeologists' work and of the value of ancient art reached remote villages on the Mediterranean Sea. And even after the word began to spread that the Mediterranean was a treasure chest, there were still innumerable technical difficulties to overcome before divers could explore its depths.

Until recently, the sea was a mysterious, hostile world, full of treachery and danger. Only experienced sponge divers and a few diving experts from northern countries dared penetrate it. In their gear they resembled heavily armored knights of the Middle Ages when they moved clumsily on the sea bottom.

They wore uncomfortable waterproof suits and large brass helmets. Their lives depended on the slender air hose that connected them with the diving ship. This hose led to a hand pump, which a man had to pump tirelessly. Should the apparatus fail or even falter, it meant the life of the diver below.

The diving profession demanded men who did not get nervous or panic. The waves of a sudden storm could kink the air hose or it might get caught on a rock overhang or piece of wreckage, thus interrupting the flow of air into the diver's helmet. If it was only a kink in the hose, which was straightened out after a few seconds, in a couple of agonizing minutes the man would have air again. But if the sharp edge of a rock cut through it, there was no saving the diver.

Helmet divers made their way warily through the mud in their heavy lead shoes. Without these lead shoes they were unable to walk: the shoes held the men's feet to the ground and prevented the divers from being carried away by capricious currents, for under water, the human body is much lighter.

Two quarter-hour periods of work at twenty fathoms was a respectable day's work for a helmet diver before the First World War. Then his comrades pulled him exhausted on board the diving boat. Deep-water work devoured a man's strength.

But what is fifteen minutes, when a job has to be done like the one near Mahdia—or Anticythera, where the greater depth reduced the diving time even further? Even in the clear water of the Mediterranean a diver's vision extends no further than 25 to 35 feet; beyond that a murky blue-green takes over.

For a long time archaeologists had to postpone any ideas of systematically exploring the Mediterranean. To be sure, there were areas such as the Gulf of Corinth, where in 373 B.C. the cities of Helice and Bura sunk, or the documented sites of ancient sea battles, which would be easy to locate and would probably yield finds. But scientists seldom have adequate funds for their work, and so a mass influx of divers was impossible.

What is more, every underwater success until lately was paid for with heavy losses in health and even human life. The mysterious diving sickness, the bends, always threatened the men who donned rubber suits and helmets and descended into the deep. If a man was lucky, he could go for twenty years before pains appeared in his joints and limbs. By the time these first signs of paralysis occurred, he might have enough money saved so that with the meager income from his small plot of land he could survive. Sometimes his son would continue the suicidal occupation and support his father. But often the sickness overcame the divers very suddenly, paralyzing their limbs, perhaps their whole bodies, or killing them outright. Caisson sickness was first scientifically observed on men who worked in caissons during the construction of the Brooklyn Bridge (1869–83) in New York. Caissons were large chambers that were sunk to the bottom of a body of water and into which air was pumped at high pressure. This pressure was necessary in order to drive the water out of the caisson, keeping it dry. Divers breathe air under high pressure which corresponds exactly to the increasing water pressure as the depth becomes greater. If a diver were to receive air at normal surface pressure, the greater water pressure would crush his chest just as air pressure crushes a thin glass container in which a vacuum has been created. But air contains more than 75 per cent nitrogen, which is assimilated by the blood in increasing amounts as the pressure increases. The blood then carries the nitrogen throughout the body and into the cells of the body tissues, which then take on much more of this gas than would be the case under normal air pressure.

At the time that the treasures of Mahdia and Anticythera were being recovered, medical science was just in the process of investigating this problem. The scientists concluded that if a diver returned very slowly to the surface his blood would have time to carry the surplus of nitrogen back out of the body. It followed therefore that the deeper and longer a diver worked, the more slowly he should return to the surface. The scientists ultimately were able to set up charts that showed the exact time necessary for the ascent. Frogmen today observe such "decompression charts," as long as an emergency doesn't require immediate surfacing.

But the old-time sponge divers did not know the cause of the bends, and it took an even longer time before this important information became known in their villages, where many people today are still illiterate. Experience had taught the divers to surface slowly. But often—especially when interest in their work had kept them down too long—they surfaced too fast anyway. Then the excess of nitrogen taken on under great pressure expanded in the cells of the men's bodies. Nitrogen bubbles formed in their tissue and blood plasma and turned them to foam—just like the carbon dioxide bubbles in champagne or soft drinks when the bottle has been opened, releasing the greater pressure inside. If it was a mild case of bends, the escaping nitrogen caused no more than an itching of the skin. But nitrogen bubbles in the fluids of the joints and in the bone marrow are especially dangerous. In severe cases the diver was paralyzed or even dead within an hour after surfacing.

And so the archaeologists could only stand before the Mediterranean treasure chest and hope that luck would favor them by leading them to further wrecks. They knew that by the time the two recently recovered ships had sunk, thousands of ships had already sailed and rowed along the Mediterranean coast before them—at least since the beginning of the third millennium B.C.

Countless ships had served as merchantmen or warships during the Roman Empire. After the fall of the Western Empire, the Goths, Vandals, Byzantium and the Arabs assumed control of the

Mediterranean. Hundreds if not thousands of ships must have been wrecked along its coasts. To be sure, only a small part of these ships were probably laden with art treasures, but even that small part would still make up whole fleets. In many wars, the victors carried off the treasures of the vanquished. After conquering Greece, the Romans packed whole villas and temples; enterprising businessmen sensed an opportunity for profit and exported works of art, expensive furniture, and construction materials in great quantities to Rome.

In 1925 a find of significance was discovered in the Bay of Marathon—a precious bronze statue of a youth which belongs among the rare originals from the fourth century B.C. Many art historians take the youth for an original from the workshop of the great Praxiteles, of whose work only later marble copies have otherwise been preserved.

The Youth of Marathon

Gerhard Kapitän

Three years later more loot was taken from the sea and again the finders were simple Greek sponge divers. While working under water off Cape Artemisium, on the northern part of the island of Euboea, one of the divers spotted a bronze arm sticking out of the sand. Further parts of a statue were not to be found. The fisherman packed the fragment in a blanket and took it directly to Professor Georg Karo of the German Archaeological Institute in Athens. Karo saw that the arm belonged to a great work of art and began immediately to organize an expedition to Cape Artemisium. He was sure there were more fragments buried there in the sand and mud and later a second arm was found.

Professor Karo induced Alexander Benakis, a Greek patron of the arts, to donate a few thousand drachmas for an expedition, and talked the Greek government into providing some naval ships. The divers again descended to the sea floor off Cape Artemisium, and after several days' search at last attached a recovery line to a giant statue of a god.

This statue depicts either the ruler of the heavens, Zeus, or Poseidon, the god of the sea. The bronze god, which stands upright

*Closeup of the statue of Zeus
found off Cape Artemisium*

Verlagsarchiv

33

and is more than life size, is casting in vengeful wrath his (lost) lightning bolt or trident. The god is naked and wears no jewelry; only a thin fillet holds back his hair. But his sublime bearing shows a god of ultimate power whose majestic pose and serenity is undisturbed even by his expression of wrath.

The god of Cape Artemisium is considered the greatest work of antique art extant. One of the most important Greek sculptors—who, we do not know—must have formed the statue of bronze during Greece's Golden Age as a symbol of a mighty god and at the same time of a free Greek citizen.

When the god of Cape Artemisium was cast around the year 460 B.C., Greece had given birth to philosophical thought; Greek citizens had conquered mass oriental armies during the Persian Wars; and the *polis*, the community of the free, had just succeeded in defending itself against the subject state.

The statue had withstood the two thousand years on the bottom of the sea in good shape. Skilled restorers were easily able to free the bronze surface of deposits and reattach the two arms.

The figure was taken to Athens to join the treasures at the Greek National Museum there. A copy of the statue stands in the main hall of the United Nations Building in New York as a gift from the Greek government, and acts as a reminder of the debt humanity owes to the Greek past.

Not far from the site where the god of Cape Artemisium was found lay the bronze statue of a riding boy and fragments of a galloping horse. At least two centuries separated the smiling little rider and the lofty statue of the god. Even so, this cheerful little work of art is a rare treasure. The divers also raised segments of a wooden ship's hull. The archaeologists waited expectantly for further finds. But one of the best divers surfaced a bit too fast from the deep and died, and the search had to be abandoned. In the meantime the exact location of the sunken ship was lost. Frogmen are still searching vainly for it.

The following years brought the discovery of a marble Aphrodite near Rhodes (1929), and a whole shipload of marble reliefs which were sunk when the ship burned in the harbor of Piraeus in

*Statue of the god Zeus
of Cape Artemisium*

*Small bronze statue of jockey
found off Cape Artemisium
not far from the site
of the statue of Zeus*

the second century A.D. The marble friezes had scarcely been cleaned of mud when the researcher became quite excited: they were copies of one of the most famous works of Phidias, whom the Greeks had honored as their greatest sculptor. This artistic genius advised Pericles in the construction of his splendid buildings, directed the creation of the sculptures of the Parthenon on the Acropolis, and himself sculpted a gigantic cultic statue of Athena out of gold and ivory. Athena's statue has disappeared, along with the mighty Zeus of gold and ivory which Phidias made for Olympia. But from ancient descriptions we know approximately how this Athena looked, and that her shield depicted the battle against the Amazons, which according to ancient legend took place on the Acropolis. However, only small Roman copies of Athena have been preserved. The marble reliefs from Piraeus are good marble copies of the battle scenes in the original size.

But the story of the most expensive underwater archaeological enterprise so far goes back to the fifteenth century. At that time the Roman Cardinal Colonna heard of two mysterious ships which were said to lie in Lake Nemi, a small crater lake in the Alban Hills southeast of Rome. It was the age of the Renaissance. The educated world of Europe had rediscovered ancient culture and was enthusiastic about Greek and Roman art. The "legend" of the sunken ships appealed to the archaeological interests of the Cardinal. In 1446 he commissioned the architect Leon Battista Alberti to investigate. Alberti had divers come from Genoa, and they actually found two ships, one of which was 210 feet long, the other almost 240 feet. They lay on the bottom of the lake at a depth of ten fathoms. Alberti had a float constructed from empty barrels and attempted to raise the ship's hulls with hooks and ropes. But either the ropes broke or loose wooden planks were brought to the surface. Alberti was able only to recover the torso of a large Roman sculpture. Nevertheless, the ships in Lake Nemi continued to attract adventurers and technicians. In 1535 the Italian, Francesco Demarchi, went to the bottom of Lake Nemi in one of the first diving suits in the world. His head was protected by a wooden helmet with a small plate of built-in glass. Demarchi saw the ships, their decks and superstructures, their precious decorations and gigantic rudders. But Demarchi also recognized immediately that the technical means of his time were insufficient to raise them. In 1827 a hydraulic engineer, Annesio Fusconi, positioned a diving bell big enough to hold eight persons over the wrecks. From the work platform scientists, diplomats, noblemen, and representatives of the Vatican followed the progress of the explorations. But Fusconi was able to raise no more than fragments. They were an indication of how exceptionally expensive the ships had been. The scholars then poked through old writings and found references to two highly decorated ships belonging to the emperor Caligula, who ruled during A.D. 37–41, and celebrated lavish festivals in his boats on Lake Nemi. But the scientists had to admit that recovery of the ships was out of the question. Experienced divers of the previous century would have had no difficulty working at a depth of ten fathoms, but ships' hulls two thousand years old cannot simply be looped with rope and brought to the surface. For although the recovered wooden planks of the ships had retained their original form, they possessed only a fraction of their previous strength. At the first tightening of the ropes the hulls would have broken into pieces. Decades passed, and the ships in Lake Nemi were almost forgotten again. Then the Italian dictator Benito Mussolini heard about them.

Mussolini dreamed of re-establishing the Roman Empire and paid much attention to the preservation of ancient monuments. The scientists still had only approximate ideas about the appearance of the ships on which the Roman legionaries had set out to turn the Mediterranean into *mare nostrum* (our sea). Mussolini therefore decided to raise the ships in Lake Nemi regardless of cost.

He abruptly ordered that Lake Nemi be pumped dry. By 1930 the work was begun. The water level dropped lower and lower, until finally in 1932 the ships were left high and dry. The divers' statements were true. On the bottom of the lake lay two splendid giant barks. Their hulls were still well preserved. Only the superstructures had not withstood the ages.

The Italian government had the ships taken to a museum built especially for them on the edge of the crater lake, where archaeologists from all corners of the earth soon collected. The finds in Lake Nemi disclosed for the first time some details of the secrets of Roman shipbuilding technique. Specialists admired especially the planking of the vessel: their Roman builders had artfully mortised the planks one into the other. Over that was a layer of wool fibers impregnated with tar and covered with a thin sheet of lead. Impregnation and lead sheeting meant an effective protection for the wood against algae, barnacles, and shipworms. Without the discoveries in Lake Nemi, scholars wouldn't have credited even the Romans with such a highly developed shipbuilding technique.

They also marvelled at the ships' outfitting. Their decks of oak beams were covered with mosaics and marble, their rooms decorated with bronze and marble statues. There were extravagantly furnished cabins and hot baths on board. It could not be doubted that the barks had been built for the emperor. Even the items found on board definitely belonged to the time of Caligula or his successor Claudius.

Unfortunately, both ships were burned in the Second World War, but fifty-foot models of the barks may be seen today on Lake Nemi. They were built by specialists of the Italian Navy from drawings and photographs that had been rescued.

"Operation Lake Nemi," however, had little significance for the progress of archaeology under water. It remained without successor, for in spite of their enthusiasm for science, even the archaeologists felt that the financial outlay had been excessive. It could only be afforded by a dictator who did not have to answer to anyone regarding the spending of tax money. Furthermore, it would be an impossible method to use in recovering ships from the sea.

During the thirties, several Frenchmen began to work on ways to conquer the deep. Vacationers on the Riviera at first laughed at the man who waddled across the beach with fins on his feet and struck out into the water. But a commission of the French Navy, to whom Louis de Corlieu demonstrated his invention in 1933, did not find it funny. For de Corlieu showed the officers that a skin diver who dives to the bottom with no more air than he can hold in his lungs can move and maneuver much faster and better than a diver with an air hose. He can make much better use of the few minutes' diving time allowed him by his limited air supply and even has his hands free, for rapid kicking with the flippers is enough to propel him.

At about the same time diving masks were put in use. They protected the diver's eyes from the stinging salt water and permitted clear, undistorted vision under water. Snorkels completed the outfitting of the first diving pioneers. Now they could swim over whole bays, watching the bottom from the surface without repeatedly having to take their face out of the water to breathe. The frogman was born. Like a sea animal he swam through the water, plummeted swiftly to the bottom in depths of ten fathoms and more—but unfortunately for only two or three minutes.

For this reason three young Frenchmen, Jacques-Yves Cousteau, Frédéric Dumas, and Philippe Tailliez, worked feverishly on the development of an "artificial lung," an apparatus that would permit a man to remain at least thirty minutes or an hour in the silent world of the sea, unhindered by air hoses that connected him to a diving boat.

Since the time of the great painter and inventor Leonardo da Vinci (1453–1519), countless inventors have occupied themselves with the problems of diving. The three Frenchmen studied all these constructions: none of them had the ability to render man independent of the world above water even for a short time.

Cousteau tried the oxygen breathing apparatus that had proved so useful to the Viennese Hans Hass in his successful and sensational advances into the world of the sea, and to navy frogmen. But he quickly abandoned his experiments when he suffered oxygen poisoning on his second try. An oxygen apparatus delivers pure oxygen to the lungs of the diver; under high pressure—below six fathoms—this becomes more than the body can take.

Finally Cousteau went to Paris to look for an engineer who could build him a practical breathing apparatus. Chance led him to Emile Gagnan, a skilled engineer and inventor. In June of 1943 the device that was to become the key to the silent world was finished—the "aqualung." The frogman now carried small compressed-air-filled steel bottles on his back. Since air can be squeezed into a small space under high pressure, the air bottles of the aqualung were filled with air at a pressure of 150 to 200 atmospheres. They could hold enough air for an extended stay under water. A valve that Gagnan invented reduced the pressure so much that it corresponded exactly to the prevailing water pressure. Through a rubber tube the diver was supplied with sufficient air at the proper pressure. The used, exhaled air escaped from the exhaust valve into the water and climbed in small bubbles to the surface. Gagnan assembled the entire valve system in a single, small box which he called the "automatic lung." The invention of Cousteau and Gagnan formed the basis for the compressed-air-breathing apparatus with which today thousands of amateur divers scout the bottoms of seas, lakes, and rivers everywhere.

Now the world of the deep could be conquered and the hunt for sunken archaeological treasures begin in earnest.

On their first excursions with the aqualung, diving pioneers discovered pottery fragments and well-preserved amphoras—ancient clay vessels. But this caused no real excitement at first, for Mediterranean fishermen and sponge divers had been finding such fragments and amphoras on the bottom of the sea for years. The fragments were usually thrown back into the water, while whole amphoras were kept as useful containers for drinking water, wine, fish, and oil.

But on August 8, 1948, Henri Boussard, the chairman of the Club Alpin Sous-Marin in Cannes made a noteworthy discovery. He chanced across a whole mountain of amphoras near Anthéor on the Riviera. A wide area at nine fathoms was covered with fragments and countless whole amphoras stuck upright in the sand, as if they had been placed in rows by hand. Thorough investigation revealed that an ancient freighter had sunk off Anthéor. But before the site could be properly explored, reckless souvenir hunters with frogman outfits had already ravaged the area and carried off the well-preserved amphoras, leaving nothing but a chaotic pile of fragments behind.

Soon reports of findings like the ones at Anthéor began to circulate. The wreck of Grand Congloué, which has now become famous, was discovered by a frogman. More than two thousand years ago there occurred a maritime catastrophe, which divers and archaeologists have since been able to reconstruct.

II

A Phoenix Rises
From the Ashes

A good dozen sea miles before the steamship from Genoa enters the harbor of Marseilles, the barren, rugged rock formation of Marseilleveyre looms up on the starboard side. A chain of islands runs parallel to its precipitous heights; they are deserted, rocky islands, as inhospitable as the mountains. The mistral wind whips around it, the islands of Maire, Jarres, Calserange and Riou, and the breakers lash at their sharp cliffs. Surf and storm have also cracked and eroded the rock of Grand Congloué, the easternmost of the smaller islands of this chain. Surf and storm pounded these rocks when Egypt still had no pyramids, and in the second century B.C., when a Greek captain sailed in the region.

We can picture him standing on the afterdeck of his heavy ship, which was listing heavily in the boiling sea. The captain had long since ordered the sails reefed, but the storm drove the large ship before it like a piece of cork. The captain's strongest sailors stuck to the rudders but were unable to steer. His eyes stinging, the captain tried to see through the thick wall with which the driving rain surrounded his ship. Where were they? Rain and sea had been pounding his ship for hours now, and it was impossible to see the nearby coastline. Winter had struck even before the ship could seek refuge in Massilia (modern Marseilles).

Suddenly a rock cliff loomed out of the darkness, white and threatening. We can picture the captain shouting an order to the men at the rudders. Too late! The bow crashed on the sharp cliffs. The heavy ship fell back. A wave threw it against the rocks once more, then it fell back again, this time more slowly and sluggishly. It sank deeper into the water, the waves closing over the deck. Then the mast, too, disappeared.

The ship carried the captain and his men with it into the deadly deep. Perhaps a sailor managed to jump quickly from the bow of the ship onto the cliff at the instant of the first impact, and eventually send word back to the owner, Marcus Sextius, on the island of Delos, that his precious cargo had gone down. The loss may have ruined Marcus Sextius.

The sunken ship was conquered by the sea, a slow, untiring process which took thousands of years. Before it sank, the ship turned and went down upright, with its bow aimed at Delos, past the rock walls covered with corals and sponges. It sank fifteen or twenty fathoms until the keel struck the gradually sloping foot of the rocky cliff. The underplanking burst under the weight of the tall, Italian wine jars. Round amphoras with Delian wine and finely glazed Campanian dishes poured out through the rupture in the ship's belly and into the open water. Containers rolled down the incline. But the deck held. The slender amphoras from Italy remained in orderly rows just as they had been carefully loaded.

The mighty hull of the ship now rested in twenty fathoms, the stern pressed against the rock wall. Great chunks of rock shielded it from sediment and the pounding surf high above.

Soon squid and cuttlefish made their homes in amphoras, piling pebbles, clay fragments, and empty clam shells to form a protective wall outside their houses. Countless porcupine fish fastened themselves to the planks, their quills extended to catch passing plankton. Thriving sponges, white and red coral followed them onto the wreck. Microorganisms gradually loosened the seals on the amphoras. More cuttlefish moved into the newly vacated containers. Sometimes moray eels beat them there, predatory fish, shaped like snakes.

In a few years the silent world had filled the wreck with a dazzling variety of life. Now it looked more like a giant rock on the bottom of the sea than a ship. Meanwhile shipworms ate away at planks and beams. A thin sheeting of lead with which the Greeks had covered the hull repelled them at first. But they entered through hatches and portholes, and soon were eating the planks from within. They gnawed at the masts and decks. While these termites of the sea were at work, mud grew thicker and thicker over the hull. This process continued incessantly over the years. Rain washed fine limestone dust from the Grand Congloué rock into the deep. This dust was mixed with countless mussels, with remains of innumerable minute organisms, with broken porcupine-fish skeletons and cuttlefish shells. On the sea floor a flat grave mound grew over the ship, protecting its wood from shipworms. New settlers could no longer find solid footing in the soft ground. The many creatures withdrew to the amphoras that still protruded from the mound. And they, too, sank deeper and deeper in mud in the course of the millennia, until only their necks still stuck out. Beyond the wreck lay strewn fragments of vessels, pots, bowls, and cups also, covered with algae and sponges until they blended with the bottom of the sea.

Another two or three centuries and the wreck could have disappeared completely in the mud and sand.

But before that happened, a diver called Christianini nearly lost his life.

Christianini was one of those men who live by retrieving booty from the coastal waters of the Mediterranean. He worked successfully as a salvage diver, and on the side gathered spiny lobsters, sponges, and corals. Christianini knew the waters east of Marseilles like the palm of his hand. But ultimately the sea was victorious in the eternal battle of the diver with the deep. In October, 1950, he was carried on a stretcher into the marine hospital in Toulon. His body was paralyzed when, after spending two hours at seventeen fathoms, he sped to the surface without observing the necessary decompression periods.

Toulon is the home of the underwater exploration division of the French Navy, and its doctors are prepared for cases of the bends. They put him into a steel chamber under high pressure. For two days the pressure was gradually decreased in order to permit Christianini's body slowly to dispose of the accumulated nitrogen. He lived, but his toes had to be amputated. He was bedridden for months and gradually had to realize that the paralysis in his legs would never fully disappear and that his career as a diver was over.

Frédéric Dumas, civilian adviser with the French Navy, visited Christianini every week in the hospital. One day the man from Marseilles shared his secret with him. He told Dumas of an incredibly large colony of spiny lobsters on the sea floor off the rock island of Grand Congloué, which he would be able to find by the number of old clay jugs lying around.

At the mention of "old clay jugs," Dumas became interested. The diver assured him they were probably ancient amphoras. He had seen so many of them in his work that he paid little attention to them any more. But Dumas wondered if there was an ancient ship sunk off Grand Congloué. It would pay to investigate the area more closely.

Dumas told Cousteau about it. Cousteau commanded the *Calypso*, a French Navy ship that had been transferred to work in oceanographic research. But for the time being, exploration of the sea floor by Grand Congloué was out of the question. The *Calypso* was already being readied for a research voyage which was to take Cousteau, Dumas, and many other divers and scientists back and forth through the Red Sea to the shores of Iran.

Perhaps the amphoras of Grand Congloué would have been forgotten again had not sport divers found other amphora fields while the *Calypso* was crossing between Africa and Arabia. At the news of these finds, the ship set out from Marseilles on a new crossing in August, 1952.

Besides the French divers, Professor Fernand Benoit, director of archaeological research in Provence and director of the Archaeological Museum in Marseilles, was on board. The *Calypso* was to inspect a whole series of sites where findings had been made. One of these sites—near the island of Maire—the divers wanted to investigate in detail under the direction of the professor.

Judging by the amphoras that had been found there, a ship had sunk near the island in twenty or twenty-five fathoms during the first century B.C.

The islands of Maire and Grand Congloué lie quite close to one another. Cousteau, Dumas, and Professor Benoit felt, therefore, that they might take this opportunity to look at Christianini's "old clay jugs." Should they go to Maire first, or Grand Congloué? The investigations at Maire might take a long time and then no time would remain to check out the site at Grand Congloué, the men reasoned. Thus they fortunately decided to set the *Calypso*'s course for Grand Congloué.

Christianini's "Old Clay Jugs"

After a short crossing through the islands, a white cliff jutted out of the haze: Grand Congloué. Slowly the *Calypso* proceeded through a fjordlike passage. Half a stone's throw from the surf-pounded cliff of the eastern end, the anchor splashed into the water. Here, under the sheer rock walls, must lie the site Christianini had mentioned.

Dumas slipped into his fins, buckled on the breathing apparatus, and adjusted his mask. He lowered himself into the water and swam toward the steep rock formation. Fathom by fathom he let himself sink deeper into the water. The rock wall got steeper and steeper, became an overhang, and began to form a huge arch. Dumas remembered that Christianini had mentioned this. The pounding of the surf grew softer and softer; the brilliant colors of the algae, sea anemones, and sponges on the rock wall were followed by the bizarre bushes of gorgon coral. A startled scorpaenid withdrew its red head into a grotto, spines extended. Dumas passed through a school of blue-black sea swallows and reached a wide rock ledge which encircled the island like a belt under the rocky overhang. But there were no amphoras in sight. Dumas checked out the rock ledge. Nothing. Only a solitary crab scurried across the sea floor and disappeared in a little nook.

Disappointed, the diver returned to the ship. Now Cousteau gave it a try. He descended near the eastern point. Maybe an ancient ship had been wrecked on this point. At thirty fathoms he hit bottom. Gradually his eyes grew accustomed to the blue-green twilight. But only a few stones lay strewn on the monotonous sand floor which dropped off gently, extending into the open sea.

Cousteau rounded the point toward the south. When he saw there was nothing there either, he swam back to the point, tired and disappointed. Almost by chance he followed the rock wall beyond the point to the west, and suddenly hit on an amphora that lay alone in a bed of sand extending otherwise uninterrupted as far as the eye could see. Cousteau stood it upright in the sand and decided to surface, for his diving time was up. A single amphora wasn't worth the risk he would run if he stayed down too long. Lone amphoras are found comparatively often along the Mediterranean coast. It didn't look as if a ship had sunk off Grand Congloué; perhaps Christianini was mistaken. Probably he had simply exaggerated a couple of amphoras into a field of them.

But suddenly he saw that Christianini had neither been mistaken nor had he exaggerated. Close to the foot of the rock wall, there was a broad, flat mound. Here and there the neck of an amphora protruded from the mud, and along its edge lay strewn clay fragments, whole vessels and jars.

A wreck! Cousteau was sure of it. But his air supply was nearly gone. Quickly he grabbed at a pile of fragments, laying hold of a chunk of something and a bronze hook, and brought them to the surface. Professor Benoit, who was leaning on the railing of the *Calypso*, saw his hand come out of the water holding three clay cups that had been welded into a single cluster by sea deposits. He took the cluster excitedly, turned it over in his hands, and exclaimed that it was Campanian.

Professor Benoit had already found specimens of these Italian dishes in other excavations. The cluster came from a Campanian workshop near Naples in the second or third century B.C. Benoit and the two archaeologists, Ferdinand Lallemand and Henri Medan, who accompanied him, flooded Cousteau with questions. Was there more dishware on the bottom, and could it be recovered?

Cousteau's short report gave the divers and archaeologists hope that the wreck on the bottom off Grand Congloué would throw significant light on ancient sea trading and navigation.

The *Calypso*'s voyage was over. Not another word was spoken about the wreck off Maire. The find at Grand Congloué was more important than all other amphora fields, for the age of the dishes told the archaeologists unambiguously that they had discovered the oldest sea-going vessel in the history of underwater archaeology.

The men stood around the diver Marcel Ichac in silence while he set up his tools and prepared to separate the cups and free them of mud. The three cups were piled one inside the other, like soup bowls, with the two handles of alternate cups at exact right angles. Ichac remarked that they must have been packed by a specialist.

Slowly Ichac freed the cups from the clump, cleaned them, and put them on the table. For the first time the divers standing around him had the feeling that they would not just be removing a large quantity of valuable, well-preserved pottery, amphoras, and bronze implements from the sea. Actually they would be taking life from the sea—life, which, though it had ended thousands of years ago, had been saved from destruction by the deep. To re-create this life from the discoveries would be their real object.

Fifteen divers from the *Calypso* went to work eagerly on the wreck. All day long baskets full of fragments, dishes, slender amphoras, and pieces of bronze were sent up to the *Calypso*. The men on board the research ship had their hands full hoisting the laden baskets with the small winch on the ship's stern and emptying them out. They also had to help the divers back on board, for they surfaced loaded down with clay vessels. And so it went for days, and the men hardly noticed the time. Toward the end of August the mistral—a cold autumn wind that comes down the Rhône valley and breaks out onto the sea between Marseilles and

Toulon—began to blow, two months too early this time. It brought the ice-cold layer of deeper water to the surface and made waves boil around the *Calypso* as it pitched and tugged at its anchor chain. In their eagerness, the divers didn't let themselves be disturbed by the weather. They put on wool underwear under their rubber insulating suits and leaped courageously into the surf. More and more baskets full of amphoras and Campanian dishes, bowls, and wine cups were emptied onto the rocking deck of the *Calypso*. But gradually the findings began to dwindle. Finally all the pottery scattered on the sea floor had been recovered. The divers tried to dig into the mound over the wreck to free more amphoras with their bare hands. The top layer of light mud was easily removed, but then came layers that seemed hard as cement. The amphoras were firmly imbedded; it was impossible to continue the excavation in this manner.

The divers and archaeologists aboard the storm-tossed *Calypso* discussed their next "plan of attack." Every empty space on board the ship was now filled with amphoras and pottery. The divers had recovered several hundred vessels and countless pieces of pottery. But this was only a tiny fraction of the amphoras in the mound, judging by its size. The men guessed that the excavation of the mound would take months, maybe even one or two years. Of course, they never guessed that divers would work on it for almost ten years. Cousteau quickly estimated what one year's exploration would cost. It was a great deal more than the underwater explorers and archaeologists could spare from their meager treasuries. Providing for the diving crew alone would cost a sizeable sum: already the divers were having difficulty supplementing their menu with fish. When divers go fishing with harpoons along a coast, the inhabitants of the sea learn to fear the weapons and keep their distance. Soon good-sized fish no longer show themselves along that stretch of the coast.

Above all, a base camp had to be established on the island by January at the latest. The *Calypso* and the researchers Cousteau and Dumas were already scheduled to explore new sites. The ship would not be available much longer for underwater excavating.

Jacques-Yves Cousteau (center) directs recovery work off Grand Congloué.

The divers and archaeologists would then need a home for the work platforms, a generator, a compressor, and drive mechanisms for the new "mud sucker."

The men knew that national sources would be sure to contribute something, and perhaps they might tap private sources. . . . But would they be able to collect enough? Even the possibility that they might have to abandon a half-excavated wreck, leaving the opened mound vulnerable to the gradual destruction of the under-water elements did not stop them: they would simply have to overcome all difficulties, for the wreck at the foot of the island was the long-sought opportunity for a major and pioneering break-through in archaeology. Far below the destructive surf, the wreck had survived more than two thousand years, and its lonely location and great depth would continue to protect it from plunderers should the explorers be forced to interrupt their work for a short while. The cliff of Grand Congloué did rise, sharp and menac-ing, out of the sea, but it provided enough of a foothold for a small base camp. All other amphora fields lay so far from dry land that they could not be explored without a ship standing constantly by. The divers and archaeologists decided that the wreck off Grand Congloué would be the first ancient sunken ship to be excavated with scientific accuracy.

Cousteau and Dumas wanted to solve the technical problems of the excavation, and Benoit wanted to do the archaeological work, as much as time allowed. The men had great hopes for the enter-prise. Of course they knew that the pioneering nature of the under-taking would mean that mistakes would be made, but they hoped, in spite of that, to establish underwater archaeology as a significant branch of archaeological science.

In the first days of September the *Calypso* again set sail for Mar-seilles, in order to unload the results of the first recovery work and take on provisions and equipment for the next work period.

Marcus Sextius' wine bottles arrived in Marseilles two thousand years late, although empty, of course, somewhat encrusted, and not all intact. The *Calypso* was tied to the wharf, and unloading began. Before the astonished eyes of a growing number of observers, the men carried amphoras out of the ship's hold and loaded them into a truck for delivery to the storage rooms of the museum in Château Boreli. The stream of vases and pottery looked as though it would never end, and the crowd doubled in size. The police finally had to ask the men of the *Calypso* to unload in the dark, since the crowd was already blocking traffic.

The next day the most important piece of equipment was put on board: the suction pump. On dry land archaeologists simply hire a large number of men when they want to excavate an old city mound. In a few days of pick-and-shovel work, large masses of earth are moved. But underwater it is impossible to swing a shovel. There, even the trowel, with which archaeologists do fine work on land, becomes a useless tool. Mud and sand simply swirl off the shovel and trowel and form a cloud.

With this problem in mind, the French had already designed and built a gigantic mud-sucking machine a few years earlier, which worked like a vacuum cleaner. A hose with a suction nozzle is lowered into the water. Just above the nozzle a smaller hose leading from a compressor on board the ship blows compressed air into the suction hose. The compressed air mixes with the water in the suction hose, forming a foaming mixture. This is lighter than water and therefore rises speedily up the hose. The machine had already had two test trials—one at Anthéor and the second on the wreck off Mahdia, which Cousteau and his fellow workers had worked on in 1948. In the first half of September of 1952 the *Calypso* anchored again off Grand Congloué with the giant pump on board. The suction hose was put in position, the compressor switched on, and the hose, guided by the diver's hand, began to eat its way into the mound like a giant snake. The upper end spat the mud into a finely meshed filter basket. An archaeologist was always on watch at this basket, for the suction hose did not just send up soft mud and sand. Into the basket also fell an assortment of corals, clay fragments, mussels, and cups. Now and then a young lobster would also plop into the basket, caught in the suction. The first lobster to land on deck startled the archaeologist Lallemand, who was on watch at the filter, and he jumped aside. As more came up,

Federico Foerster-Laures

Vacuum cleaner

The "mud sucker" or vacuum cleaner in action

he grabbed them deftly and deposited them in a container that had been set up for just this purpose, for on the Mediterranean coast octopods and squid are considered great delicacies.

The nozzle of the suction hose loosened the thickest mud deposits and soon exposed the first amphoras; their beautiful, classic forms rose from the mud like the statue a sculptor carves from stone.

Divers sent them up with a basket and the other men received them and emptied them, shaking their heads, for every amphora contained handfuls of small clay fragments, clam shells, and pebbles; some were even filled to the top. But the mystery was soon solved. More and more amphoras came up with small octopods in them that either fell out or had to be pulled out when they resisted. In the course of the years the wreck had become an octopod colony —a regular city. The octopods had learned that the amphoras made good hiding places and settled in them one after another. They had collected all kinds of rubble at the entrances which they had piled up with their claws when danger threatened. In the process much of the matter had fallen into the amphoras, mixed with countless clam shells and remains of octopod meals, until finally some of the amphoras were filled to the brim.

Amphoras from the wreck
off Grand Congloué

Meanwhile the autumn storms raged. The *Calypso* threatened to tear loose from its anchor chain and to be tossed against the rocks.

But here good fortune was on the side of the divers and archaeologists. General Marie Eugène Aimé Molle, commander of the southern military district of France, visited them at their work, dived down to the wreck himself, and was so thrilled that he promised them support. He kept his word. A few days later a young lieutenant with six soldiers from a pioneer unit arrived on the scene. Working in surf up to their waists, in three days the soldiers erected a platform at the foot of the island for the compressor, and a beam for the hoist. The hoist beam was over sixty feet long and was cemented into the rock of the cliff and anchored with steel trusses. On a float similar to a landing barge the men of the *Calypso* transported the compressor and equipment to the platform, while the soldiers began constructing a roomy sheet-metal barracks for the divers and archaeologists in a niche in the rocks. From now on the operations had a base, and the project could be continued without the aid of the *Calypso*.

The press and radio spread word of the men and their work near the tiny island all over France. Government and private concerns were enthusiastic. Aid from the Ministry of Education, the Navy, the Harbor Administration of Marseilles, and prefect of the Bouche-du-Rhône Coastal Department poured in. The Chamber of Commerce of Marseilles gathered money, and the American National Geographic Society, a private American organization of many millions of members which conducts or supports explorations throughout the world, sent a representative. Besides the flag of the NGS, he also brought along a big check. The continuation of the research activity was assured.

The hose from the suction pump now hung from the beam which extended far out over the waves. The excavation plan was to dig out the wreck almost exactly as archaeologists do a tell—a city mound in the Orient.

The divers wanted to dig a shaft into the mound and make a cross section through the wreck. As they lifted one layer of slender Italian amphoras out of the hole, they hit upon another. Under it lay a third.

The amphoras stood upright and close together, just as they had been loaded two thousand years before.

A Sip of Lucius Titius' Wine

The men aboard the *Calypso*, which visited the island regularly and lay at anchor there, were astonished when the divers sent up the first amphoras that were still unopened. The mouths of the vessels had been sealed with pozzolana, a volcanic natural cement from the slopes of Vesuvius. Beneath the seals were corks. The last cracks between the corks and the clay sides had been carefully caulked with pitch. The seals bore a stamped impression of Roman letters, which the archaeologist Lallemand started to decipher immediately. This was not hard, for the seals had withstood the time under water very well.

Bringing amphoras up to the surface

57

The letters were L. TITI C. F.—Lucius Titius Caii Filius—a well-known family, which had owned huge vineyards in the Sabine mountains near Rome.

It was a discovery that was to take on great significance in the reconstruction of the fate of the sunken ship.

Even more significant was a second group of letters, which numerous amphoras bore on their necks, stamped into the clay: SES. These three letters were followed by the sign either of an anchor or a trident, the weapon of Poseidon, god of the sea.

Closer investigation, however, showed almost all the remaining unopened amphoras to be empty. A small hole in their necks gave the explanation but at the same time posed a new puzzle.

Again and again Lallemand inspected the clean boring in the clay sides. It was not the work of sea animals. He could find only one explanation: crew members of the sunken ship had secretly bored into many of the amphoras and drunk their contents during the voyage. Perhaps storm, rain, and waves had not been responsible alone for the sinking of the ship. Had the poor navigation of a drunken crew and an equally intoxicated captain also contributed?

When the first wine-filled amphora was brought on board the *Calypso*, Lallemand and Cousteau poured themselves some of the wine. With great ceremony and anticipation they raised their glasses of wine, two thousand years older than the oldest and most expensive wine in the port cellars in Portugal. Lallemand was cautious and spat the stuff out onto the deck. Cousteau had taken a large swallow and with a contorted face enjoyed a liquid from which alcohol and bouquet had long since evaporated.

The suction pump ate further and further into the grave mound of the wreck. The divers brought up more clay dishes. Soon some pieces showed up that had been so well encased in mud that the encrustation had not been able to destroy fully their black glaze. Lallemand eagerly awaited the first totally glazed pieces.

It wasn't long before a shiny black bowl fell into the filter basket. Lallemand grabbed hold of it and then stared in amazement at his black fingers and the ancient bowl. A diver had played a trick on him by smearing the dish with black shoe polish. But

Lallemand's disappointment did not last long. The suction pump had in the meantime eaten down to the first planks. Along the way it had sent up many small, interesting objects that had been overlooked by the divers on the bottom. Lallemand, who was taking Fernand Benoit's place in the exploration, at first only fished out lead weights from fishing nets. Then he recovered numerous objects of bronze, knives, an ancient finger ring, and fishhooks.

Sea animals had gnawed away the major portion of the hull, but a few significant parts had been preserved by the mud—sturdy planks of Aleppo pine fastened together with dowels of hard oak and olive-wood, and covered with a sheeting of lead. Even the long bronze nails with which the ancient shipbuilders had nailed the planks and beams together were coated with lead, proving that the master shipbuilders of antiquity already knew about the physical phenomenon of contact corrosion.

This phenomenon occurs because of an electric current flowing between two different metals in an electrolytic solution (such as the salty water of the sea). One of the metals disintegrates very rapidly in this process. All the ancient bronze nails found by Grand Congloué bore a coating of lead, which prevented sea water from getting between the lead sheeting of the ship's hull and the bronze of the nail.

Deep in the bowels of the ship the divers found wider, rounder vessels than they had seen thus far. These were of an even nobler and more beautiful form, like those made in ancient times on the islands of Rhodes, Delos, and the Cyclades. Now Lallemand's dreams came true—to an excess, in fact. Deep inside the ship were more Campanian dishes, bowls and cups, neatly packed one inside the other according to size, shiny black just as they had left the

Campanian dishes: Grand Congloué

workshop in Italy thousands of years before. Not just a few, but literally hundreds of them were quickly dug out of the ship, and the divers estimated thousands of them might still be lying on the sea bottom.

Lallemand had his hands full inspecting, sorting, and registering the materials. As the pile continued to grow, he was able to draw a scientific conclusion. The Campanian dishes were surprisingly regular. Many dishes and bowls were identical, but none showed signs of the forming hands of the potter. Closer scrutiny revealed that the potters had worked with wooden forms which had permitted them to produce a large number of similar vessels in a short time—the mass-production methods of the potter two hundred years before the birth of Christ were only slightly different from those of a modern porcelain factory today.

Lallemand's work threatened to become too much for him; but compared to the mountain that still had to be brought up from the bottom—the mound still measured over 120 feet in length and 30 to 36 feet in breadth—he was making real progress. The work speed suffered considerably because each diver could stay under water only a short time. Cousteau and Dumas, who took turns directing the diving activity, strictly observed the change-of-shift times. Each diver was permitted to go down three times a day: eighteen minutes the first time, fifteen minutes the second time, and the third time only twelve. At a depth of twenty-three fathoms a diver could not take more than that in one day without observing long decompression stages while surfacing, or risking the bends. Even with these carefully reckoned diving periods the men sometimes suffered from a mysterious intoxicating sensation at the end of a work day. One diver on the platform continually had to keep track of the work periods of his comrades below. Should a diver forget to surface on schedule, a rifle was fired on the surface, and the sound of the shot penetrated into the deep, warning the diver to come up.

The strict discipline protected the men from serious accidents, until one night the float holding the suction hose broke off in a storm. The anchor had come loose from the bottom and the float had drifted until the anchor caught again somewhere and broke the chain. All day long the divers searched the sea bottom without finding the valuable anchor. Jean Pierre Servanti, a young Navy frogman who had finished his military service and then joined the Grand Congloué expedition as a volunteer, suggested following the track left by the dragging anchor in the mud. He was one of the best divers of the *Calypso* and was ready to take up the search in depths of thirty fathoms and more.

Cousteau warned him that he might not find the anchor in one dive, and gave him a cork buoy to take along. He told Servanti to tie the buoy to a rock when he got tired, so the next diver could go on from there.

Servanti disappeared into the sea. Cousteau checked his watch. Ten minutes passed. He waited for Servanti to surface. Instead, the air bubbles from his exhalation—the life sign of the diver—suddenly ceased. Albert Falco, the best diver on board, went down immediately. He found Servanti unconscious, his hand on the anchor.

Three divers recovered the victim. He was placed immediately in the decompression chamber aboard the *Calypso*, which steamed full speed ahead for Marseilles. At the wharf a fire truck, equipped with a decompression chamber, was waiting to speed the unconscious man to the large decompression chamber at the hospital. It had been notified by the ship's radio. After five hours, the doctors gave up their attempts to revive the man. Servanti was dead. Overexertion had probably made him unconscious, and then he had suffocated.

Servanti's death brought the excavating to a stand-still. Cousteau considered halting it altogether. He did not feel that he could be responsible for continuing and thereby possibly endangering more divers.

But volunteers, amateur divers, offered to take Servanti's place, and aid in the digging without pay. With a heavy heart, Cousteau finally gave the signal to resume work. "We decided," he later wrote, "to continue the work which cost Servanti his life—as he would have wanted it."

Now Cousteau himself went down. In two difficult dives he found the anchor and tied a rope to it.

The next accident soon followed.

One night in December a storm swept the work platform from the cliff into the sea. All night long the divers worked in the surf to recover the valuable suction pump and to secure the long boom.

Days passed before the three men could recover the compressed air bottles and breathing devices and refasten the work platform— this time well above the water level.

The exploration went on without a winter break. By spring several hundred more amphoras and Campanian dishes had been collected in the island station. Finally the men could no longer resist the temptation to try out the ancient dishes. They held a large banquet, for which several theaters lent the costumes.

The banquet was actually intended as a show for press photographers and movie people, but it turned out to be more than that. The cooks served bread, meat, and fruit in Campanian bowls. They poured wine out of amphoras thousands of years old, and the men drank it from ancient wine cups. When fruit shone against the shiny black glaze of the bowls, it became evident to some of the divers just how superior ancient esthetic taste had been. The black-glazed clay set off the foods better than the finest china.

The scholars, too, found pleasure in the ancient dishes. Between 1952 and 1954 the divers brought to the surface more than six thousand dishes—more Campanian dishes than all land digs together had produced up to that time. The archaeologists distinguished 137 forms. They were amazed at the active trade of two thousand years ago and at the surprisingly high level of table culture in Gaul at that time, which the cargo indicated.

The findings did bring sorrow to one person, an Italian scholar, who after years of excavating and studying, wrote an article on Campanian dishes. Then he came to the island, inspected the findings, and sadly shook his head. His work had already been superseded.

But the archaeologists on the excavation also had their steady stream of new problems to solve, such as the mystery of the black pebbles and the secret of the lead pipeline.

The suction pump started spitting out the black pebbles as the divers approached the keel of the wreck. There were black, pea-sized volcanic pebbles that could not have been carried down from Grand Congloué by rain or storm, for there is no volcanic rock anywhere in this area.

Had the little stones served as ballast for the ship? Were they mosaic pieces, a trade item which the ship carried?

A lead pipeline caused the archaeologists even more head-aches. The divers discovered yard after yard of it. Did the ship have a pump system in case of a leak? Or did the pipes belong to the freight? The scientists considered it possible that the Greeks had equipped their ships with a complicated pump system.

On May 15, 1953, the keel of the wreck was found. The Greeks had hewn it from oak. It was the keel of a sailing ship that must have measured several dozen yards in length.

Dr. Jean-Loup de la Brunière, the medical doctor of the research group on the island, found one of the ship's anchors a short time later as he was swimming along the rock ledge in search of red gorgon coral. To be sure, the sea animals had long since eaten away the wooden parts of the anchor, but the remaining shaft of lead gave a good idea of its original size.

On the Trail of Marcus Sextius

In 1954, when Cousteau left and passed the direction of the re-maining excavation (which continued, with a few interruptions, until 1960) on to Yves Girault, the Secretary General of the French Office of Deep Sea Exploration, Professor Benoit had al-ready delivered the wreck from anonymity. He had figured out the ports of its last voyage, the time of its sinking, and even identified the ship's owner—two thousand years after the catastrophe. The story behind the ship wrecked off Grand Congloué was the result of a painstaking study in detection that matched the best work of the Sûreté—France's famous secret police.

In fact, Benoit had a more difficult job than a criminologist. He could not question witnesses or find fresh clues—all his clues were more than two thousand years old. The wreck contained no human remains and no log or other written material. The only clues were amphoras, clay dishes, and fragments. He had to make these speak to him, and let the story of the ancient ship unfold from what they told him.

Benoit had two good starting points for his work: the form and construction of the amphoras and dishes and the letters and insignias they bore. The amphoras fell into two distinct groups. One came from Italy, the other from the eastern Mediterranean. Amphoras of the second variety had been produced primarily on the islands of Rhodes and Cnidus. The Italian amphoras had been stacked on top of the Greek ones and had therefore probably been loaded later.

Professor Benoit was able to place the first little flags on his map of the Mediterranean. The destination of the ancient voyage had certainly been Masilia, a Graeco-Gallic *polis* on the site of modern Marseilles, for centuries the most powerful city in the western Mediterranean and from time immemorial the terminal of important trade routes. The ship set sail in the eastern Mediterranean, loaded amphoras in Syracuse, passed safely through the Strait of Messina toward southern Italy, took on more cargo in Latium and Campania, and followed the old navigation routes along the coast of Italy and France. That must have been in the second century B.C., for the major portion of the amphoras and dishes showed typical signs of this period.

More than that could not immediately be deduced from the form of the recovered pottery. But there were still the letter groups on the amphora seals and the amphoras themselves. Obviously they were abbreviations of Roman makers, for they were Roman letters. And Roman writing and the Latin language were of little significance in the second century B.C. Hardly any peoples but the Romans used them, for the universal language of the time was Greek.

Benoit had good reason for deciding that the abbreviations stood for makers. He knew that brand names were already used in ancient times—especially for wines. And the practical-minded Romans used as many abbreviations as we do today.

Thus he deduced that the letters "L. TITI" on the seals of Italian amphoras probably stood for Lucius Titius. His vineyards in the Sabine mountains near Rome lay on the ship's course. And the letters "SES" found on many amphoras' necks? Did they form the name of a large pottery manufacturer employing hundreds of slaves in the mass production of pottery? Many such factories did exist. But every "SES" was followed by the sign of an anchor or a trident. An anchor and trident would scarcely have been chosen by a potter as a trademark—"SES" with anchor or trident could only be the mark of a shipping firm or a very rich man who owned more than one ship.

Now, if Benoit's theory was right so far, it wasn't necessarily impossible to identify this "SES" even more than two thousand years after his death.

In antiquity men were not so preoccupied with bookkeeping as in our own time, but a politically or economically important man could not easily pass away without leaving some written clues behind. Archaeology has discovered and preserved an amazing number of such clues. With scientific methodicalness even the most improbable inscriptions on clay fragments, tax lists, grave markers and many other things have been collected by generations of archaeologists, photographed, sketched, and published in scientific journals. The result is an enormous body of knowledge regarding some aspects of ancient life—primarily Roman. Especially good sources of information were provided by the works of ancient philosophers, poets, and authors, whose writings of course were preserved and passed on through the years.

Another discovery strengthened Professor Benoit's hopes for success in his search. In reading scientific publications on excavations in Burgundy and Alsace he came upon pictures of amphora fragments that bore the sign "SES" with anchor and trident. Thus

"SES" was doubtless an important entrepreneur of his time, whose wine journeyed up the Rhône as a welcome precursor of the Graeco-Roman culture.

Now Benoit and his assistants in France and Italy set to work searching through the names of ancient families. In the process he hit on the name Sextius, an influential Roman family.

Was "SES" the abbreviation for "SESTIUS" (or Sextius)? Benoit consulted the annuals of the Roman historian Titus Livy, which tell the history of Rome from its legendary founding in 753 B.C. Here he found proof.

Livy mentions a certain Marcus Sextius, prominent wine dealer and shipowner from Fregallae near Naples. According to Livy, Sextius had settled on the island of Delos, built himself a luxurious villa there, and in the early part of the second century B.C. assumed local citizenship.

In 1873 French archaeologists began work on that barren little speck of land and dug out "Holy Delos," the island which, according to Greek legend, Zeus found floating in the sea. He chained it down and chose it as the birthplace for his son Apollo. The French are still working today at digging out the once flourishing city, for Delos was a city without peer. While the Greek city-states ravaged each other in endless wars, Delos flourished more and more, for Delos, the holy city, was spared from war. No one was permitted to die on Delos, and no child was born there. Expectant mothers and people near death were taken to the nearby island of Rhenea. All peoples respected the holy city of life; even the Egyptians brought sacrifices to Apollo. And so the destination of pilgrimages gradually made the island into an asylum for merchants and a sort of free port.

Long before the barbaric plundering of the city in 88 B.C. by a fleet of Mithradates, king of Pontus on the Black Sea, a large part of the sea trade from Asia Minor and Egypt to Greece, Italy and the western Mediterranean passed by the holy island. Delos was considered by far the richest and most beautiful city in Greece. Luxurious villas sprang up one after the other, richly designed with columned hallways, mosaics, and baths. Already toward the end of the third century, when Rome began to expand its power to the east and coerced some Greek cities into league with it, the first Roman merchants appeared in Delos. When Marcus Sextius arrived, they had already made themselves well at home, and had established a Roman quarter which was especially luxurious. According to Livy, Sextius, too, settled in this quarter.

It was Cousteau who got the idea of looking for more clues on Sextius in Delos. And so the *Calypso* retraced the last route of the large ship, between Scylla and Charybdis, over the Aegean, to the Cyclades. She lowered anchor outside the entrance to the holy harbor and the trade harbor, which were now filled with sand.

In Delos' best years thousands of slaves often embarked and disembarked in a single day.

The *Calypso*'s lifeboat carried the men to shore, where they were received by Jean Marcadé, the director of the French excavation activities on Delos. He led them to the Roman quarter at the foot of Cynthus Mountain, on which the Apollo temple stood, and to the street with the most lavish villas. Here they chanced upon a villa with a colonnade like the one Livy reported Sextius had built for himself. The divers combed the house in groups, looking for any sign that might give information pertaining to Sextius.

Suddenly one of the men let out a cry of joy. The others rushed to him and crowded around a mosaic which depicted a porpoise curved around an anchor. The anchor was exactly like the one that decorated the amphoras found in the wreck off Grand Congloué and were followed by the letters SES. While one group stood around discussing it, others made an even more significant discovery. They found a mosaic picture of a trident.

The stamp found
on the amphoras
off Grand Congloué

James Dugan, one of the divers, knelt down and traced out one of the ribbons on the point of the trident and read "S," then he traced along the trident itself: "E," and finally the second ribbon, "S."

While Cousteau wandered through the villa deep in thought, he noticed a few black mosaic pieces lying in the dust. He bent over, picked them up, and found black, volcanic pebbles in his hand—pebbles just like those he had found by Grand Congloué. Jean Marcadé watched silently, and then gave his opinion: it was the ruin of a luxury villa—a villa which had never been completed.

The divers and archaeologists searched through the museum of Delos for more clues to Marcus Sextius and found proof of Livy's claim that Sextius had lived on Delos. A list of names belonging to a legal document of naturalization cites among the naturalized citizens one "Maarkos Sestios Maarkou Phregellanos"—Maarkos Sestios (Hellenized form of his Latin name), son of Maarkos, from Fregellae.

For Professor Benoit and many other scholars that did not conclude the chapter on "Grand Congloué." Much of the reconstruction of the story of the ship was from a scientific point of view still hypothetical. Further research provided scientifically sound proofs for many things—and even some totally new, unanticipated facts. The amphoras were again submitted to the most exacting scrutiny. It turned out that some of the vessels originating in Rhodes and Cnidus were a good seventy years older than most of those made in Delos and southern Italy.

Pioneer Research

Men in ancient times even had clay vessels which lasted at least two or three generations. Had the ship been loaded with some amphoras with especially valuable old wine, as freighters today sometimes transport crates of century-old port wine from Portugal to England?

Some of the scholars formulated another theory: Two ships had lain by Grand Congloué. Marcus Sextius's sailing vessel had sunk

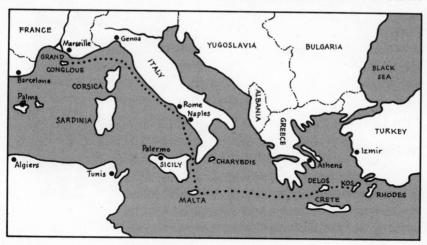

The route followed by Marcus Sextius's ship on her last voyage

on top of the wreck of an older vessel from Rhodes or Cnidus. Although this theory could not be proved, it was equally impossible to disprove it.

The research at Grand Congloué left some mysteries unsolved. Mainly responsible for this were mistakes made during the excavation, in spite of all the precautions that were taken. The worst and most important mistake was that the divers dug out the wreck without first having photographed, measured, and drawn it, and without taking measurements during the excavation.

In the scholarly altercation that followed, the archaeologists and divers who took part in the excavation at Grand Congloué were severely criticized. But these men rightly argued that they had been doing pioneer work and were forced to develop and try entirely new techniques. Under such circumstances, mistakes are inevitable. Exact scientific methods can only develop gradually.

Despite shortcomings, the exploration by Grand Congloué did achieve its main objective. Underwater archaeology was established as a new branch of archaeological research, and took the place of aimless underwater hunting for art treasures.

III

The Coast
of the "Thousand Wrecks"

Ile de Riou, Iles du Frioul, Cape Ferrat, Cape Antibes, Le Dramont
—each of these names is a location where divers have found ancient
wrecks. And almost every month Professor Benoit is able to draw
a new "X" on his map, denoting still another.

Professor Nino Lamboglia from the Instituto Internazionale di
Studi Liguri in Bordighera on the Italian Riviera, Italy's specialist
in underwater archaeology, has meanwhile registered the wrecks
discovered along Italy's coast and islands.

All along the ancient shipping channels in the Ligurian Sea, divers have been discovering sunken Greek and Roman ships since the
late forties. At first just a few were found, then dozens, and then
more and more. The wrecks discovered now total almost a thousand. Time and again amateur divers chasing a fish through tall
sea grass or scouting an underwater cliff or dark grottoes chance
upon a ship which has been sunk for thousands of years. Before
them a fishing boat may have dragged its nets over this spot, or a
steamship taken soundings with sonar, or other divers swum here—
without seeing anything. For an ancient wreck does not look
like the ships in the fantastic tales of old sea dogs, with sails hoisted
and a cabin clock still ticking on the sea bottom. It has long since
become a ship's grave.

Bell found in the sea off the island of Giglio

The sailor of antiquity had neither compass nor sextant. He steered his ship along the coast on a route learned by experience, utilized such sailing handbooks as the *Stadiasmos*, and hated to venture out on the open sea where he had only the sun and the stars for bearings.

But the nearby coast only gave the ship and its crew a false sense of security. Often sudden storms would drive the heavy sailing ships onto reefs and rocks. Along some stretches of the coast strong currents gave the captains a bad time. But they were especially wary of the capes, which were constantly buffeted by changeable winds and on which the Greeks and Romans built temples to placate the gods and to warn passing ships. There were only a few lighthouses to warn sailors that treacherous reefs lay slightly below the water's surface. Discoveries have revealed that reefs have sent countless ships to the bottom.

71

Whenever an ancient captain crossed bays he could not see completely, he had to be especially careful. They provided hiding places for pirates who at times made whole oceans unsafe.

The history of medieval seafaring cities reveals many more dangers which must also have threatened the ancient sailors, such as faulty rudders. Fire on board could turn a wooden ship into a flaming torch. In addition to these, there were many sea battles fought in which hundreds of ships were sunk by iron-tipped battering-rams. No harbor in the world could contain the fleet of merchantmen and warships that have sunk in the Mediterranean from the beginnings of sea travel to the Middle Ages.

The condition in which a diver finds a wreck is the result of the manner in which it sank, the underwater landscape in which it came to rest, and its construction and cargo. Thus for a specialist no two wrecks are alike, and each newly discovered one means a new scientific and technical problem that must be solved.

Sometimes an ancient wreck looks at first glance like the ship by Grand Congloué; often another consists of nothing more than a few remains, or a third is so well preserved under deep layers of mud and sand that its condition far exceeds the expectations of scientists.

Total destruction was the fate of all those ancient ships that caught fire or were repeatedly hurled against cliffs, or those that got caught in flat surf areas where the waves soon pounded them to pieces. Divers today can only find a few scattered amphoras, clay sherds, and maybe an anchor or some fragments of wood from these ships.

Probably the greatest part of the ancient warships were also destroyed. Triremes (ancient three-ruddered warships) and small Liburnian galleys (brigantines) were either set afire or rammed to pieces by the iron-covered bows of enemy ships during sea battles. Free of the weight of amphora cargoes, they did not sink immediately to the bottom, but became corks on the waves that finally pounded them apart. The helmets, armor, and weapons of the drowned soldiers were strewn over a wide area in the process, as were the many lead anchors, the iron parts of the battering-ram,

Verlagsarchiv

Relief of a Roman warship, in the Vatican Museum

and the clay vessels containing provisions. All organic parts of the ship—bodies and clothes of the warriors, sails, food, and the ship itself—were soon devoured by sea animals, and the last remains were taken care of by bacteria and other microorganisms. For these reasons divers and archaeologists have not succeeded in finding a single sunken warship. Heavily laden freight vessels suffered the same fate when they sank along shallow coasts, where high waves would break up the ships and scatter their cargo.

Even wrecks that are considered well preserved were usually damaged in sinking. The storm snapped the masts and carried away the sails, or the anchor ropes were broken, leaving the heavy anchors strewn along the bottom of the sea while the ship itself drifted away.

If a sailboat was driven against a treacherous reef, the bow usually broke open, pouring part of the cargo over a wide area. As the ship sank it was subjected to the laws of the altered gravity in the

73

underwater world. Heavy pieces sank fast. Light objects drifted away and came to rest far from the wreck.

But heavily laden merchant ships full of amphoras sank rapidly and settled firmly on the bottom. Then the geological characteristics of the sea bottom at this spot determined further damage of the ship.

Shipworms and microorganisms always went to work immediately on the hull until the weight of the amphoras finally burst it open like an egg shell, and the sides pushed outward. But at the moment that the wreck reached the bottom, the weight of the cargo pushed the keel deep into the protective mud. A layer of oxygen-deficient water directly over the bottom, which water animals avoid, protected an additional section of the hull from destruction. Slowly mud and sand piled up and put an end to the sea animals' feast. Only the amphoras still protruded. The sea could only encrust them and surround them with mud, for fired clay holds up indefinitely in sea water.

Sometimes sand, mud, and sediment would cover a wreck so quickly that the sea animals never got a chance to eat it to the extent that the sides of the ship gave way and the amphora cargo spilled out. Frogmen today find the ancient vessels as closely stacked as they were two thousand years ago when longshoremen loaded them. Some ancient ships immediately sank so deep into the mud that even a good part of the wooden hull remains intact. Of course, in these cases the sea buried them so deep that they are very hard to discover. But underwater archaeologists hope soon to be able to uncover completely one of these few well-preserved ancient ships.

A Roman sailing ship that sank in the days of Caesar had already become a mound by the time Emperor Nero set fire to the city of Rome. Then the sea gradually—half an inch a century—spread a cover over it. It became an oasis of colorful maritime life. Lobsters, moray eels, and octopods settled in the amphoras of the deck cargo. Mollusks, corals, sponges, and algae fastened themselves to clay vessels, scattered lead anchors, bronze implements, and rocks. Hard sea sediments encrusted the amphoras and baked them together into a single mass.

If the wreck landed on one of the endless meadows of tall sea grass, which cover sandy stretches of the Mediterranean floor, then time began to stand still for the ship. It stood still—for many wrecks it continues to stand still—until one day divers scouted through the thick sea grass jungle and found an island shaped like a ship on the blue-green plain. Most of the wounds that wrecks have inflicted on the sea floor have been slowly healed up. Mud covers the colorful oasis until finally only a few amphora necks protrude—or the encrusted end of an anchor shaft, a chunk of marble, partly eaten away, or a piece of bronze. Often a few amphora fragments lie scattered around, but nothing more can be seen of the ship's cargo.

Countless ancient wrecks may be lost forever because thoughtless amateur divers have removed as trophies these sole indications

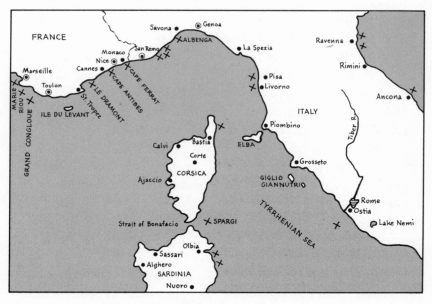

The coast of the "thousand wrecks"

of their existence. Even when the finders report afterward that they found pieces of amphoras in a certain bay, but took every last one of the fragments, the situation is almost hopeless. Only exact information regarding the location can assist the scientists. Under water it is very difficult to determine an exact position. Sonar would register the flat mound of a ship only on a level bottom. But there are few places along the Mediterranean coast that are not covered with hills, rocks, and valleys.

Thus chance often led to the discovery of the first amphora ships. The French diving pioneers were the first who learned to search the coastline of Provence for ancient wrecks and find sunken ships in places where before them no one had seen anything but an untouched underwater world. Then in the large French and Italian diving clubs on the Riviera more and more men became interested in spending their free time searching for underwater archaeological treasures. Discoveries occurred frequently, as diving became more popular.

Sometimes fishermen along the coast of the Ligurian Sea guided scientists to places where they had brought up amphoras in their nets, or where they had seen amphora fields through their glass observation boxes. The divers can locate the spots easily if the directions of the fishermen are precise. Frogmen can search out amphora fields using torpedo-like vehicles that pull them along the bottom at a speed of several knots. Often, too, they are pulled by boats using an aquaplane. This device was developed from simple boards connected to the boats with long ropes. The diver holds on to two handles on the board and determines his course by tipping the board. A slight turn of the board and he shoots to the bottom—or to the top. An aquaplane has the same function as the elevators on a glider. Nowadays a diver usually lies flat on a large board which is pulled by a motorboat. A plexiglass bubble protects him from the wash of the water, and he determines his depth with his own movable rudder.

In searching for unknown wrecks buried in mud, the divers usually choose places along ancient shipping channels that were especially dangerous—rocky areas and reefs. But first even the reefs have to be found. Modern sea charts rarely note them any more, for these days ships sail farther offshore.

The divers' job is not unlike that of prehistory scholars who have to seek out Bronze Age grave mounds in uneven heath areas. The jungle of maritime life covers rocks, mines, the rusted remains of a car body, amphoras, and Roman marble with an equally colorful carpet. The diver must often be able to recognize the location of a sunken ship from minute indications, such as a dark coloring of the sand in one place, or a too-rectangular stone that, under scrutiny, proves to be a marble building block. Often amphoras become visible only after the diver has wiped away the mud with his hand. Even amphora fragments lying out in the open, covered with encrustation, disappear all too easily in a marine landscape.

Thieves at the Bottom of the Sea

Since diving has become a widespread sport, archaeologists have been hampered again and again by chance discoverers of wrecks, who have torn amphoras out of fields, often using knives, hammers, and hatchets to break them loose, and who have, in the process, destroyed many other vessels and partially demolished the sites. Lone anchors or amphoras are of little value to science; as art they are insignificant—like boxes and crates today. It is only what they can tell us about the past that is important.

Isolated finds can lead scientists to conclude that a ship once sank on that spot, and an entry is then made on the charts. But science also needs to know what ship sank, where it came from, and where it was headed, what its cargo was and what it looked like. One or two amphoras can hardly provide this kind of information. Scholars find the answers only at the sites themselves, where they can carry out exacting research with methods developed since Grand Congloué. In these studies the location of each individual amphora is important. The removal of a few items out of hundreds or even thousands can significantly alter the appearance of a site and make the archaeologists' job decidedly more difficult.

For this reason archaeologists and underwater explorers try to impress amateur divers with their responsibilities. But usually they have little success. Many discoverers of wrecks feel no obligation to science, but rather view the ship they have discovered as a welcome source of profit. They recover the best amphoras and sell them on the black market as antiques. Scholars then get at best only a few of the more poorly preserved vessels, or hear accidentally about the wreck and then find the site in a state of chaos. What is more, an increasing number of antique dealers themselves have taken up diving. To the horror of the scholars, amphora hunting has become a favorite sport of millionaires and their friends, carried on from luxury yachts along the Riviera.

But underwater archaeology's greatest problems come from the many diving schools and clubs that have opened up along the coast of the Ligurian Sea in recent years. Each little school, every club, has its own wrecks, of which the scientists rarely ever get wind. In the fall the *moniteurs*, the diving instructors, who are often experienced in underwater work, search for new wrecks which their students may then strip down in the coming season for an appropriate remuneration.

Archaeologists and underwater explorers are almost powerless to do anything about this situation. Plundering of wrecks is illegal in all countries, but only a few countries actually prosecute offenders.

The wrecks off the French coast are "protected" by an edict proclaimed by Jean Baptiste Colbert, the influential minister of Louis XIV in the seventeenth century. But of course it is impossible to oversee all the wrecks along the coast of the Ligurian Sea. Even though the divers in the French Navy, the respected diving clubs of Marseilles and Juan-les Pins, the Club Alpin-Sous-Marin of Cannes, and the divers of the Italian underwater exploration ship *Diano* patrol amphora fields regularly, they often find that amphora fields become empty in the course of a summer. For amphora thieves even work at night, using underwater searchlights on the sea bottom.

A Munich amateur diver described the fate of a wreck in the

following way: "We set out from the Italian island of Giglio in a rubber raft. Our destination was Giannutri, the tiny little neighboring island. We anchored near Punta Scaletta. An ancient marble staircase led from the Tyrrhenian Sea up to the walls and columns of a Roman villa, the estate of a wealthy warrior or senator. This splendid structure was erected over two thousand years ago. . . . We donned our breathing apparatus and dived in, finding a sunken ship in twenty-three fathoms! The sailing vessel had carried amphoras. Piled in rows, they now stuck out of the mud. But our

Cargo of an ancient ship wrecked off the island of Giannutri

S. Köster

greatest discovery was the deck cargo on top of them: plates, dishes, finely glazed Etruscan ceramics. Almost a thousand pieces of the precious containers lay on the bottom, still neatly piled and unbroken! We recovered a few ceramic samples and presented them to an archaeologist: he dated them at the second century B.C. But word of our find traveled fast. When we came back a year later, the wreck had been plundered. Every last piece of the dishes had been carried away by amateur divers, and only a miserable heap of fragments remained."

The one way for the archaeologists to save ancient sunken ships for science would be to raise them immediately after discovering them. But previous excavations underwater have shown that this problem is insoluble. Even if archaeologists were to employ all available forces and financial means, sacrificing progress in land archaeology in favor of underwater work, it would still mean decades of hard work before the known wrecks could be explored. Frédéric Dumas, doubtless the most experienced wreck diver in the world, estimated in 1960 that it would take twenty years to investigate the wrecks known at that time. And every year since 1960 has added numerous new discoveries to the list. The excavations by Grand Congloué took years, admittedly with a few long interruptions, but the refined research methods and techniques developed since then require even more time.

Digging and retrieving in underwater work alone account for an enormous amount of labor. A medium-sized ancient merchant ship was laden with three thousand amphoras. Its wreck presents a mass of about four hundred tons of findings, mixed with at least two hundred tons of sand and mud. In addition, another six hundred tons of sand, mud, and rocks must be removed if a wreck is to be explored with the most modern scientific methods, excavated and brought up. The divers then have to move at least 1,200 tons in a depth of fifteen to twenty fathoms.

But at such depths a good diver can work only ten to fifteen minutes, three times a day. At more than twenty-five fathoms the work becomes so much more tedious and dangerous that so far no one has ever dared to attempt systematic excavations of finds at these depths.

Of the 1,200 tons, only a portion of the mud may be removed with large suction pumps. On land, when the rough digging has been accomplished, the archaeologist reaches for his trowel and finally his brush. The underwater archaeologist has to discontinue use of the large suction pump, which is destructive to some things with its strong suction, and replace it with a smaller pump with less suction, and finally with a spray hose and manual work. The spray of a water hose under water is soft as a brush and carefully washes the mud away from the objects. The most gentle method is fanning with a hand. The frogman uses his flattened hand in such a way as to wash water over an object, wafting away layers of mud without clouding his view. Work by spray hose or hand doesn't move any large masses of mud, but exacting research methods demand that even the tiniest finds be photographed, sketched, and entered in a chart while they are still in position before they can be removed. This photographing, measuring, and sketching underwater, before the excavation is begun and after each phase of the work, costs additional diving time.

Thus the crew of an underwater expedition must include not only archaeologists, conservationists, and experienced and hardy frogmen for the digging and recovery work, but photographers and artists as well, who work underwater in frogman suits under the direction of the archaeologists. Underwater excavations therefore make much greater demands on specialists, technical means, and money than land exploration. Furthermore, Europe has very few archaeologists who are able to get around in swim fins, diving masks, and breathing apparatus. Archaeological work underwater requires perfect health, untiring diving training, and much underwater experience.

For this reason almost all expeditions so far have been remote-controlled by the scholars. The scientists had to wait on board the diving ships until the divers brought them reports and findings. At Grand Congloué an underwater television camera was of some help. It sent impressive pictures up to the receivers on the *Calypso*. This camera had been lent to Cousteau by a British firm along with a few technicians. But generally archaeological institutes are too poor to be able to afford such television setups.

Gradually, underwater explorers are developing more and more highly refined techniques. Along with Grand Congloué, special highlights in this development have been the recovery of wrecks by Albenga, Ile du Levant, and Spargi.

The Successful Fishing Trip of Albenga

Albenga is a small town on the Italian Riviera between Genoa and San Remo. In ancient times the Roman harbor of Album Ingaunum was located here. In 1925, fishermen a nautical mile out from the city set out their nets. All hands on the boat had to help pull them in again. The take was extremely heavy. The men were already exulting over their catch when they noticed that two Roman amphoras had got caught in their net. The fishermen took the amphoras to the city museum along with all the other fragments they pulled in while fishing over that area on other trips.

When Professor Nino Lamboglia heard about them, he attempted without success to talk the Italian government into providing him with the necessary materials to investigate the sea floor on that spot and recover the finds. In those days not even the Italian amateur divers were interested in doing archaeological work underwater, and they refused to help the scholar. Finally Giovanni Quaglia, president of the Genoese Salvage Company Sorima, volunteered his help gratis. Quaglia was an experienced salvage specialist who in 1925 succeeded in recovering 800,000 pounds of gold from the steamer *Egypt*. Quaglia sent the salvage boat *Artiglio II* with equipment and divers to Albenga.

The boat was outfitted with a special grappling crane, which even at great depths could rip steel plates from the hulls of sunken ships, and with an underwater observation chamber from which a man could control the movement of the grappler. This observation chamber was lowered into the sea off Albenga. As it slowly neared the bottom, the man inside excitedly reported seeing hundreds of amphoras in a pile a hundred feet long, which rose a good six feet above the flat sea bottom. Helmeted divers went into the water immediately and brought several of the amphoras up on board. Professor Lamboglia dated the finds around the end of the second and beginning of the first century B.C. Many other amphoras that were scattered were raised with ropes. The major portion of the ship's cargo, however, stood upright on the bottom, cemented together by sea sediment.

The grappler cut into the amphora field with steel teeth, shattering hard sediment and clay vessels. Still, a part of the vessels remained unharmed. In this way 728 amphoras were recovered from twenty fathoms of water in twelve days, and with them came black glazed dishes, wooden remains of the ship, part of the ship's equipment, some of its lead covering, and the remains of three bronze helmets.

A lead wheel with the remains of rope, which was found in the midst of the amphoras, still has scholars puzzled to this day. No similar object dating from antiquity has been found. Did the wheel belong to a pump system to remove water from the ship in case of a leak? Was it a steering wheel for the rudder? These and other possibilities have already been considered by scholars, who can only hope that one of the still untouched wrecks at the bottom of the sea will reveal a similar device in its original position.

Professor Lamboglia kept an eye open for some amphora stoppers, but in vain. Instead he found pine cones stuck in the necks of several of the amphoras. The bottoms of three amphoras were still covered with hazel nuts. Amphoras full of hazel nuts did not need airtight stoppers, so the ancient shippers in Albenga had them stopped up with pine cones, which were cheaper.

The professor's search for stamps or inscriptions on the amphoras was equally in vain. But the forms of the amphoras and dishes soon dated the sinking of the ship between 80 and 60 B.C. The helmets, too, were similar to those worn by Roman soldiers as shown on reliefs of this era. Finally Professor Lamboglia's conclusions were verified by carbon-14 tests. The underwater explorer

James Dugan took a wood splinter from the hull of the wreck to the radiocarbon laboratory in the State Museum of Arizona.

The carbon-14 test developed by Professor Willard F. Libby of the University of Chicago makes it possible to date finds of organic material such as wood, bone, leather, or cloth with some accuracy. This test, which is very useful to archaeologists, is a result of atomic research. It employs a radioactive isotope of carbon, namely, C^{14}, whose radioactive decay proceeds with perfect regularity. After 5,360 years, only half of a given starting quantity of C^{14} still remains. In another 5,360 years the material will have reduced itself to a quarter of the original quantity, and in 53,600 years the radioactive carbon will have reduced itself to one one-thousandth of its original quantity. By measuring the carbon-14 accompanying the normal carbon present in all organic matter, or by measuring its state of decay by means of a geiger counter, the age of any organic substance can be determined within a few hundred years. With the C^{14} test, for example, the age of an ancient sunken ship, often impossible to date otherwise, can be estimated. In the cases of the wrecks by Albenga and Grand Congloué the dates arrived at by other means were verified by carbon-14 tests.

A few years later, when Italian divers again went down to the wreck by Albenga they found that it had not loaded two or three thousand amphoras but at least twice that many. But more important than the finds and the research information gained at Albenga was the experience in the salvage operation. Except for a few thousand amphoras, the steel grappler of the *Artiglio II* left behind a heap of rubble on the sea floor. For that reason such crude methods were never used again in archaeological undertakings. Professors also never needed helmet divers again, for the finds by Albenga inspired Italian amateur divers to go looking for amphora ships themselves, or to help on the professor's expedition as volunteers. Italy also finally acquired a research center, the "Centro Sperimentale de Archeologia Sottomarina," which was founded in Albenga under the direction of Professor Lamboglia. Because the Italian Navy has been lending the institute the corvette *Diano* with a crew every summer since 1959, it has already been able to undertake significant diving expeditions.

It was the French who succeeded in excavating the third significant amphora ship. Frigate captain Philippe Tailliez, the long-time commander on the underwater research group of the French Navy, tackled it in the summer of 1957 near the Ile du Levant by Cape Antibes on the French Riviera.

Dr. Piroux's Secret

Dr. Jacques Piroux of the "Club de la Mer" in Antibes had discovered the wreck in 1948 while on an underwater hunt from his boat. Near the lighthouse *Titan,* he was pursuing a large perch when he found an untouched amphora field at a depth of fourteen fathoms. Piroux hooked his anchor through a handle of one of the amphoras and pulled it up. It took all his strength to get the ancient vessel aboard. It was almost as big as his eight-year-old daughter, who was watching her father from the boat.

The wreck lay somewhat beyond the island, so that a swimmer would not be likely to discover it by chance; and Piroux told only Professor Benoit and a few of his best friends about it. The amphora field remained untouched until Professor Benoit and Philippe Tailliez with several divers cruised up to the Ile du Levant on the research ship *Ingénier-Elie Monnier* of the French Navy. The sloop lowered anchor near the cliffs of the island which face east, a stone's throw from the lighthouse, where the wreck was supposed to lie. Tailliez and three divers got ready and were lowered into the clear water. Slowly they sank deeper, over a bizarre landscape of deep, winding gullies and ravines. Light-colored sand filled one of these valleys. It shone from the bottom like a narrow river that suddenly extends into a sand lake enclosed by rugged rocks.

A dark island grew out of this lake. Algae, sponges, and sea deposits covered it as they did the other rocks. But upon closer inspection the men recognized amphoras, countless vessels, piled closely together, sticking up out of the dark island. Using all their strength, the divers forced their way against the strong water current from rock to rock down past amphora fragments, colorful algae, gorgon and other corals, past sponges and small sea animals, which disappeared into their hiding places, until they reached a narrow gully in the sand sea. Here everything was still. High rocks of fifteen to twenty feet surrounded the sand lake and protected it and the wreck in its middle from the current. No surf or other sound from the surface penetrated to the ancient wreck.

A silvery mackerel, as long as a man's arm, and two perches swam slowly away from the ship's mound and down into the depths of the sand valley. Schools of sardines and rainbow-colored girellas played around the wreck. Between the amphoras bright red scorpaenids waited, bizarre fish with a prehistoric appearance. Moray eels had populated the amphoras, and they stuck their snakelike heads out threateningly.

The divers chose four amphoras out of the uppermost layer of the cargo. The crane on the sloop *Elie-Monnier* brought them up one at a time amid loud cheering from the crew. Professor Benoit was able to date them immediately: the vessels must have been produced in the first century B.C., in the age of Augustus Caesar, judging by their appearance. The professor himself was no diver and therefore had the wreck described to him exactly. He was determined that this wreck would not become the victim of amphora thieves.

Larger and older wrecks had been located since the find at Grand Congloué. But none of the other wrecks was so well preserved. Lucky chance had led the ship into a quiet, protected hollow. Time had turned it into a mound, but the rock walls had protected it from waves and currents. Every nail and oil lamp from the ship would be preserved in the sand lake. Beneath the encrusted amphoras there probably lay more, undamaged and tightly packed just as they had left an ancient harbor. And further down they would find more cargo, ship's equipment, and finally the bottom of the hull. As it later turned out, the divers and Professor Benoit had guessed right.

But there was only one way to save the wreck from plundering by amphora thieves: they would have to explore, excavate, and recover it as quickly as possible.

Tailliez hoped to get the agreement and support of the Navy for this. He had his sloop equipped with a suction pump and returned shortly to the Ile du Levant for a thorough inspection. Tailliez did not begin immediately with the digging, for he had learned from the mistakes made at Grand Congloué. First he himself made the necessary underwater photographs. It was impossible to get the whole wreck on one picture. Therefore he hung at a depth of five fathoms and took several partial pictures that could then be combined later to form a single complete picture. The pictures were like aerial photos taken by land archaeologists with the aid of airplanes. But Tailliez encountered a difficult problem: if the photographer alters his distance from the bottom—or the camera is tipped slightly—then pictures result which can no longer be joined to one another, owing to the varying distances between camera and object, or various angles of photography. Such photo mosaics remind one of a wrinkled patchwork quilt, as the American archaeologist George F. Bass once remarked. Air-reconnaissance pilots have it easier. If a plane is flying at an altitude of 30,000 feet and there are altitude variations of up to 300 feet, they still only amount to one per cent. Besides, these planes are equipped with devices which record each variation exactly, and the pictures can be corrected later on. But the diver has to fight changing currents constantly, and even a slight current can alter his depth by three feet in each direction. Assuming a wreck to be five fathoms below him, that already makes a considerable variation of ten per cent. And Tailliez had none of the air reconnaissance instruments for correction. But he wasn't discouraged. Finally he hit upon a simple solution: he attached a lead plumb to his camera which just touched the wreck while he was photographing and a bubble level to his camera in order to keep it perfectly stable. In this manner he was able to achieve the first usable "aerial photo" of a sunken ancient ship. While Tailliez took pictures, two divers with measures and compass measured the sandy basin surrounded by rock and the ship, and in several dives charted it exactly with soft chalk on a slate of roughened plexiglass.

In the first operation with the suction pump, the purpose was to inspect the wreck. The divers dug a ditch in the sand from the rocks to the wreck. Only later did it become apparent that cross-sections used in land excavations are not functional underwater.

For hours the divers worked in shifts. On the beach, meanwhile, others sorted the first finds: amphora stoppers, bronze ship's nails, wooden remains, water-worn rocks, and mollusks. But it soon became apparent that a boat as light as the *Elie-Monnier* did not offer the right working platform for exploration at the site. In spite of heavy anchoring, it moved around too much in the wind and currents.

So Tailliez went to the Navy docks at Toulon and picked out a flat float lying still and heavy on the water, giving the wind very little surface to blow against. Float 26, as it was simply called, was not needed elsewhere, and Tailliez got permission to use it for his exploration. In the spring of 1955 the float lay in the harbor of Toulon, equipped with suction pumps and compressors. But in France, too, officials work slowly, and by the time he finally got permission for his expedition it was already too late. Tailliez was an active Navy officer, and in the summer of 1955 he had to take command of the French Rhine flotilla, in Koblenz. The wreck became the victim of amphora thieves.

When Tailliez again took up his exploration activities in April, 1957, he inspected the ship closely. The amphora thieves had torn holes into the mound and removed about three hundred amphoras. But the prosecution of two of the plunderers seemed to have scared off others. Between the holes and around the cargo, the sand was untouched, and the second, lower level of amphoras was still intact in the mound. Tailliez now decided to act fast. He went to Toulon, found the float again, had it re-equipped, had the old permits renewed, and rounded up a crew of experienced Navy divers, some of whom had accompanied him on his earlier expeditions.

In early July everything was in order and the expedition put up its tent in a pine grove on the island by the lighthouse *Titan*.

They would have only a summer, not quite three full months, for the excavation. The Navy could not do without Tailliez and his divers for longer than that. In that time the wreck had to be explored and excavated, and the finds had to be raised. And Tailliez didn't even have two dozen men for the work underwater and for the hardly less fatiguing work of cataloguing, sketching, preserving, and stowing the finds on board the boat, which was constantly heated by the sun and shaken by the sea and clattering compressors. The men soon saw that they had not gone on an underwater vacation, but were involved in a kind of peaceful sea battle which had to be fought day in, day out, against the sea and the scorching sun. Only an ingenious work schedule and iron discipline in diving could lead to victory, to a completion of the exploration and recovery work.

The eight-hour workday for the men began at seven in the morning. While some were busy getting the old compressors going, the first ones to dive made themselves ready. The day's work had been laid out the night before. Each man knew what he had to do and on what part of the wreck he was to work. Two or three twenty-eight-minute periods under water per man per day were safe, according to Tailliez's calculations. If a diver overstayed his time a rifle shot reminded him to surface. Slowly the divers removed sand and mud with the suction pump. But before a find could be removed from its original position, it first had to be measured. For this purpose Tailliez had a measuring tape stretched from one end of the rock hollow to the other, passing over the sunken ship from bow to stern. The divers measured the position of single pieces with respect to the longitudinal axis of the ship, and reported the results of their measurements to the excavation leader on board the float, where they were entered on a chart.

It was with great enthusiasm that the Navy frogmen struggled to work with archaeological methods. Of course their enthusiasm could not replace the archaeologist, who would have investigated each find more thoroughly before removing it, and would immediately have drawn conclusions from its location. But there were no archaeologists who were willing to descend to the floor of the sea. Tailliez and his men had to expect the destruction of an occasional unapparent but important detail, and be happy that they were at least rescuing the major portion of the wreck from amphora thieves.

Tirelessly, Tailliez himself went time and again to the bottom to take photographs and movies. Meanwhile some of the divers were busy placing the freed amphoras along the rock wall. To raise hundreds of amphoras would have taken too long. They would be taken up later in a basket. But the divers found not only amphoras. All sizes of copper nails lay in the mud, along with Campanian dishes, which apparently belonged in the ship's galley, and many other small finds. Professor Benoit, who had taken over the scientific evaluation of the findings, gave special attention to a modest little oil lamp of red clay. A similar oil lamp had aided in dating the wreck by Mahdia, and the professor saw immediately that this lamp, too, was typical for a very specific time: the first years of the reign of Augustus Caesar. That jibed well with the indications provided by the amphoras and the Campanian dishes. Hundreds of amphoras were ready for removal when work on them was begun on July 31, 1957. They were tall, slender vessels with long necks of two kinds. Each amphora was slightly different. Whereas the uniform amphoras of Anthéor, Grand Congloué, and Albenga had been formed by slaves in factories, these were shaped in the hands of individual potters in small workshops. Some of them were still unopened, but the sea had destroyed the caulking material of volcanic earth and filled the amphoras with sand, mud, and water. The vessels weighed almost a hundred pounds each, with their thick clay walls and their contents of rubble and mud. The divers loaded each basket with sixteen of them. Shining brown, red, and white, they broke through the surface. Two men pulled them out of the basket, which was then sent back down.

Divers who were not busy on the bottom went to work cleaning the amphoras and emptying their muddy contents—and sometimes also inhabitants—out onto the deck of the float. These contents were carefully searched through for finds, and then thrown back into the water.

The first unopened amphoras came on board. The men emptied them out, and saw, besides sand and mud, some brown stuff pour out onto the deck. It was mixed with fibers and chunks and turned out to be fish bones, scales, and vertebrae from large fish. Some divers with good noses thought they detected the odor of olive oil. An analysis of the fish remains in a laboratory in Marseilles determined that the ship had carried preserved fish: bonitos, a kind of tuna fish in olive oil. There were at least a hundred tons on board.

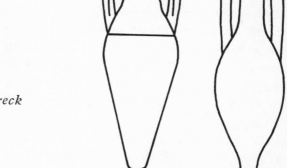

Amphoras from the wreck off the Ile du Levant

Soon so many amphoras had been raised and cleaned that Tailliez was able to send a ship load of them to the marine museum in Toulon.

Impatiently, Tailliez followed the removal of the amphora mound. For he anticipated making an even more important discovery beneath the cargo, in the lower part of the ship itself. The ship appeared to have settled undamaged onto its keel.

By July 16, 1957, the divers had discovered a piece of wood. It probably had been part of the stern of the ship. The wood had become soft, but it had retained its shape well.

Later, more dark wood became visible beneath the amphoras.

On the third of August the suction pump exposed three ship's ribs. Tailliez had the suction pump replaced by one with less suction, in order not to damage the soft wood while removing the rest of the sand and mud from the keel, ribs, and remains of the planking. Only the upper ends of the ribs had been eaten by sea animals; the lower ends were still securely fastened to the keel on the bottom. The keel and ribs resembled a huge fish skeleton.

Even so, the find was a scientific sensation. It was the first time that the sea had given up the perfectly preserved keel of an ancient sailing ship complete with ribs. Tailliez had the parts of the ship measured exactly, and he filmed and photographed them from all sides. From this well-preserved ship's skeleton archaeologists would be able to draw many conclusions regarding the size and construction of the ancient sailing vessel. Tailliez himself could already determine the dimensions pretty closely just from the measurements. The ship must have measured 75 or 80 feet from bow to stern. It was smaller than the wreck at Grand Congloué and therefore had a cargo of only around three thousand amphoras. According to what we know today, a cargo capacity of three thousand amphoras must have been about average for a merchant ship in ancient times.

To the great disappointment of the scientists, it was impossible to raise the ship's skeleton in a single piece. The soft ribs and the keel would have fallen to pieces in the process. The divers carefully dismembered the skeleton, sawed the keel in half, and reinforced the fragile pieces with boards and beams. A special transport vessel from Toulon loaded the many tons of remains from the ancient ship.

In Toulon they didn't know what to do next. While they knew how to preserve wood that had lain in fresh or only slightly salty water, archaeologists and chemists are still experimenting today on preservatives for wood that has lain in the sea thousands of years. As soon as the wood begins to dry in the air, it starts to shrivel up. Professor Benoit suggested wrapping the pieces in wet cloth and letting them dry very slowly in crates of sawdust. By this method the wood retained at least its approximate shape. In the first days of September, 1957, the expedition was finally over. It had taken seventy days. Exhausted, the men took down their tent in the pine grove near the lighthouse *Titan*. Many of them were suffering from boils, which often resulted from too long and strenuous diving activity. But they were all happy; by their untiring efforts they had not only recovered huge quantities of material in a very short time, but they had also accomplished some respectable research in underwater archaeology.

Techniques of Recovery from the Sea Floor

No less admirable than the achievements of the divers in the explorations of Grand Congloué, Albenga, and the Ile du Levant is the scientific achievement of Professors Benoit and Lamboglia and a few other scholars who dedicate themselves to underwater archaeology. Besides the huge quantities of finds from the large, official expeditions, a steadily growing stream of discoveries made by amateur divers and fishermen has been flowing into the research labs of scientific institutes. The archives are filled with reports, photos, drawings, and charts. This material must be thoroughly studied and evaluated before the findings can be seen in their proper place in the still incomplete mosaic of ancient and early sea travel and commercial life. A number of scholars work hard on these problems.

Whereas a few decades ago archaeology was primarily concerned with works of ancient art, today it attaches much importance to the exploration of the economic life and especially the sea traffic and trade of the ancient peoples. Archaeologists have found that these studies reveal a great deal of knowledge regarding the development of ancient culture and civilization, religion, and even of art and philosophy. In particular the Mediterranean Sea connected its peoples more than it separated them. Not only was the Graeco-Roman way of life carried to all parts of the Mediterranean world by ship, but all known superstitions and religions of the time up to the teachings of Christ came to Rome on ships. But ancient writers rarely wrote about matters of everyday life such as trade or seafaring. Everything connected with work in those days was considered appropriate for slaves and the lower class and not worthy of written documentation. The free citizen dedicated himself to sport and battle, art and politics. Therefore archaeologists are generally restricted to rather meager finds from the earth for their information in these matters. But the sea, on the other hand, supplies a wealth of material.

The amphoras, those that have been present, at least in fragments, at every underwater research site so far, are considered the most important pieces in the mosaic picture of ancient sea travel. They played a role in the daily life and trade of the ancient peoples for thousands of years.

Amphoras were first made in prehistory. The oldest ones known, which were formed in Canaan thousands of years ago, were used chiefly for carrying water from the well. Their distinctive beetlike shape made them fit well onto pack saddles. Even the point had a use. It gave the vessels additional strength. They did not break so

Amphoras recovered from ancient wrecks

Freddy Knorr

easily when they were set down hard on the ground. In later developments of the amphora the pointed end doubtless also had its utilitarian purposes. Along many coasts, crude carts were used instead of pack animals, as is still the case in southern Spain. These carts had bottoms of woven reeds. The amphoras were placed in them with the points imbedded in the reeds and were thus suspended in a padding which prevented them from striking together even on the roughest roads and paths. In sea trade the form proved even more practical. What good is a flat surface when the ship is tossing in a storm? The amphoras were stuck into precisely cut holes in special racks. Stacked close together as they were, not even the severest storm could move them.

Sea trade became very important around 1500 B.C., at the latest—probably even earlier. It enriched the Minoans on Crete, and brought a high standard of living to the Mycenaean rulers of Greece and to countless cities in Asia Minor, Italy, Africa, and the western Mediterranean. Besides metal, the main item of trade in the early times was wine. For more than a thousand years it remained one of the most important trade items, until the Romans started making their own wine in the northernmost provinces of their empire. The wine was spiced with honey, aloe, thyme, and bay; resin was added as a preservative, then it was thickened to a syrupy liquid, and transported in amphoras sealed with a special clay. Some of this tradition of wine processing has been retained down to the present time: Greek *retsina* is still made in a similar manner. But the ancient wine drinkers mixed the drink in a bowl with water, thus producing several containers of drinking wine from one amphora of wine extract.

At the time of Greek colonization in the interior of Gaul, a slave is supposed to have been valued at one amphora containing twenty or thirty liters of wine syrup. This ancient report is credible, for as a result of the countless wars among the princes of Gaul there was a surplus of slaves. By contrast, delicious wine from Delos and the Greek homeland was rare, for on the average, only three out of four merchant ships ever reached their destination.

With the expansion of trade, amphoras spread throughout the

entire Mediterranean area. Phoenicians, Etruscans, and Romans produced these handy vessels and used them in increasing quantities for transporting oil, grain, preserved meat, fish in oil or salted, vegetables, honey. Toward the end of their culture, the Greeks began importing luxury items from the Orient, as did the Romans toward the end of the Republic. Soon large quantities of preserved fruits, expensive perfumes, textiles from all parts of the ancient world, silks from China, and amber from the Baltic were sailed across the Mediterranean.

Amphoras followed the development of ancient cultures. Decades ago the German scholars Dressel and Leschke concerned themselves with exacting studies of their forms, their structure, and the composition of their clay. The result of Dressel's work was the extensive *Corpus latinorum inscriptorum*, whose tables have been expanded in the light of underwater discoveries of recent years. Dressel did not have access to well-preserved amphoras in large quantities, but had to struggle with countless fragments from the rubbish of Rome. Thanks to the work of Dressel and those who followed him, it is today possible to determine quickly the origin and age of almost all newly discovered amphoras.

Some trade customs that developed in classical antiquity made the work of the archaeologists easier. Prominent wine growers or dealers had begun to cork the amphoras with stoppers bearing the marks of their firms. In this way, wine became one of the first brand-name products in the world. Even then there were wine counterfeiters. Archaeologists discovered in southern France— in the harbor of Arles—amphora stoppers which, judging by the materials used, had been produced there but bore imitations of well-known wine trademarks. On some amphoras, brush and ink markings indicated the names of the consuls who had been in office the year the wine had been bottled, the names of the exporters, the loading weight, and the weight upon arrival. Occasionally an "R" followed the weight figures: the sign of a slave who had tested the weight and found it correct—"recte." Such marks were found on numerous amphoras by Grand Congloué.

Grand Congloué was not the first time that marks on amphora stoppers led to noteworthy conclusions. Divers at the wreck by Anthéor had taken stoppers of pozzuolana to Professor Benoit. The type of volcanic earth immediately pointed to southern Italy. The inscription was Oscan, an orthographic sys-

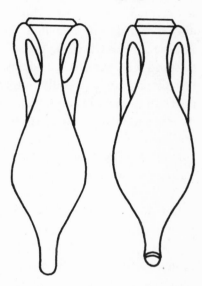

Amphoras from the ship sunk off D'Agay Anthéor

tem that goes from right to left like Hebrew. The writing specialist Jacques Heurgon deciphered: Caius Lassius and Marcus Lassius. These names said a great deal. Archaeologists are well acquainted with the powerful Lassius family who lived in Campania and kept vineyards on the slope of Vesuvius and the hills of Sorrento in the first century B.C. Although it was strange that the Lassii should write their names on the vessels in Oscan, at a time when Campania had long been under Roman rule and Roman writing had replaced Oscan, one explanation may be that the familiar, typical writing was supposed to assure the purchasers that they were really getting precious wine from the sunny slopes of Vesuvius.

Evaluation of clay items found on the sea floor must be conducted very carefully. In some places along the Mediterranean coast the bottom is literally covered with fragments of ancient clay vessels. The manner in which the pieces are strewn and their various origins usually tell the specialist immediately that he has not discovered the site of a wreck but an ancient anchoring place. These sites lie on flat banks at sea or in protected bays, where ancient seafarers waited at anchor until the dawn of the new day or until a storm had ended. Often they stopped to carry on trade with small coastal settlements. Objects probably fell overboard during transfer to a smaller boat, or the ship's cook threw broken dishes into the water, or the sailors lightened the ship's load in order to stand a better chance against storms and currents. Such anchoring places are especially interesting to archaeologists, for sometimes they can reveal more about ancient sea trade than a wreck. These anchoring places were passed on from one seagoing generation to the next, and were generally used for centuries. Therefore every clay fragment removed by a souvenir hunter can mean a serious loss to archaeologists.

Another discovery was made by the Spanish officer and underwater explorer Delgado. He was curious about the many amphoras, all with broken bottoms which lay in the sea by Cartagena, not far from Barcelona. When he had entered the locations of a large quantity of these amphoras on a sea map and connected them with lines, he found that they produced raylike lines from all directions, converging at the harbor of Cartagena. He concluded that these amphoras were offerings to Poseidon. The sailors on ships arriving along the various shipping lanes to Cartagena had broken them open and dropped them into the sea so that their contents could mix with the water of the Mediterranean.

At first, science was rather puzzled by another sort of find that appeared in almost every wreck: roofing tiles.

But finally frescoes in the ruins of ancient buildings in Ostia, the ancient seaport of Rome, cleared up this problem. The frescoes show ships whose captains' cabins are roofed with tile. Of course, tiles and stone building blocks were also sometimes the cargo of a ship. French divers discovered several freight loads of ancient tile along the bottom of the Riviera.

The legendary "millstones" found in the shallow coastal water off St. Tropez are probably sunken ancient building blocks which were intended for the reconstruction of the monumental Roman temple of Narbonne, destroyed in the city fire of A.D. 149 and no longer extant. And the noted German underwater archaeologist, Gerhard Kapitän, with German and English divers, investigated colossal marble blocks along the eastern coast of Sicily, which came from ancient ships that had sunk near the Isola delle Correnti, near Marzamemi, and at Cape Taormina.

The finds of ship's parts that might indicate type and size of the sunken vessel are usually rare: ship's nails, small pieces of bronze, lead, and wood.

Anchor remains are found at nearly all wreck sites. They are massive pieces of lead, almost always weighing several hundred pounds. Archaeologists have registered chunks of almost a thousand pounds, and one huge one found near Cartagena weighed 1,570 pounds. This anchor must have been lost by an unusually large ship. The lead in the Greek and Roman anchors has endured the millennia underwater so well that sponge divers along the Turkish coast rarely report anchor finds to the authorities, but melt them down instead and sell the scrap. By contrast, the wooden parts of these anchors rarely survive in more than fragments. Therefore much research was necessary before scholars figured out how ancient shipbuilders had constructed the anchors for their vessels. The anchors themselves were made of wood and tied to thick ropes. The use of iron anchor chains was first introduced by Caesar's soldiers during the English campaign in 56 B.C., when they saw such chains being used by Breton seamen. We know this from Caesar himself who notes in his work *De Bello Gallico:* "The Veneti [a Breton tribe] tied their anchors with iron chains instead of with ropes."

In order to get these wooden anchors to sink and dig into the ground, ancient shipbuilders had to weight them with heavy pieces of lead.

Ancient anchors of iron are seldom found. Iron doesn't hold up long underwater. But some iron objects were covered with thick coatings of limestone and schist soon after sinking. While the iron decomposed rapidly, the encrustations remained intact. Their form resembled roughly that of the object they had once covered. If

Anchor parts from an ancient Roman wreck

they are sawn apart carefully, two halves of a form are apparent. A plaster casting then exhibits the original form of the object. The diving pioneer Georges Barnier discovered encrustrations in sediment which had collected around an ax in his recovery work on the wreck of Anthéor. When encrustations resembling anchors were found near a Roman wreck in 1956 near La Ciotat in southern France, the men remembered the ax of Anthéor. Instead, the encrustations formed the mold of a Roman iron anchor.

Reconstruction of a Roman anchor made of lead and wood

Divers along the Riviera have also found stones, shaped by human hands and provided with holes. These are stone anchors which were used for two thousand years in the Mediterranean area, until around 700 B.C., when it became more common to make anchors of lead and wood. In recent years stone anchors or anchors of highly varied forms have been found, mainly along the coast of the eastern Mediterranean. It took a long time before the original purpose of these strange-looking stones was discovered. Isolated finds, which had been made before underwater archaeology became a science, landed in museums as "cult stones." But the numerous finds of such stones with holes in them on ancient anchoring grounds have clearly shown that they served as anchors. The purpose of the holes and the forms of the stone was explained when the ancient stone anchors were compared with the equipment of native fishermen along various Mediterranean coastal areas. The old stone anchors usually were in the shape of a triangle with three holes. Clearly the upper hole was where the rope was fastened. But what were the lower holes for? The answer was provided by the stone anchors still used today by men in the Spanish Balearic Islands for anchoring their nets; they resemble the ancient ones in every detail. Through the lower holes were shoved pointed sticks which drove themselves into the sea floor.

Like amphoras, anchor finds provide extensive information about ancient sea travel. The number and size of the anchors, lead or stone, can indicate the size of the ships and the one-time prevalence of ship traffic. The types of particular anchors, on the other hand, indicate to scholars when the anchor and ship were constructed.

Rarely do more than fragments of the keel, ribs, and bottom planking remain from the hulls of ships. Yet in spite of this, science has been able to gain significant clues to the appearance of ancient merchant vessels. Before archaeology began underwater research, we had only a very vague picture of these ships, provided by ancient depictions, mosaics, frescoes, or reliefs. The pictures usually show sailboats and galleys stylized almost beyond recognition. Underwater finds so far have not given us a complete picture. Not only is the poor condition of the wrecks responsible but the still inadequate research methods used underwater. The French diving pioneer Frédéric Dumas therefore developed new methods, by which the fate and approximate size of ancient wrecks could be determined from ship mounds and the exact appearance of the ships.

Underwater explorers prior to the "Dumas method" always began with sample diggings. They succeeded a few times in digging cross sections through ancient wrecks, but they never succeeded in determining the structure of the entire wreck mound on the basis of cross sections which change every few inches. Yet only the knowledge of the overall structure of the mound and the location of all finds can give scientists a basis from which to calculate the size and appearance of the ancient ship. The use of traditional exploratory methods is futile because of the unique problems posed by the underwater world—especially the apparently altered weight of finds, which may be washed out of place by light wave action.

Cutting narrow, vertical trenches in a wreck mound proved nearly impossible. As in land excavations in loose, dry sand, the walls would cave in immediately, forming a funnel-shaped cavity with a large opening. Just a small sample digging suffices to turn an organically formed wreck mound into an unrecognizable heap.

Underwater archaeologists using the method developed by Dumas dispense with the sample diggings. They begin their work with a thorough investigation of the wreck mound. It is charted and carefully searched over for single, small finds which are not immediately removed, but first entered on the exact-location chart. As an aid in this procedure, a grid square is laid over the mound by divers, if the expedition is not using the sounding method devised by Dumas.

The French diving pioneer worked on the problem of measuring exactly the structure of a wreck mound for a long time. Then he hit upon a simple aid, used by geologists for a long time: a sounding device. Such a sounder is in principle nothing other than a steel pipe bored into the ground, pulled back out, and laid open. The geologist now has the exact earth layers before him and can determine the kind of layers and their actual thickness.

Dumas concluded that one would only need to bore into the mound at regular intervals. The excavation would begin only after the exact location of the wooden remains and the cargo, and therefore the extent of the wreck and its load, had been determined by specialists on the basis of the soundings and a thorough study of their research. Divers would dig a deep, wide trench around the wreck and peel the mound out of its surroundings. As the mound became more and more separated from the sea floor, the size and shape of the ship would become apparent. Finally the excavation of the mound itself could begin. The divers would remove one layer after the other.

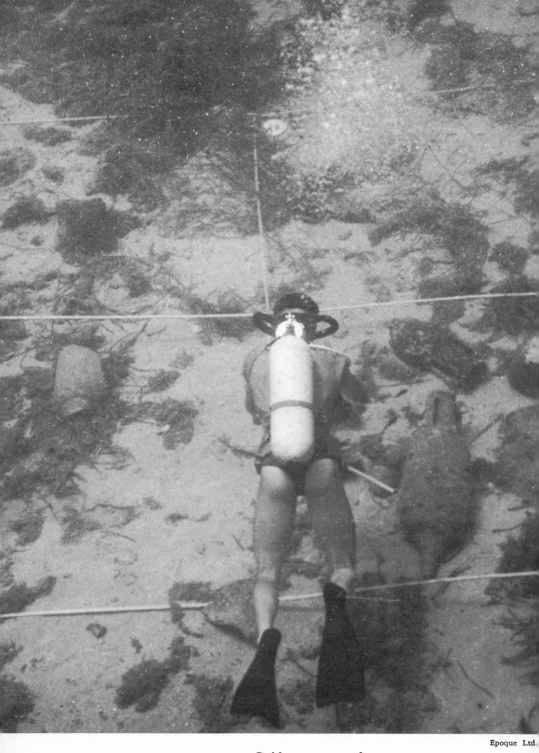

Grid over a wreck

But as promising as Dumas' methods seemed to be, they have not met with success along the coasts of the western Mediterranean owing to the lack of the enormous sums of money necessary to finance them. An expedition from the University of Pennsylvania, however, has used Dumas' ideas along with a few additional inventions and improvements in the underwater excavations by Yassi Ada on the Turkish Mediterranean coast.

While Dumas was developing his new methods, the Italian Professor Nino Lamboglia was busy making a thorough study of the problems of underwater archaeology, and the result of his work was a method not unlike that of Dumas, although he had to dispense with many necessary technical aids owing to limited funds.

The Find at Spargi. The Story of "Luigi"

A chance to use Professor Lamboglia's method came in the fall of 1957 when Italian amateur divers discovered the wreck at Spargi. The site promised more than any wreck discovered previously. For the discovery of this wreck, science owes thanks to the Navy diver Lazzarino Mazza, who was supposed to repair the anchoring of a buoy on a reef off Corsica.

Spargi is one of the tiny islands around La Maddalena in the Strait of Bonifacio between Sardinia and Corsica. Directly off the island, at a depth of eight to ten fathoms, lies the sand bank of Secca Corsara, out of which a confusion of rocks protrude, one of them almost at the surface. Today a light buoy warns ships of this dangerous place.

The discovery of the wreck of Spargi is associated with this light buoy. When in 1939 a severe storm damaged the anchor cable and threatened to wash the buoy away, the naval command in La Maddalena commissioned the diver Mazza with the job of its repair. Mazza, a helmet diver, had hardly touched bottom when he shouted excitedly into the telephone that there were amphoras down there, thousands of them.

On board the diving ship his report produced incredulous astonishment. But it proved true. Mazza brought up ten amphoras in all, but later, when he wanted to recover more of the ancient vessels, the amphora field seemed to have disappeared. In spite of long searching, he didn't find the spot again. He was sure it lay at twenty fathoms. Navy divers combed the sea at a depth of fifteen or twenty fathoms, and fishermen tried their luck with nets, but the amphora field remained lost—fortunately for science.

The inhabitants of the islands, however, did not forget the story of the amphora treasure on the bottom of the sea. The journalist Gianni Roghi heard it from them while on vacation there. Roghi was an avid amateur diver, and he decided to look into the matter with some of his friends. On September 1, 1957, he and four diving comrades set out in a small boat from Sestri Levante and soon reached the Secca Corsara. The agile frogmen needed no longer than an hour to find the amphora field, after the helmet divers had searched for so long. The sixteen-year-old Rudolfo Riva, the youngest of the group, discovered it in nine fathoms of water. Lazarina Mazza had erred in his judgment of the depth, thereby sending his colleagues from the fleet on a wild goose chase. But his words "thousands of amphoras" were scarcely exaggerated. Before Roghi and his friends an amphora field of fifty to sixty feet in length extended into the thick, green meadows of algae.

Beneath the uppermost layer of closely packed amphoras, still more could be detected. Initial estimates were placed at two thousand amphoras. Later investigations raised the figure to three thousand.

Only the top layer of vessels seemed to have become disordered in the sinking of the ship. The next layer was still neatly packed, and as Roghi reached between a couple of amphoras with his arm, he felt wood—wood from the ship's side!

The ancient sailing ship had run onto the most dangerous protruding rock of the Secca Corsara and sunk slowly at a slant to the bottom. Single amphoras that had fallen to the bottom as it descended showed the path it followed. Dr. Roghi and his friends found them while investigating the amphora field. About a hundred yards beyond the rock the ship landed on the bottom, keel down, listing somewhat. The place seems to have been favorable —free of destructive bottom currents, and covered with loose sand into which the keel and lower portions of the hull were pressed by the weight of the wreck. Sand had further covered the sailing ship, thereby protecting it from the gnawing of shipworms and microorganisms.

The divers carefully removed a few of each of the two types of amphoras of which the cargo consisted, and a few plates and bowls they found on the east end of the amphora field. These dishes seemed to come from the ship's galley and thereby gave an initial indication of how the ship lay.

The finds, together with exact descriptions of the site and underwater photographs, were placed before Professors Lamboglia and Miro Mirabella, who is the government overseer over ancient remains of Lombardy and Liguria. Both scholars agreed that the wreck could be dated at 100 or 120 B.C. They considered the discovery very significant. Never before had anyone discovered such a well-preserved cargo, still in its original position and under such favorable conditions, along the Italian coast. The minimal depth of nine fathoms would permit extensive explorations without much danger. In particular Dr. Roghi's report of feeling wood under the first layer of amphoras interested the archaeologists. Had they finally struck the preserved hull of an ancient ship? Professor Lamboglia and Dr. Roghi began immediately to prepare an expedition, to which Mirabella gladly granted permission. Roghi won over his publisher, Angelo Rizzoli, the editor of the illustrated magazine *L'Europeo*, to the project, as well as some diving enthusiasts from Milan who volunteered their help. In seven months the expedition was equipped. The expedition ship, the twenty-eight-ton *Medusa*, lay ready. On April 23, 1958, they sailed from La Maddalena to Secca Corsara.

This time the site of the ancient freighter was not hard to find. Ships of the Italian Navy had marked the place with buoys, alongside which the expedition ship was able to moor and hold its place above the amphora field even in rough weather. A few divers began immediately to stretch a net of plastic cords over the wreck.

It was fastened to iron pegs hammered into the sea floor. This net was to serve as a system of coordinates. Yellow cords formed squares of two meters to a side, while black cords divided these into four smaller squares. Each square on the net had a number corresponding to one on a chart of coordinates, which was drawn to scale 1:20.

While the other divers busied themselves removing sea grass and mud from the area, Dr. Roghi began with the underwater photographs. He had to photograph each square individually from a height of four meters, and then groups of four squares from a height of eight meters. One of Professor Lamboglia's assistants on board the *Medusa* then drew in the exact position of each amphora onto the chart on the basis of the photographs.

Before the divers could begin digging, all the finds had to be numbered on the sea bottom and on the chart, so that later, after the pieces had been raised and inspected, it would still be possible to know from what part of the wreck mound they had come.

The divers therefore tied small, bright plastic number tags around the necks of the amphoras with wire. But one day something strange happened. Overnight a whole row of these tags disappeared.

The diver Pederzini reported with a concerned expression that the wires were still there, but there was no sign of the tags. What had happened?

The men looked at each other helplessly until Dr. Roghi suddenly shouted cheerily: "Luigi! That was Luigi!" Roghi had noticed that a few days before, in a similarly mysterious manner, a net bag of flash bulbs had disappeared from the place he had put it on the bottom. When he looked around, he had caught a glimpse of Luigi disappearing into an amphora. He had pulled him gently back out and recovered the bag of flash bulbs from him. Luigi was the largest of all the cuttlefish that inhabited the wreck. At the beginning of the expedition he shied quickly away from the divers when he sighted them in his vicinity, but soon he became friendly. The diver Pontiroli went immediately to the bottom and the reluctant Luigi again had to leave his home. And sure enough—Luigi, who like all cuttlefish loved shiny things, was sitting on the number tags. He was a bit hurt as he watched Pontiroli take away his loot. Finally the divers gave him a few burned-out flash bulbs, which reconciled him.

When the numbering was completed, they were able to begin with the much anticipated digging. The men put the suction pump to work on the amphora field. Its trunk quickly ate up sand, mud, and sea deposits, exposing one surprising find after the other.

Once they discovered a salve jar in the stern of the ship. It was of blue-green glass, decorated with gold, and so finely formed that it fit in the palm of the hand. Another time divers brought ship's dishes from the stern of the wreck to the *Medusa*. When Dr. Roghi wanted to separate them from one another, he found that they were stuck. But the adhesive was neither sand nor mud. It was the remains of a meal, thousands of years old!

The stern of the wreck produced even greater treasures. Here the men discovered the ship's altar. First they found the pediment of a slender Ionic column, then an artistically wrought bronze lamp, and underneath, the heavy altar stone of Carrara marble. Stone borers had defaced it but it was still recognizable. Professor Lamboglia succeeded in reconstructing the small ship's temple, while men on the bottom dug in the bow of the wreck and made another surprising find: Campanian dishes and cups, stacked together as they had left the factory over two thousand years ago. The professor immediately classified them as being dishes of the rare type B. The dates of the ceramics agreed with that of the amphoras, so the ship had sunk almost certainly between 120 and 100 B.C., laden with Campanian ceramic goods which had been stored forward, and with three thousand amphoras of wine and oil amidships.

In the stern, on the other hand, were located the captain's cabin, the ship's temple, and maybe a few cabins for passengers.

Then the removal of the first layer of amphoras began. They were taken up four at a time in a basket. Slowly, portions of the ship's hull became visible. Already on the third day of the expedition, the diver Ferandi had felt a piece of wood through a hole at the edge of the amphora field; he beckoned to Dr. Roghi, who pulled off his glove, reached into the dark opening, and detected a board wall with his fingers.

Now more and more of the boards of the bow came into view, strong ribs and thick planks covered with white, glittering lead, high in silver content. With reduced suction—in order not to damage the ship's hull—the men worked on. Section after section was cleared, until the divers could construct a plain picture of the size and appearance of the ship. The twenty-eight-ton *Medusa* looked like a nutshell compared to the ancient freighter with its thirty-meter length and its cargo capacity of between 150 and 200 tons. The divers would have been more than glad to follow the board sides into the deeper layers of sand and expose the hull in its entirety. But the time and funds of the expedition were used up, and furthermore the divers could have done nothing else than turn the hull over to shipworm by freeing it of the protective sand.

Whereas wreck after wreck has been found along the coast of Italy, France, and Spain, only occasionally has word of a significant wreck come from the coast of the eastern Mediterranean. For the most part they remain unexplored, for there are but few amateur divers there. But about three years ago news came from the coast of Anatolia which excited even the specialists: the young American journalist Peter Throckmorton had in a short time discovered almost forty sunken ships of the period 1200 B.C. to A.D. 1700.

IV

On the Trail of Odysseus

Peter Throckmorton started. Hadn't somebody mentioned *bakir*, the Turkish word for copper? The sponge diver Kemâl Aras and a steamship captain from Istanbul were discussing finds made on the sea bottom, and Throckmorton had only followed the conversation sleepily—until he was jolted by the word *bakir*. He turned to his friend, the amateur diver Mustafa Kapkin, and asked what they had said. Mustafa Kapkin replied that Kemâl had discovered a few pieces of bronze stuck to rock.

Throckmorton then asked Kemâl, who told him he had found objects of bronze on the bottom of the sea while hunting sponges off Cape Gelidonia on the Anatolian coast the year before. He had seen large, flat metal bars, all stuck tight to the rocks, in about fifteen fathoms.

Amca Seytan, one of the crew of the diving boat, had raised a few of the pieces and sold them as scrap metal, Throckmorton was told. But salvage operations would hardly pay, Kemâl said, for metal in that condition brought a low price. For a moment Throckmorton lost interest in the matter. They were probably ingots from a merchant ship of the eighteenth or nineteenth century, and therefore of little significance. Yet a detail in the story bothered him.

Throckmorton had many years of experience as a salvage diver and had often pulled copper two or three hundred years old out of the sea. He knew that the sea needs thousands of years to destroy copper and bronze. Only once, in a museum, had he seen badly corroded bronze from the sea. It was a bronze apparatus from ancient times recovered from the Mediterranean.

That night he lay awake for a long time in his hotel room in the sponge-diving village of Bodrum on the Anatolian coast. He thought more about the ingots. Somewhere he had read that seamen of the Bronze Age had traded with flat bars, more than a thousand years before Christ.

Early the next morning Throckmorton flipped through his books and found a picture which was a reproduction of a painting from an Egyptian grave from the period around 1500 B.C. This painting depicted Cretans offering tribute to a Pharaoh—and underneath them were flat bronze ingots.

Thus begins the story of the discovery of the oldest high-seas sailing vessel known to man. Peter Throckmorton found it when he followed the directions given to him by the sponge diver Kemâl Aras.

The young American journalist already had a great deal of experience. Near the death reef of Yassi Ada, he had found eighteen shipwrecks.

The story of the reef begins with the discovery of Demeter of Izmir (Smyrna) by the diver Amca Ahmed Seytan of Bodrum. Amca Seytan is considered unique among the sponge divers of Bodrum, for he is already over fifty years old, has been diving for almost forty years, and has survived countless shipwrecks and diving accidents without harm. At fifty most divers are usually at rest beneath simple wooden crosses, or are at least partly lame. But Amca Ahmed is one of the most active divers in the town. The villagers are sure he is in league with the devil, which is why he received his not ill-intended nickname "Seytan."

In 1953 Amca Seytan came upon the over life-size bronze statue of Demeter. He took it to Bodrum, where it was propped up on the beach with a block of wood. When the Turkish newspapers reported on the find, Professor Bean, a philologist of ancient languages at the University of Istanbul went immediately to the sponge-fishing village. After a four day trip through Anatolia, the bus lurched into the village. The sponge divers led the professor to the beach where he saw the bronze image of a goddess of a rare and austere beauty. Seytan had only found the upper three-foot section of the seated goddess, but the sea had preserved it in excellent condition. The metal was free of patina. Light encrustations covered the clothing of the statue, but the face was flawless, with a sad countenance partially covered by a veil. The semi-precious stone eyes had been lost, but that only deepened the peaceful, distant gaze of the goddess. Even if she cannot compare to the triumphant, superhuman godheads of Olympus, the statue can still be classified among the great works produced by the earth cults of the earliest peoples of Greece and Asia Minor.

Professor Bean remembered a marble statue in the British Museum in London which had been excavated by Cnidus in the vicinity. It is a similarly veiled sorrowing goddess—the earth goddess Demeter, goddess of fertility, of agriculture, of marriage, and culture. The sorrow is for her daughter Persephone who has been led away to Hades.

The professor reflected on the fact that this goddess had been worshipped as the giver of eternal life in the secretive Elysian mystery rites, and that still today remains of the Demeter cult survive in many parts of Anatolia in annual harvest feasts of thanksgiving.

Finally the bronze statue was taken to the museum of Smyrna. There it was seen by the young American journalist Peter Throckmorton when he, almost accidentally, came to Anatolia some years later in 1958.

Throckmorton had begun his career as a salvage diver in the Pacific. Later he became a newspaper photographer—a war correspondent in Korea—traveled in India for a while, and finally drove an old jeep from Afghanistan to Turkey. There he not only saw the impressive Demeter, but he also met with Mustafa Kapkin and other divers of the small but enthusiastic "Kurbaga Adamlar

Kulubu," the frogmen club of Smyrna. These divers told Throckmorton the story of Demeter and spoke of the remains of a
few other wrecks they had found in their free time.

Peter Throckmorton was interested and decided to search on
his own. Mustafa Kapkin declared himself ready to accompany
Throckmorton and suggested they ask the advice of the Bodrum
sponge divers. With frogmen's equipment and a small compressor
they set out for Bodrum.

Bodrum stands exactly over the ancient site of Halicarnassus.
Surely a few ancient ships had sunk off the city, for the whole of
Anatolia has an ancient history. Thousands of years before
Christ tribes built cities and city-states on the ground of modern
Turkey—cities of which we know scarcely anything today. Later
the Hittites ruled over Anatolia, the Trojan War was fought there,
and many a powerful empire was founded. When Halicarnassus flourished, the Persians already ruled over it, a mixture of
tribes, and numerous Greek cities. Halicarnassus nevertheless became famous because of its important citizen Herodotus, the
father of written history, and the tomb of the Persian Satrap Mau-
solus, who ruled the surrounding province of Caria from until 353
B.C. His wife, Artemisia, had the most famous tomb in the history
of the world built for him; ancient peoples considered it one of the
seven wonders of the world. It became the prototype for all
other "mausoleums" to be built in the following two thousand
years from the Asiatic Samarkand to all corners of the earth. In
those days, in the time of Alexander the Great, Halicarnassus was
a metropolis. As the Romans extended their power over Asia
Minor, it was reduced to a provincial city. In the high Middle Ages
the Crusaders, Knights of St. John, recognized the superior stra-
tegic position of a Byzantine fortress which had stood for a number
of centuries on a small island in front of the city. They tore down
the already dilapidated walls and columns of the tomb of Mau-
solos and used them to complete the fortress, which they then
called "St. Peter."

All the storms of time, from Alexander's army to the hordes of
Ottomans and Knights of St. John, could not efface Halicarnassus.

Today one still walks on the deeply worn cobblestones that were laid thousands of years ago by Lydians, Greeks, Persians, or even by Romans. A large portion of the houses of modern Bodrum rests on ancient foundations. Often only specialists can tell which wall or which column of a house is Persian, Roman, medieval, or modern. Warships and merchant vessels have been using the harbor of Halicarnassus for thousands of years. All these factors made it highly probable that ships had sunk off the harbor.

On their arrival, Throckmorton and Kapkin went immediately to the sponge divers' tavern on the waterfront where divers congregate who are not at sea taking part in the sponge harvest. Kapkin and Throckmorton were lucky. The sinister-looking man who sat down at their table was Captain Kemâl Aras—the captain of the *Mandalinci,* which a few years before had brought the Demeter to Bodrum. They sat together for four hours and the captain told them about the work of the sponge divers, of the dangers which threaten them, and stories of unusual things he had seen at the bottom of the sea.

No, besides the Demeter there were no bronze statues in the waters that he knew of, but if all they wanted was old jugs, he could show them plenty. He ended by inviting the two men to accompany him and his crew for a month on the *Mandalinci* along the Anatolian coast.

At first glance the *Mandalinci* did not look terribly safe. She was a sailboat of scarcely thirty-six feet in length with a decrepit, spitting-and-knocking auxiliary engine; a boat that seemed to be overloaded with the air pump, helmet divers, provisions for one month, the divers Kemâl Aras, Amca Seytan, a few others, and two ship's boys. But Kapkin and Throckmorton already knew these proven, agile, and seaworthy little sailboats, which resemble very closely prototypes thousands of years old, and accepted the captain's invitation with pleasure. They were sure he had exaggerated when he spoke of countless jugs in numerous places. But he would certainly be able to point out a few wrecks.

On board ship Throckmorton suddenly caught sight of a large jug which the Turks had tied to the base of the mast. It was a jug with a slender form, two handles, and a narrow neck, and was slightly encrusted with sea deposits—an ancient amphora. It contained the drinking water for the *Mandalinci*.

Kemâl explained to the American in an indifferent tone that the old jugs were made better than the modern ones, and besides they didn't cost a single piastre. All the divers had to do was pick them up off the sea floor.

The Death Reef of Yassi Ada

The two ship's boys untied the *Mandalinci* from the dock, and the boat set a course for the Karabagla Islands in the Chuka Channel, two sailing hours from Bodrum. Kemâl held a course for Yassi Ada, one of the tiny rock hills in the Aegean and the most desolate of these uninhabited islands. Just two stones' throws from the shore of the island of Yassi the sail was lowered. The diver Ciasim Arslan got into the only diving suit which the crew of the sponge boat owned. Ten minutes later the signal line jerked. Ciasim had found the place Kemâl wanted to lead the two frogmen to.

Throckmorton slipped into his fins, took his mask and snorkel, inhaled deeply, and pushed for the bottom. He did not need to dive deep. Only four fathoms beneath him stood Ciasim in the middle of a huge heap of amphoras and clay fragments. Mustafa Kapkin followed on Throckmorton's heels. Astonished, they swam in the crystal-clear water around the diver and the large amphora field. When they returned to the surface for air, Captain Kemâl signaled for them to return to the boat. He had still more to show them. Ciasim was pulled up, and Ali Zorlu took over the diving suit while the clattering auxiliary motor pushed the *Mandalinci* to the southern tip of the island.

A few minutes later Ali Zorlu and Peter Throckmorton, who had strapped on a breathing apparatus, met at around twenty fathoms by another ancient wreck. This time Throckmorton saw a whole mountain of amphoras. But before he could take a closer look, the Turk pulled him away—to a third wreck. The cargo of this one consisted of large, pot-bellied, almost round amphoras which Throckmorton had never seen. In some places he saw encrusted pieces of iron, among them some anchors.

The discovery trip on the sea bottom continued. Before twilight Throckmorton had already recorded more than a half-dozen wrecks sunk off the island of Yassi.

All these ships had collided with the same, tricky, razor-sharp reef. Scarcely a hundred yards from the island, it ascends in a gradual slope to a long hill with a sharp rock ridge. Like a giant knife blade it cuts off a wide path of the sea.

Today seamen's charts warn sailors about this place. But the ancient captain was dependent solely on his eyes; in a quiet sea he could see the reef shimmer through the water, but if there were heavy seas, or if the ship was sailing against the sun so that helmsman and crew were blinded, it meant a deadly danger. With their bows slit open, many ships sank immediately on either side of the

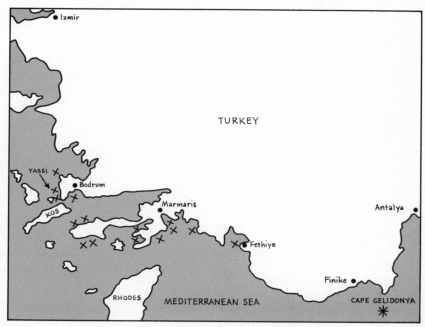

Locations of wrecks off the Anatolian coast

reef in depths of only a few fathoms. But others struggled a few lengths farther on and landed in a depth of fifteen or twenty fathoms.

In the days that followed, Kapkin and Throckmorton figured that the death reef had dragged at least eighteen sailing vessels to the bottom. Two wine freighters, whose remains had survived the ages, interested them in particular. A huge area of broken amphoras remained of the first; the other had become a ship's mound, out of which the uppermost layer of five thousand amphoras still protruded. It was later learned that these two wrecks, to which the Turks had first led Throckmorton and Kapkin, were from the Byzantine era. They were freighters from the sixth and seventh centuries, a significant discovery for underwater archaeology. All previously discovered wrecks were from the period ranging from the end of the third century B.C., to the end of the third century A.D.—much to the sorrow of the scientists, for we are about as much in the dark regarding the Byzantine era as we are regarding the period of classical antiquity.

The last large ship to wreck off Yassi Ada was a Turkish frigate. She was broken apart by the knife edge of the reef, and the waves then pounded her to pieces and spread them about. But the cannonballs had rolled down both sides of the ridge and had gathered in pockets. There they still lie today, in large piles. A Turkish diving boat landed on one of the piles of cannonballs only a few decades ago, also a victim of the death reef.

The two frogmen could see that this reef alone would be able to supply research material for well equipped expeditions for years to come. But the sponge divers had to move on, to places that promised sponges for them and more wrecks for the frogmen.

Under full sail and with motor chugging, the *Mandalinci* passed the countless islands, bays, and peninsulas which made up the rugged coast of Anatolia. As soon as the divers detected from the sound of the waves that their boat was sailing over rocky bottom they dropped anchor and the sponge diving began. Each of the divers worked on the bottom for one hour, then he would give the suit over to the next one. The pile of black, shiny sponges around the mast grew. Throckmorton and Kapkin helped the sponge divers with their work when they were not busy seeking or photographing wrecks or supplementing the skimpy menu by shooting fish and catching lobsters.

The number of wrecks grew almost faster than the pile of sponges. The Turks always had still another to show them, and sometimes the crews of other sponge boats passing by were able to direct them to still more. The story of the two "slightly crazy" young fellows who were looking for "old jugs" had spread along the coast. Kapkin and Throckmorton couldn't even follow up all the tips, but they came again the following year with more divers, and by the end of the next summer they had identified thirty wrecks—wrecks of the Graeco-Roman and Byzantine eras, ships from the fleets of the Seldjuk Turks and the Ottoman Turks who followed them.

It was at the end of the first year that Throckmorton heard the conversation about *bakir*. Kemâl Aras had invited Mustafa Kapkin and Throckmorton to spend an evening with him and a friend, a steamship captain from Istanbul. But Throckmorton was so tired that he left most of the conversation in Turkish up to the two seamen, and soon he could hardly follow it any more. They had begun "shop talk," and as a result had come to speak of the bronze finds.

By the time Throckmorton began to realize what the sponge divers might have found, Captain Kemâl Aras was already back on the high seas in his *Mandalinci*. But Throckmorton could no longer shake the idea that he was now on the track of a wreck that was more than three thousand years old. Patiently he waited in Bodrum for the return of the *Mandalinci* in order to find out more about the find from Kemâl and his divers.

In response to Throckmorton's eager questioning, one of the divers remembered seeing two small bronze containers. He had picked them up because he had hoped to find gold in them. When he saw that they only contained a black, greasy substance he threw them in a high arc back into the sea, for they had been severely corroded by the sea and were ugly, he said.

Amca Seytan had also brought up a few finds. He said hesitatingly that one of the objects looked like a spearhead, that he had also found a knife and something similar to a sword. All the objects were made of bronze.

Throckmorton asked excitedly, who had bought them, but Amca Seytan could not remember; he had sold them as scrap.

Seeing Throckmorton's disappointment, Captain Kemâl told him not to worry because next year they planned to blast that stuff loose from the rock so that a salvage operation would pay. He would save him a chunk.

Throckmorton was horrified. He grabbed Kemâl by the arm and made him promise that he wouldn't touch that bronze until he had seen it. He would pay Kemâl twice the value of the metal.

Kemâl Aras agreed, shaking his head. Just what Throckmorton wanted with those old hunks of bronze he couldn't quite understand.

Wanted: Adventurers and Sportsmen with Money

Summer was over and Throckmorton returned to the United States to face a difficult question: how do you find a man willing to invest his time and money in the exploration of a possible wreck of uncertain age?

If Peter Throckmorton had taken this problem to a large archaeological institute, the young man who claimed to have found a ship from the first millennium B.C. would have only aroused a chuckle. A wreck from the time of the Trojan War? That was impossible; so far only a few remains of ships from the fourth, fifth and sixth century B.C. had been discovered—along the Riviera and by the island of Chios. Thus scholars would scarcely have taken Throckmorton more seriously than they once took Schliemann, the discoverer of Troy.

Fortunately Peter Throckmorton met Drayton Cochran, through the American archaeologist Virginia Grace.

Cochran, a New Yorker, owned a seaworthy yacht more than seventy feet long, and was as excited about the idea of an expedition as were his son John and the latter's friends, John Richter and Stan Waterman. Cochran and Richter had already gathered some underwater experience as amateur divers, and Waterman worked as a professional diver and underwater photographer. Four experienced divers, joined by another amateur diver, Susan Phips from Florida, would suffice for an exploratory trip. Mustafa Kapkin, who wanted to go along, also acquired the participation of Hakki Gültekin, the director of the Archaeological Museum in Smyrna, and in June of 1959 Cochran's yacht the *Little Vigilant* lay in Piraeus, where it was equipped.

From Bodrum, the cruise from wreck to wreck began. The divers utilized the opportunity to revisit all the wrecks which Throckmorton and Kapkin had discovered the previous year, and found even more.

Cape Gelidonya, on whose extreme end is perched a dark spot —the lighthouse—looked like a pale streak on the horizon reaching far into the sea. Off its sheer cliffs lie tiny islands, strewn like chunks of rock thrown maliciously by a mighty titan of prehistoric times—the Adalar group. The wreck was supposed to lie in the narrow passage, no wider than two stones' throws, between the two outermost islands, where it had grounded on the rock ridge that connected the two islands. The ridge was a confusion of jagged rock, hills, and small sand hollows which varied in depth from one and a half to eighteen fathoms. Just one step beyond the ridge, the sea bottom dropped off to depths of twenty-five fathoms and more.

By evening the *Little Vigilant* lay at anchor over this ridge. The next morning the divers could hardly eat breakfast. They hurriedly jumped overboard and swam in all directions along the ridge between the islands. But the initial eagerness did not last long. The men and Susan Phips found nothing but an old rusty cooking pot at first.

The afternoon brought nothing but a stone that Mustafa Kapkin had picked up at a place which fit perfectly Kemâl Aras' description of the location of the wreck. Bronze patina had given the stone a greenish hue.

Kapkin wondered if someone had worked with dynamite at the site. A feeling of deep depression spread over the boat. Throckmorton was the most disappointed. Had sponge divers beat him to it after all and blasted the bronze ingots from the rocks? Nevertheless he and Mustafa Kapkin protested vigorously when, next morning, the others wanted to weigh anchor right after sunrise. Finally the two of them were able to persuade their companions to stay one more morning. When this morning also brought no success, departure was set definitely for early afternoon. A half hour before sailing time, Throckmorton and Kapkin, fearing that they wouldn't soon get another chance to visit Cape Gelidonya, a place rarely frequented by sponge divers, put on their diving gear for a final desperate dive. John Cochran and Susan Phips decided that they would take one more dive, too, although not to look for the wreck, for they had given that up as hopeless long ago. Cochran wanted to take a few more underwater pictures.

Kapkin and Throckmorton again found nothing, finally gave up, and returned exhausted to the *Little Vigilant*—where the entire crew was waiting excitedly for them. As fast as they could, they clambered aboard and saw that John Cochran had accidentally discovered what they had been looking for: he held two shapeless chunks of bronze in his hand, heavily encrusted and covered with a lacework of color.

Throckmorton began immediately to scratch off the sea deposits from one of the pieces. The archaeologist Hakki Gültekin worked on the other one. In a few minutes they had uncovered two spearheads, rough weapons of bronze. Gültekin said they were at least three thousand years old.

According to John Cochran, there was a lot more bronze weapons down there, and a pile of large, flat metal bars that looked like double-bitted axes.

Throckmorton shouted with joy, for he knew that the inhabitants of Cyprus in the late Bronze Age had often cast the metal mined on their island in ingots of that shape. Scholars had excavated a few of these bars in Mycenae and on Sardinia. They were from the period between 1600 and 1200 B.C.

The wreck lay near the place where Mustafa Kapkin had found the rock covered with verdigris. Some of the divers must have swum very close to it without noticing the remains of the wreck, because it had been covered and changed so much by the sea.

But the divers tugged on the bars in vain. Sea sediments and verdigris had welded them together and to the rocks through metal oxides released during the slow process of corrosion.

Luckily they had a crowbar on board the yacht. It took hours of pounding and prying before the men had broken one of the bars loose and were able to lift its fifty-pound weight on board. In the excitement of their success they almost overlooked what lay in a hollow in the rock—pieces of wood from the sunken ship, clay fragments, bronze battle-axes, pickaxes and spearheads—even a ship's rope braided from tough reed grass lay in the hollow.

Meanwhile the weather worsened. The *meltem,* a wind that at this time of year often whips the surface of the eastern Mediterranean and beats the water into sharp waves, blew from the north. Breaking waves poured between the two islands, and the current became so strong that a swimmer could be carried off immediately. But no one spoke of returning. The divers carried a rope from the *Little Vigilant* to the bottom and made it fast to a bronze bar. The men were able to work their way down this rope without being carried away by the current. At the depth where the wreck lay, the water was quieter. But two divers who didn't hold on to the rope tightly enough were carried quite a distance by the current. Each time, some of the other men had to strain every muscle on the oars of the lifeboat to pick up the swimmers and bring them back. In spite of it all, the men and Susan Phips worked tirelessly for two more days.

Now it was a matter of making precise sketches and photographs of the Bronze Age wreck and collecting some characteristic finds to present to archaeological institutes in order to persuade one of them to undertake a new expedition. The wreck off Cape Gelidonya had to be explored under the direction of an experienced archaeologist. Even the enterprising members of the expedition crew agreed on this. They were now certain that between the two unfriendly islands off the cape lay a wreck from the era in which the Greeks had stormed and besieged Troy. Not a single nail must be lost from this exceptional find.

Two days later the *Little Vigilant* again set sail. The expedition had achieved its main purpose. The notebooks of the divers were filled with drawings; they had photographed the site in detail, and in the hold of their boat lay carefully selected sample finds, among them bronze ingots, battle-axes, spearheads, farming implements, bronze mirror and parts of amphoras from the Mycenaean era—in all, thirty clay fragments and fifteen bronze items.

The yacht again sailed into Bodrum, and the men carried their finds into the Castle of St. Peter, for Turkish law declares all archaeological finds government property and forbids their export. Throckmorton and Kapkin left the *Little Vigilant* and set up their workshops in the citadel with the finds. Day and night they wrote reports and sketched and photographed the artifacts. The reports and pictures were sent immediately to archaeological institutes and journals. The most important reply came from Dr. Rodney Young, the head of the Institute for Classical Archaeology at the University of Pennsylvania and the University Museum. Dr. Young found the bronze bars "typical and characteristic for the late Bronze Age" and decided to send an expedition to Cape Gelidonya.

Weapons for Troy

A year later, in the spring of 1960, when the small expedition fleet neared the confusion of islands off Cape Gelidonya, Throckmorton suddenly began to doubt his discovery. Was it really a ship? After all, he had found no recognizable mound—just thousands of fragments scattered over sand and rock. Perhaps it hadn't been a ship at all, but only a place where Bronze Age seamen threw their heavy cargo overboard in rough weather to save the ship.

But Dr. Rodney Young had trusted his conclusions enough to get together a good deal of money and form the best expedition team that had ever worked on an underwater site. Archaeologists, underwater photographers, artists, conservationists, and divers from five countries had gathered at Bodrum, among them Frédéric Dumas. The Turkish government had sent Hakki Gültekin and the archaeologist Lufti Tugrul. Those among the men and women who had not yet learned to use mask, fins, and breathing apparatus had quickly learned to dive—including the expedition leader George F. Bass of the Archaeological Institute and Museum at the University of Pennsylvania, who had taken a thorough diving course from the "Philadelphia Depth Chargers." The expedition consisted of fifteen selected specialists, not counting a few Turkish sponge divers. Now they all sat expectantly aboard the *Mandalinci* and the doubly large *Lutfi Gelil*, piloted by Kemâl Aras' friend Nazif Goymen.

The *Mandalinci* dropped anchor and Throckmorton could hardly contain his impatience. The harm caused to the progress of underwater archaeology if the expedition to Cape Gelidonya proved a farce was simply more than he could bear to think about. It would surely discourage all those scholars from taking part in underwater archaeological research who up to now had been skeptical, and who believed that the results were not worth the outlay. The discovery of unrelated bronze finds on the bottom of the sea instead of the shipwreck Throckmorton expected to find would certainly mean just such a failure. Bronze ingots and tools alone do not give science much to work with. In equipping his ship for the expedition, Dr. Young had counted on finding a ship from the time when Agamemnon, Achilles, and Odysseus led their armies on ships into the Trojan War—from the period around 1200 B.C., one of the darkest periods of world history.

Throckmorton and Dumas were the first to dive. Throckmorton led the diver to isolated finds in a sandy hollow which spread out between a reef, a huge block of rock, and a rocky platform, and then to the pile of bronze ingots he had found on the platform. Dumas surveyed the bottom closely, touched a stone with a remarkably round hole, and scratched at it with his knife. Then he returned to the ship. Throckmorton and the others watched him expectantly as he swung himself on board and removed his mask.

They knew that Dumas, with his experience, didn't need long to decide with relative certainty what it was.

Dumas nodded affirmatively and quipped that he believed they were on the trail of Odysseus. Then he said earnestly that it could easily be a ship, but they would have to move tons of sand and stone before being certain.

The site did not resemble any of the wreck mounds on which the underwater explorer had previously worked. It was more like a clearing in a jungle into which an airplane has crashed. And the expedition's job was not at all unlike that of aeronautical experts who have to hunt up, uncover, and collect thousands of fragments long since covered by jungle growth, and then determine from them the type of some totally unknown airplane.

In fact, the job facing the members of the Cape Gelidonya expedition was even tougher. Not only were they dealing with objects thousands of years old, but the divers had to work with heavy hammers and chisels in fifteen fathoms of water. Later on, not even hammer and chisel were of much use.

Still, the crew began work eagerly, for a ship from the days of Odysseus would surely compensate their greatest efforts. An hour's sailing distance from Cape Gelidonya lay a narrow beach, skirted by high rock walls with a clear spring. Here the expedition set up its camp. Some of the men set up tents while others built a dam of broken rocks and sand across the stream from the spring. The pond formed behind this dam was for washing off finds that had lain centuries in the salt water and had to be cleaned immediately to prevent them from becoming brittle and fragile. Joan du Plat Taylor of the Archaeological Institute at the University of London, a bronze specialist, set up a small laboratory and got ready the chemicals that were needed for the preservation of the valuable finds. The photographers and artists set up their darkrooms and drawing rooms. The work on the wreck could begin.

Every morning fifteen to twenty persons climbed aboard the *Lutfi Gelil*, which sailed out to the Adalar Islands under full sail and with engines chugging. There the divers scrambled down the rope stretched between a firmly anchored buoy on the surface and the bronze bars, for the current was sufficiently strong to carry off a person, if he was not holding on. The Turks, on the other hand, swore by their traditional diving methods with heavy helmets and lead shoes, until one day the current caught Ciasim Arslan. In their heavy equipment the sponge divers could not pull themselves down the rope, and usually it wasn't necessary, for the weight of their helmets and lead shoes carried them quickly to the bottom. But on that day the current raced through the gap between the two islands with exceptional force, and suddenly it carried Ciasim Arslan off. The crew of the *Lutfi Gelil* noticed him just in time. The men pulled him back to the boat by his lifeline just as one lands a hooked fish. Ciasim Arslan came up cursing. Captain Kemâl Aras jokingly accused him of trying to sneak off to the neighboring coastal town of Finike. But then he became serious. He knew that his diver had just escaped grave danger. If the air hose had got kinked, Ciasim Arslan would probably have died an agonizing death.

Kemâl Aras was now finally convinced that he had been wrong in thinking of frogmen equipment as playthings for tourists, and gradually the Turkish sponge divers learned to use fins, masks, snorkels, and breathing apparatus. Every morning the quiet ocean floor off Cape Gelidonya was transformed into an excavation field. Artists sat on rocks everywhere. Groups of divers took measurements of chiseled finds from the rocks or removed obstructing sea grass. Among them swam photographers and fish. Huge sea bass looked over the artists' shoulders as if they wanted to inspect the drawings, and just as crows in spring hop along behind the plows to pick the seeds, small fish swarmed everywhere around the divers hoping to eat any small sea life that might be knocked loose in the process of chiseling and digging.

Now and then the *Lutfi Gelil*'s winch brought up a basket with bronze items or an ingot. In just a week all the visible finds had been uncovered and raised—but still the divers had found no definite evidence of a ship. Initial enthusiasm threatened to give way to deep disappointment. Dumas' only advice was to wait.

For several days now an overhang on the rock platform had

struck him as peculiar. He went to work on it with his pointed hammer—and disclosed a corner of a bronze bar. With astonishment the divers discovered that half of the rock platform was not rock at all, but bronze, great piles of bronze bars covered and joined together by layers of rock-hard deposits up to two fingers thick. And Dumas noticed something else. Between the platform and the huge rock block lay a stone of unusual shape in the sand. He gave it one hard tap with his hammer and a green cloud of verdigris drifted from it. Dumas had found another location of bronze objects. Closer inspection revealed that the gap between the stone block and the platform was filled in places with bronze bars and implements over a meter deep.

So the expedition was working on the sinking site of a Bronze Age ship after all! At least two thousand pounds of bronze lay on the bottom. This much metal could only result from a shipwreck, for no crew could throw so much overboard in one place even in the gravest danger of a storm. Furthermore, ingots and implements thrown hurriedly into the water would have been scattered over a considerable area, and not stacked neatly. No, this was the site of the sinking of a sailing vessel from the time of Odysseus! The same day, the *Mandalinci* sailed the twenty nautical miles to Finike. She took along enthusiastic telegrams which were to carry the news to Philadelphia, London, and all the cities from which the expedition had received support.

But by evening when the archaeologists convened around the campfire, the enthusiasm had somewhat waned. It was a gigantic job, and they all agreed that using hammer and chisel, it would take many summers to break the bars loose. Then Dumas suggested that they use a hydraulic car jack.

At first the members of the expedition were dumfounded, then relieved. The solution to the problem had been found. In a garage in Finike they found just such a jack. Three days of hammer and chisel work and it was in position under an overhanging pile of ingots. Two of the divers worked the handle. With three tons' force the device separated the pile of ingots from the rocky floor. It cracked a few times, then a cloud of verdigris rose, and a whole stack of ingots was raised from the bottom, inch by inch. The *Lutfi Gelil's* winch groaned as the stack was hoisted up, but it held. And stack after stack left the sea floor. On land, where neither pressure nor confined working space hampered the men, the stacks were quickly separated. With hammer and chisel the sea deposits were removed from the bronze. Even the most stubborn encrustations broke loose after treatment with an electric vibrator and a few well-placed blows of a hammer.

The last bars were just swinging onto the boat when one of the woman divers surfaced and excitedly reported to the expedition leader that beneath the cargo lay parts of the sunken ship. George F. Bass hurried below and investigated the discovery. There was no doubt about it—there were wooden remains of a ship, so poorly preserved that it was impossible to determine what had been ribs and what had been planks. Even so, the find roused hope of making further discoveries.

But days passed, and the chart of the sites of finds gradually showed the general outline of a ship—yet the longed-for ship's remains still did not appear. The hopes of the expedition waned. But every day the quantity of bronze finds grew. The divers not only brought up bronze ingots and weapons, such as spearheads, stone war axes, hatchets, and knives but a collection of household items, plowshares, farming implements, tools—hoes, shovels, picks, needles, and bronze bows—and copper and tin cast in the form of discs. In addition to all this was a complete smithy's outfit—a bronze forging block for fine work, whetstones, polishing stones, hammers, and a 175-pound stone anvil of the kind used in the Bronze Age.

At first the divers were amazed to realize that many of the tools and farming implements were scarcely different in form from their iron and steel counterparts presently used in Turkey. Peter Throckmorton was busy cleaning a long bronze needle when Kemâl Aras joined him. Throckmorton asked the Turk what he thought the peculiar instrument was.

Kemâl Aras replied that it was a *shish,* a skewer which could be found in any Bodrum kitchen.

On several occasions the members of the expedition were surprised by similar replies from the sponge divers. The similarity between the shapes of implements from the Bronze Age and modern times is not evidence of backwardness in contemporary Anatolia, but of the astonishing height of Bronze Age culture, which developed even hand implements to such perfection that they can't be improved upon today.

All finds were carefully cleaned and thoroughly studied immediately after being brought up. George F. Bass and the other archaeologists sat far into the night in the glow of sooty kerosene lanterns, hunched over drawings, photographs, and artifacts. There were a thousand questions to answer. Where had the ship come from? What did it look like? Who owned it?

These questions were balanced by thousands of clues. But the latter were not in order, and even contradicted one another occasionally. The archaeologists had to solve the contradictions and piece together evidence like the pieces of a giant jigsaw puzzle.

It was mental labor which demanded tremendous patience of George F. Bass, Joan du Plat Taylor, and the others, not to mention extensive knowledge of vanished Bronze Age cultures in the Mediterranean area. During the first few weeks of excavation, before the "Captain's treasure" was found, the wreck seemed to pose fewer questions than afterward. In these days Bass drew a circle on his map of the eastern Mediterranean around the island of Cyprus and connected it with a line to Cape Gelidonya. The ship had doubtless carried a precious cargo of metal from this island which in the second and first millennia B.C. had possessed the most important copper mines of all the Mediterranean lands. Cyprus was not only indicated by the forms of the handy double-bitted ax-shaped bronze ingots and the eight-pound copper discs, but the archaeologists also found that many of the weapons and tools resembled those found in excavations on Cyprus. Finally they also found markings stamped into many of the recovered implements—writing in the Cypriot-Minoan style used around 1200 B.C., and still not deciphered.

But what were the anvil, smithy tools, and stone hammer doing on the merchant ship? Today scholars are quite certain they have found the answer in the profession of the ship's owner. He was simultaneously both a bronze smith and a merchant who sold bronze weapons and implements, taking old, broken things in trade —not unlike the coppersmiths who still go around Anatolia with their jugs and pots today. For the divers found large quantities of bronze scrap carefully packed in willow baskets, the remains of which still lay on the bottom. One diver suggested laughing that it was a weapon factory and supplier for the Trojan War.

But as an archaeologist pointed out: if the ship hadn't sailed to the bottom, with a good wind she would have been in Troy in a few more days. The wreck lay on the route between Cyprus and Troy.

When Captain Kemâl Aras heard that the divers had recovered scrap, he shook his head and laughed. He couldn't understand why anyone would dive to the bottom of the sea to recover scrap that was three thousand years old.

The "Captain's Treasure"

July of 1960 passed. The sun had dried the thin, prickly grass on the hills around the camp and turned it brown. A searing heat hung over the narrow strip of beach—and still no connected piece of the hull of the sunken ship had been discovered. The men cursed and groaned under the heat and the plague of flies. A diver would barely reach the surface when flies would attack him on cuts and scratches that were constantly reopened by the salt water.

The generator on the compressor burned out. The compressor was taken to a repair ship, and meanwhile the frogmen had to work with air hoses, which were hooked up to the old-fashioned pumps on the diving boats. It was tedious and dangerous, for often an air hose became kinked, and then the diver was without air for seconds. The engine of the *Lutfi Gelil*, decrepit with age, ran only occasionally. Captain Nazif Goymen injured his hand severely while throwing an anchor. Ciasim Arslan spent a whole night making repairs on the engine of the *Mandalinci*, and then threw himself onto his bunk, dog tired—forgetting to refill the engine with oil. The next day when Captain Kemâl Aras started the engine it ran only a short time before the pistons, glowing hot from lack of lubrication, bonded themselves firmly to the cylinder walls. At the same time the photographer Herb Green was caught by the current above the wreck. Luckily he was able to pull himself out of it quickly, but he lost his valuable underwater camera in the murky depths in the process. The men were secretly entertaining ideas of calling it quits and did their work grudgingly since it promised no new results.

Then one afternoon the diver Waldemar Illing clambered aboard the *Lutfi Gelil*, his face beaming with joy. With a triumphant gesture he held up a little piece of black stone, the thickness of a pencil and about an inch long.

George F. Bass saw it and shouted for joy. Then the others left their work and crowded around Illing, who held the little black stone in the sunlight. And suddenly the mood of the expedition crew changed. Illing had found a treasure—a seal from the eighteenth or seventeenth century B.C. A North Syrian artist had at that time carved an image of a goddess and two worshippers into the polished stone. Thousands of years before the birth of Christ, in Syria and Mesopotamia, such small works of art were used to seal freshly written clay tablets which were still soft. By the time the seal went down with the ship off Cape Gelidonya in 1200, it was already at least five hundred years old—probably still in use, but even then already a rare treasure.

But the crew of the *Lutfi Gelil* was just happy about the small stone itself. They took it as a good omen, for seafaring people are always a little superstitious, and after many long weeks at sea with seamen and fishermen, even an occasional scholar becomes infected.

The archaeologists and the divers returned to their work with renewed vigor. With the aid of a suction pump the divers now began to dig out sand between the rocks—and they found more treasures. They discovered the captain's cabin, and next they uncovered three finely carved scarabs, a scarab plaque, an oil lamp, then three sets of balance weights, and finally even remains of food carried by the ship. The scarabs were already real treasures by the time they sank. They were ancient pieces created by Syrian or Egyptian artists—perhaps old family heirlooms of the Bronze Age captain or valuable travel souvenirs and good-luck charms. Scarab amulets are replicas of the scarab beetle held sacred by the Egyptians and the peoples of Palestine. This beetle was considered a symbol of fertility and continued life after death. Egyptian officers took them on campaigns as talismans, as did wealthy merchants on business trips, and all rich Egyptians carried them to the grave.

The scarabs, which Throckmorton had found in a small wooden chest, were passed around from hand to hand. An almost reverent silence reigned until George F. Bass, who had been inspecting the falcon-headed god Re on one of the talismans, gave his opinion that the scarab was carved during the Nineteenth Dynasty in Palestine, the dynasty of the great Pharaoh Ramses II, who ruled from 1301 to 1234 B.C., erected the mightiest palaces along the Nile, and established Egypt's domination over Palestine.

Throckmorton shook his head over the bronze from Cyprus, the seal from North Syria and scarabs from Egypt and Palestine. He wondered where the weapon merchant came from.

Joan du Plat Taylor suggested that the owner of the ship was probably a man whose trade extended over the entire eastern Mediterranean, and Bass agreed.

Not even an hour had passed before proof of this hypothesis lay on the deck of the *Lutfi Gelil*: weights of bloodstone, an ore of iron, which apparently had once belonged to a wooden hand balance.

The archaeologists began sorting the weights right away. They turned out to be from three sets. One set of uniformly shaped weights was quickly identified, for the smallest piece weighed exactly 9.3 grams—this was precisely the weight of the Egyptian *quedet*. The origin of the other two sets is still undetermined. But so much is certain; they did not correspond to any Egyptian weight system, and therefore were probably used in trading with peoples who were not under Egyptian rule. The ship's owner apparently had used the weights for weighing bronze bars and scrap. The divers had already found halves and quarters of bronze bars on the bottom.

A few days later Peter Throckmorton came up from a dive and climbed aboard the *Lutfi Gelil*. Bass, seeing that he held something in his hand, asked him what it was. Instead of answering him, Throckmorton asked him what he thought the captain of the bronze freighter ate for lunch.

The leader of the expedition gave Throckmorton a blank look. But the latter opened his hand and held out a small pile of olive pits and bones from fish and fowl. Covered by sand and sediment, even these unlikely remains of the ship's food supply had survived 3,200 years on the bottom of the sea.

Hopes among the expedition crew of finding a piece of the ship itself were beginning to dwindle when in the first days of August the divers discovered another chunk in the sandy stretch between the rocks.

At first their faces were long. The chunk, which had been broken loose only with great effort, was nothing but rock covered with copper patina. Then they checked into the sand under the chunk, removed it with the suction hose, and uncovered a square yard of the ship's side. And not only that. Below it lay ballast stones which had been placed in the hold to give the ship some depth and a low center of gravity for stability. The positions of the stones were recorded, and they were weighed after they were raised. From these figures and from the location of the bronze cargo they had already raised and its weight, the archaeologists were able to estimate the size and cargo capacity of the sunken ship: it must have had a length of twenty-seven feet and a beam of six feet. Along with its 230 pounds of stone ballast, it had carried about one and a half tons of bronze and copper. In those days that much metal must have represented tremendous wealth, for the mining of ore was a tedious business. A good bronze sword cost as much as a strong slave.

The divers chiseled for three weeks before they freed the pieces of siding and its ribs from the bottom and raised them. But for science this fragile piece of wood is of more value than the gems of the captain's "personal treasure." It is the first tangible proof of the ship builder's art of the early seafaring peoples who, in contrast to the Egyptians, had long had seaworthy ships with a sturdy frame of keel and ribs—while the Egyptians' ships were of such construction that they didn't dare venture out into the open sea.

The planks of the ship were neatly dovetailed; the inner side of the hull was insulated with twigs and brushwood. This discovery solved a mystery in the *Odyssey*, in which Homer gives a detailed description of a ship's construction. No one had been able to explain so far what Odysseus used the brushwood for that is mentioned in the work.

A few days later the divers and archaeologists returned to Bodrum. The true significance of the find was first realized during scientific evaluation of the research findings.

First the age of the ship was once more tested: brushwood and timber from the wreck were submitted to the radiocarbon test. This test indicated a sinking date for the ship between 1250 and 1150 B.C. When the archaeologists once again took a look at the scarabs from the captain's cabin, they made an interesting discovery. The pieces were not genuine Egyptian, but rather Syrian-Palestinian copies of the originals. Furthermore, the captain's oil lamp, the battle-axes, and two stone mortars were definitely identified as Syrian-Palestinian. Among the personal effects of the captain and the bronze dealer not a single Greek item was to be found. The seaman was therefore from Palestine, a member of the people who dwelt along the Palestine coast—a Phoenician. But that contradicted what was known so far about the seafaring habits of the Phoenicians. Almost all history books will tell you that the Phoenicians of this time carried on trade with Egypt, and only after the turn of the millennium did they venture up the coast of Anatolia, Greece, and finally the western Mediterranean. To be sure, Egyptain tomb paintings depict offerings of bronze bars in the form of a double-bitted axe even before the turn of the millennium. But scholars had always assumed that Minoan seamen or, later on, early Greeks of the Mycenaean epoch, had brought these tributes to the pharaohs—and had also traded with Sardinia, where such ingots have often been found. Now a large number of grave paintings was scrutinized once again. And in fact the earlier assumption was proved false. Even the bars brought to the pharaohs were almost always Syrian-Palestinian tributes.

With the discovery of the 3,200-year-old Phoenician wreck at Cape Gelidonya one of the most crucial arguments for dating the writing of the *Iliad* and the *Odyssey* later, after the turn of the millennium, was greatly weakened. Homer often mentions seafaring Phoenician merchants, and scholars had argued that if Homer knew Phoenician merchants then he could not have lived before the turn of the millennium. This argument is no longer valid. The Phoenician captain of the ship of Cape Gelidonya was a contemporary of the Homeric heroes. At the same time the wreck provides a positive argument for the age of the great epics: the perfect agreement, even in details, between the ship's construction and the description of such a ship as it appears in the *Odyssey*. Homer must have actually seen the construction of such a ship, for such technical details are never passed on down verbally through millennia. Now the underwater archaeologists have to find out how ship construction developed after 1200 B.C. If it could be shown that soon after 1200 a more modern design replaced the one depicted in the *Odyssey*, then the age of this passage in the great epic could no longer be in doubt. Of course, to show this, further discoveries of more recent wrecks along the bottom are necessary. Perhaps the investigation of the vast, still unexplored areas of the eastern Mediterranean will soon provide the answers.

V

Voyages of the Past

A stranger visiting Piraeus, the harbor of Athens, in the summertime in the fifth and fourth centuries B.C., was witness to a fascinating spectacle. Merchants who had steered their heavily laden ships between the two jetties bordering the narrow entrance to the harbor and then were towed to an unoccupied place along a pier by a harbor boat had first to submit to an unpleasant procedure: government officials came on board, estimated the value of the cargo, and assessed a two per cent tax on it, regardless of whether the goods were to be sold in Athens or the ship had only landed to restock its provisions and water or to take on additional cargo. Treasury officials followed on the heels of the harbor officials. They collected the harbor fee, as it is still done today in harbors throughout the world. Captains who wished to avoid taxes and fees therefore often pulled into a small bay not far from Piraeus, but still outside the area of jurisdiction of the Attic customs office —the "harbor of thieves" as it was called in Piraeus. But the sea merchant who intended to sell good wares in Piraeus was not hurt much by the taxes and fees. He knew that he would get a good price. Athens was rich, and its wealthy citizens loved to buy luxuries from all parts of the earth.

If a shipper had fine carpets from Carthage, purple robes from the Phoenician coast, papyrus from Egypt, select wines and cheeses from Sicily, nuts from Asia Minor, gold jewelry, or coveted amber from the Baltic, all he had to do was have his wares taken to the *deigma,* the bazaar of the harbor. And if his wares did not attract a local merchant he was sure to find a trader from another country who would buy from him—a Phoenician, Etruscan, or Illyrian, for all the Mediterranean languages could be heard buzzing around the bazaar. When the sea merchant had sold his wares, he had to look around for a return cargo that was in demand in his own country. He had a large selection. He could do business with other foreigners, purchase slaves, expensive woods, incense, pigs and cattle, or load his ship with the most sought-after Athenian export goods—such as olive oil, jugs of wine or honey, weapons, and other products of Attic handicraft.

Or perhaps our sea trader stood thoughtfully in front of the largest by far of the five great columned halls on the Piraeus waterfront and considered the possibility of tying up here on his next trip with a different cargo—grain. Grain was unloaded in huge quantities, in front of the columns of this hall, weighed, and sold to Athenian merchants who took it to the city. Athens would always buy grain, for Attica's poor soil could no longer begin to feed the three hundred thousand inhabitants of the metropolis. The city-state would have to unload eight hundred shiploads of one hundred thousand tons each, annually, if even the poorest citizen was to have his daily bread and customary porridge-like dish. The grain trade was in the hands of many independent enterprisers who often managed to rake in tremendous profits, but who also sometimes had to bear up under severe losses. The purchasing price varied according to the harvests in southern Russia, Egypt, and Sicily, and the size of the supply in Athens determined the selling price.

Should our merchant decide to try his luck with grain, he would then sell his small ship and look around for a spacious grain freighter, which he might buy used, or have made in the shipyards of Athens or some other coastal city. While his ship was being readied, or built, as the case might be, he had time to gather up the necessary additional funds. If he was an honest and respected man, his problems were few. All he had to do was go to a bank, such as the "Antisthenes and Archestratus Bank and Finance Company," which after the Peloponnesian War came into high esteem under its owner, Pasion.

If he did this, Pasion would discuss the matter a while with him, decide whether he could be trusted, and finally call a scribe to write up the usual contract on fine papyrus—including of course the interest to be charged, which normally ranged around twenty-five per cent. The captain would then receive the sum in Athenian drachmas with the famous picture of an owl or in foreign notes. He would be provided with recommendations from the bank addressed to its associates, and be wished good luck by Pasion. The neophyte grain merchant could use both—Pasion's recommendations and luck.

En Route from the Crimea to Britain

In his letters of recommendation Pasion begged his associates to be as helpful as possible to his new customer in all emergencies, be they difficulties with petty officials or severe storm damage to the ship. That meant that the door was open to the grain merchant in all the larger commercial cities in the Mediterranean area—in the grain harbors of southern Russia, Egypt, and Sicily as well as along the coast of Spain, in Massilia, Carthage, Sidon, and Tyrus. For the business ties of Athens' largest and most respected banker reached just as far as the network of shipping lanes which connected Kerch, on the eastern shore of the Black Sea, Aquileia in the northernmost corner of the Adriatic, Massilia on the Tyrrhenian Sea, and extended beyond the columns of Hercules, which is what the Strait of Gibraltar was called, and on up to southern England. At the ends of the shipping lanes they connected with trade routes which led to the Baltic Sea, the interior of Russia, or to the Red Sea and the Persian Gulf and thereby to other harbors where goods were loaded for shipment to eastern Africa, India, and China.

For the grain merchant these worldwide trade systems also

meant that he had to be especially careful with his purchases so that he would not pay a high price for wheat in Sicily where the harvest had been poor while other merchants were flooding the Greek market with wheat purchased in Egypt or southern Russia at a low price owing to a bountiful harvest.

As far as the quality of the merchant ships was concerned, we know from the few extant drawings, but especially from the findings of underwater archaeology, that the ancient shipbuilders were equal to their counterparts in the Hanseatic League, Spain, and Portugal. The shipyards of the fifth and fourth centuries B.C. produced freighters usually of a 130 ton capacity, but sometimes with a capacity of 250 tons. When a good wind filled their large, rectangular sails, their classic curved bows cut the water at a good four to six knots. At this speed it took a ship two weeks to sail from Athens to Syracuse. Of course the eighty-ton "tramps" took much longer, for they used to sail from harbor to harbor, selling a little of their wares and taking on new cargo everywhere.

These tonnage figures were calculated by shipping archaeologists using ancient records. The tax records of Piraeus were especially helpful. The American scholar Lionel Casson went further and even calculated the lengths of the sailing vessels on the basis of the tonnage figures: the length of a merchant ship must have been about seventy-five feet.

The fact that sometimes only three, or even only two, out of every four voyages were completed is no indication that the ancient sea captains were unskilled. The rate of loss among merchant ships of the Hanseatic League in the twelfth, thirteenth, and fourteenth centuries was at times little better. In ancient times, just as in the Middle Ages, every fourth ship that left harbor fell victim to pirates. Pirates were interested primarily in plundering coastal towns and collecting slaves in the process, but they did not turn down a chance to make booty of a freighter. Autumn winds, such as the mistral in southern France or the bora along the Yugoslavian coast, sudden winds and storms, all affected the sailor severely when he was following one of the many lanes in sight of land past dangerous capes and between hidden reefs.

The medieval fleets of the Venetians and the Arabs avoided these dangers. Instead of following the shipping routes along the coast, they simply sailed over the open sea. But the captain of ancient times could only choose this method when a prevailing wind in a particular season gave him certainty of being carried in the desired direction, for what he lacked in nautical instruments in contrast to the medieval seaman he could compensate for neither through daring nor experience. The magnet had not yet been discovered; the seaman of antiquity had neither compass nor sextant. At sea he navigated with the sun by day and the stars by night. He dreaded extended periods of bad weather, for then he could only guess at the stretch already covered. There is a tendency to credit ancient seamen, because they seemed closer to nature, with more skill than sailors today, who are able to estimate stretches already traveled with astounding accuracy. But this is a mistake, for the navigator of ancient times lacked a most important requirement—an exact measurement of time. Like everyone in the ancient world, he divided the period from sunrise to sunset into twelve equal parts. Thus, from season to season the hours varied in length, and places in different latitudes measured time in correspondingly different units. An hour in the longest day of the year in Rhodes, for example, contained seventy-two of our minutes, while in Massilia the hour was seventy-six minutes long.

Accordingly, writers of antiquity described the speed of the ships of their time quite differently. Herodotus figured that a freighter of his time, given a good wind, could sail seven hundred stadia (furlongs), about seventy nautical miles, between sunup and sundown. Skylas, the adviser to the great Persian King Darius I estimated about five hundred stadia, and Marinus, at about the same time, calculated a day's run for a freighter at about a thousand stadia, or one hundred nautical miles.

Owing to the reduced hours of daylight in the fall, captains had little choice but to discontinue travel on the open sea in that season. Then Piraeus was a sorry sight. Until the next spring only small coastal freighters and military patrol galleys still sailed. These vessels held so close to the coast that their commanders could take refuge in a protected bay or beach on the sand on a moment's notice.

From the earliest times rulers and city-states made efforts to eliminate some of the dangers connected with coastal shipping. Besides erecting temples on protruding points and capes, they built lighthouses, the largest and most famous of which, on the island of Pharos near Alexandria, was considered one of the wonders of the world. Most harbor managements established pilot services, and the first canals with locks and the first adjustable wet docks came into existence. One was built where today the canal at Corinth saves ships the trip all the way around the Peloponessus.

A complicated system of differential pulleys and roller runways which turned in wooden bearings was employed to help galleys and light sailboats over the land. While slaves were constantly busy lubricating the smoking bearings with olive oil to keep them from burning, oxen were pulling the ship up to the watershed, and on the road alongside, the boats' cargoes were transferred in carts. Then, when in Hellenistic and Roman times ships were made larger and larger, this *diolkos*—"pull-through"—lost much of its significance, though it continued to be used for a long time. Today, travelers in Greece can still see its remains.

The *diolkos* of Corinth lay on one of the traditional ancient trade routes, knowledge of which was passed down from generation to generation. This word-of-mouth tradition was a good substitute for sea charts and descriptions, for a man was able to pass on pretty exact information regarding the coastal markings he used in determining his location. Thus the beginning seaman learned, for example, that toward the end of a voyage to Egypt he was only a day's journey from the mouth of the Nile when the sounding lead brought up mud from a depth of eleven fathoms. And the seaman who traveled regularly to India knew that he was close to Barygaza, one of the most important Indian ports, when he first sighted large black sea snakes, and then small green ones. Scientists also tried to help the seafarers. In the middle of the fourth century B.C., the geographer Skylax the Younger wrote the first extant sailing handbook. Like the *Stadiasmos,* the "guide to the Mediterranean," which followed, it listed all the ports and river mouths and the distances between them, described the harbors, and didn't omit a single coastal marking—in short, the captain found everything in it which could be important to a mariner on a voyage.

For instance, for the stretch from Leptis on the African coast to Carthage the *Stadiasmos* had: "93. Coming from the sea you will sight flat land, before which lie small islands. When you get closer, you will see the city on the coast, a white dune and the beach. Also the whole city has a bright appearance. It has no harbor. You may anchor safely near Harmaion. The city is called Leptis.

"94. It is 15 stadia from Leptis to Hermaion, a harbor for small ships."

And further down in the text the author writes:

"113. It is 170 stadia from Thapos to Leptis-Minor. It is a small city. There are underwater banks, and the approach to the city is difficult. . . ."

In paragraph 124 of the book he makes a concluding observation about the route to Carthage: "It is 120 stadia from Galabras to Carthage. It is a very large city with a harbor. There is a castle in the city. Anchor to the right of the sand bar. All in all it is 3,550 stadia from the Lotophagian island of Meninx [modern Djerba] to Carthage." That is, about 355 nautical miles.

Soon similar manuals were available for all seas which freighters traveled; for the Red Sea as well as for the trip through the Persian Gulf to India. Sold in countless copies, they were not only an aid to ancient navigators, but to medieval and Arab seamen as well. Some of them were so good that they were in use as late as the previous century, such as the *Periplous Pontou Euxeinou* of the Greek Captain Artemidor, who gives directions for travel in the Black Sea. Since all the sea charts of the preceding century proved to be inadequate, admirals of the English and French fleets in the Crimean War—1853-1856, in the age of steamships—turned to this ancient work. The copies of these ancient sailing manuals that have been preserved are also treasure chests for the scholars. They cite towns, cities, fortresses, and city-states whose names are no longer known today, but which played a very important role in the cultural development and the history of antiquity.

But as far as shipping and matters of trade are concerned, the sailing manuals provide only a general picture. Which ships traveled the routes mentioned, what they carried in their holds, and how significant shipping between individual ports was, were not discussed in the manuals.

The Battle against Pirates

By the second century B.C. ships were still crowding into Piraeus from all corners of the Mediterranean, but most of the ship houses in the adjoining military port were empty. Athens' proud galleys either lay destroyed at the bottom of the sea or sailed in the fleets of the Diadochi. In 322 B.C., one year after the death of Alexander the Great, the city-state had attempted to shake off Macedonian domination and had sent its warships against the Macedonian navy. In a huge sea battle by Amorgos, Athens lost almost its entire fleet, and soon the commercial enterprises of other powers began to surpass that of the Athenians. Sea trade experienced a sizable expansion, but the additional and larger ships crowded into the ports of Alexandria and Rhodes. While Alexander's successors pursued the art of fortification to its limit, the speedy galleys of Rhodes kept the shipping lanes of importance to it relatively free of pirates. During periods of exceptional plaguing by pirates, freighters sailed in flotillas with escorts of navy galleys.

The average sailing freighter of the time carried a two- or three-hundred-ton load. Sailing ships were developed that had a capacity of over a thousand tons, according to Professor Casson. Other scholars have not been convinced of the capabilities of the Hellenistic shipbuilders, but finds made in the last few years seem to support Casson. Judging by the size of the cargo and the length of the keels, ships with a load capacity in excess of several hundred tons were already common centuries before the birth of Christ.

Constant battling against the pirates resulted in a significant upsurge in the importance of the small island of Rhodes. Trade and shipping flourished as never before. Old records show that the customs officials of Rhodes estimated the value of the wares brought into the harbor at fifty million drachmas in a year's time, and correspondingly each year they took in one million drachmas in gold and silver—the customary two per cent. What the ships of that time carried in their holds can be read in old customs records, which were kept with exceptional painstaking exactness by the Egyptians. In the dry, desert sands of Egypt import and export lists on papyrus from the time of Ptolemy have survived the millennia. Besides huge quantities of grain, olive oil, and wine, they also mention a host of luxury goods such as pearls and gems from India, Baltic amber, Chinese silk, cosmetics, and spices—primarily pepper, myrrh, and incense—and of course the products of Egypt's trade allies in the Mediterranean area. The demand was great for expensive furniture, fine table settings, and rare, select foods for the upper crust of the Hellenic empire and city-states.

The customs declaration of two tiny coastal freighters that tied up at one of the wharves of Alexandria in 250 B.C. includes sixty-three amphoras of table wine, ten jugs of dessert wine, seven jugs of honey, ten jugs of dried figs, one jug and three baskets of nuts, one jug of cheese, ten jugs of wild pork, two jugs of venison ragout, and two jugs of the meat of young goats. A vague idea of the variety of trade items in Hellenistic times can be got from a sheet of papyrus which is among the possessions of the Berlin Museum. The strip of papyrus contains the text of an ordinary contract for that time, which was made in 150 B.C., in Alexandria. Five Greeks, one of them from Sparta, a second from Massilia (Marseilles), planned a merchant voyage through the Red Sea and needed credit. The creditor was also a Greek who required five men with sureties. One of them came from Carthage, the other four served as soldiers in the garrison at Alexandria and wanted to earn some interest on their savings. The money matters were handled by a bank. The banker was a Roman.

To the sorrow of the archaeologists, almost no ancient written material has been found to date which pertains to the Hellenistic Age. To be sure, finds made on land have provided some valuable clues—still, a map of the water trade routes of the time, until just a few years ago, showed chiefly empty spaces, and the few entries on it were considered questionable, and remained so until the large freighter of Marcus Sextius was found and further discoveries of amphora fields followed.

Until the end of the second Punic War (201 B.C.) the Greeks of Sicily and southern Italy, seamen of the Italian tribes, and the Romans themselves confronted again and again competition from the superior Carthaginians. Then Carthage fell, and the captains of Italy and Sicily could sail unhindered to the columns of Hercules and beyond, into the Atlantic, and gradually also into the eastern Mediterranean. Roman merchants first appeared sporadically, and then with increasing frequency in the flourishing commercial cities of the East. They were especially attracted by one "ware" that was abundant in the time of the great wars of the Romans against the Eastern powers: human beings. Hundreds of thousands of prisoners of war, not only soldiers, but women and children, too, were loaded on huge freighters that usually took them to Italy, where they were sold to large plantation owners as farm workers or to factory owners.

The citizens of Rhodes observed this with displeasure, but they were powerless to do anything about it. It was not the slave trade itself, but the fact that it was not carried on via their island that bothered them. The main center for slave traffic in the eastern Mediterranean was the tiny island of Delos, the "Holy Island of Apollo," which also became a common port for freighters carrying luxury items.

By a stroke of genius on the part of the Romans, Rhodes lost its position as the leading Mediterranean trade port in the matter of a few short years. This occurred, furthermore, without the loss of a single drop of blood. Rome had received control of the small island of Delos, and in 167 B.C., turned it over to its ally, Athens.

The gift had one small string attached: no duties or taxes were to be collected in the Delos harbor. The Roman senate could hardly have landed a more telling blow against the obstinate, proud citizens of Rhodes. Delos became a flourishing free port which attracted more and more ships, and Rhodes's annual revenues dropped from a million drachmas to a mere 150 thousand in the first year of the free port's existence. Grain trade was about all that was left to Rhodes.

Phoenician, Spanish, Arabic, Egyptian, Jewish, and Greek seamen now convened with Italians and Romans on the island of Delos. Some of the latter, among them Marcus Sextius, had long since settled there as a sort of Roman "bridgehead" in the eastern Mediterranean. Shops and attractive villa quarters sprang up in Delos, and thousands of slaves were sometimes embarked there in a single day. But the decline of Rhodes, which had made Delos great, was also destined to destroy it again. Rhodes no longer had the money necessary to maintain its famous fleet. The armada, at one time the dread of the pirates, disintegrated. Piracy grew worse and worse. The freebooters operated in fleets, established castle-like fortresses on the coast of Cilicia and laid waste to large expanses of land. In 69 B.C., Delos was attacked for the second time by a fleet of pirates. It never recovered from the blow.

Rome, too, suffered more and more at the hands of the pirates. Along many routes, shipping came almost to a standstill, until shortly after the beginning of the first century B.C., when pirates ventured into Rome's immediate vicinity and cut off the grain supply from Egypt and North Africa, so vital to the masses. Prior to that time, some senators voted against measures directed against the pirates, for they in turn kept the Roman property owners supplied with slaves. And, since the end of the great wars, slaves were a scarcity item. But the Romans were forced to act in the face of the crisis and gave Gnaeus Pompeius, Julius Caesar's rival, the job of routing the pirates. Inside of 120 days, not a single pirate ship could be found between Gibraltar and the Dardanelles. Shippers could undertake new ventures in all ports, for until the migration of nations the Roman navy kept the Mediterranean free of pirates.

The Art of Shipbuilding in the Roman Era

Ancient texts have given scholars some information about the merchant shipping which in a few decades, in the era of Augustus Caesar, quickly surpassed the best years of the era of the Diadochi. But here too, discoveries made in the last few years on the sea bottom have led to new knowledge: scholars have found that even liberal estimates as to the size and significance of water traffic in the Roman Empire fell short of the mark.

Fortunately the Romans also left us with more pictures of ships than did their predecessors. We find them on frescoes in Pompeii, in Herculaneum, Ostia, on mosaics and gravestones. To be sure, these pictures are very stylized, but they permit the ship archaeologist to form a basic idea about the ships of the Roman era, especially when he can also consult the reports on finds made underwater. And in addition, the vessels of this era provide clues to those which plowed the Mediterranean Sea centuries before them. Ship-

Mosaic from Ostia showing a slave transfering amphoras to a Roman river boat

Fototeca Union

builders are conservative. In the days of antiquity they were even more so than in the Middle Ages or modern times. Significant changes in the design of freighters occurred gradually over a period of centuries. In the field of shipbuilding the Romans could hardly be classified as innovators. Insofar as shipbuilding and sea-faring were even carried on by native Romans, they adhered closely to the traditions of the Hellenistic seamen. The merchant ship in the time of Augustus must therefore have differed very little from that of the Hellenistic period, except that it was more lux-uriously equipped. It ran under a large rectangular sail of Egyptian linen, reinforced with ox leather. Occasionally a freighter had an auxiliary mast on the forward deck, with a foresail like a small bowsprit sail. Large ships also had a triangular topsail on the mainmast above the square sail. The captain and two helmsmen— the ship had a steering rudder on either side—had their places on the rear deck. There was a large, lavishly decorated cabin for the captain, the owner of the ship, or an especially important passenger. Sometimes its tiled roof was supported by slender marble columns. Somewhat smaller cabins were available for other wealthy passengers, while the crew lodged beneath the foredeck or had to sleep on the deck under the open sky. In the mid-deck, just above the ballast of sand or rock, the cargo was stowed.

The ship's hulls were masterpieces of ancient skill. The builders didn't simply nail planks to the rib framework. Each board was mortised to those on either side as well, and the finished hull was then tarred, given a coating of fiber, and finally covered with a skin of lead as protection against shipworm. The decor of the ship was afforded special care. The bow was graced by a bronze figurehead and the stern ended in the figure of a mighty mythological animal. Gold, silver, and colors covered the wood of the sailing ship, and flags and pennants fluttered from its masts.

In a strict sense, one cannot speak of "the" ship of the Roman era. Specialists distinguish pictures of ships from that time among a number of types whose names are found in ancient texts. According to the coast they came from and the purpose for which they were to be used, they were built with slight differences. All these types could be admired in the final years of the Roman republic and during the reign of the first emperors in Puteoli near Naples (today Pozzuoli). This beautiful natural harbor became at that time the focal point of Mediterranean sea trade. Most of the freight for Rome was landed there until Claudius Caesar had a new artificial harbor built at the mouth of the Tiber river in A.D. 42, since the river continually filled the old outgrown harbor of Ostia with sand and mud.

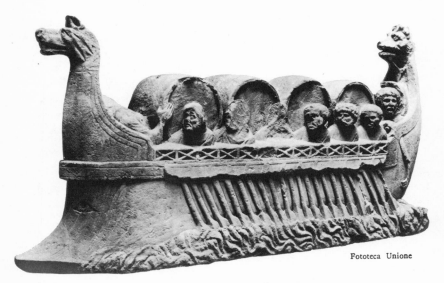

Fototeca Unione

A Roman river boat

One wharf was reserved for grain transporters called *corbitae*, freighters with two masts and an especially wide beam. They carried grain over from Egypt, North Africa, and Sicily all summer long.

At the entrance to the harbor a Liburnian galley was on patrol, an especially light, fast and maneuverable galley with a row of oars, an invention of the Illyrian pirates. The Roman navy used them for coastal patrols, on rivers and for fast reconnoitering missions. The heavy galleys of Rome's large Armada were stationed somewhat beyond Naples at the naval support base of Misenum (Miseno).

The Giant Ships of the Caesars

The largest merchant ships of the Hellenistic Age and the Roman Empire reached a displacement of seven hundred to eight hundred tons. But by the time Emperor Claudius had work begun on the new harbor at the mouth of the Tiber, they had long since ceased to be the largest merchant ships on the Mediterranean. The first giant ships of the framed grain fleet had already left the docks. The creation of this mighty wheat armada was an accomplishment of Rome that ranks alongside the construction of the great roads, viaducts, and amphitheaters. To be sure, the ships were still piloted by Phoenician and Greek captains. But the order to build the armada came from Rome, and the organization of the grain transport was also a product of Roman effort.

At the time of Christ's birth more than a million people lived in the villas, tall buildings, and housing projects of Rome. Italian agriculture could feed only a small portion of this great population, for in those times they knew neither of rotation of crops nor artificial fertilizers. The Romans ate bread made from imported grain, fish caught near Gibraltar, drank Spanish or Greek wine, and in the kitchens of the city, oil from North Africa or Greece fried in pans made of copper from Cyprus or Iberia. The population's basic food was bread. To feed Rome, more than half a million tons of grain had to be ground and baked in a single year.

All summer long freighters sailed from Sicily, North Africa, and Spain to Puteoli, later to Ostia, and back. They managed to deliver around three hundred thousand tons of wheat from these grain elevators of Rome, but that wasn't enough, for another ten thousand tons were brought to the city from other sources. Egypt was able to supply the additional hundred and fifty thousand tons needed annually. The fields of the old pharaoh kingdoms, fertilized as they were with the rich mud of the Nile, produced heavy harvests. But the shipment to Rome was not without difficulty. A steady north wind carried the sailing ships from Italy to Alexandria in two weeks. The return ship against a headwind, however, took from fifty to seventy days.

Fototeca Unione

A Roman relief from the second century A.D.: *the busy harbor of Ostia*

Heavily laden, the freighters sailed from Alexandria along the coast of Asia Minor, battled their way from Rhodes to Crete, and from there steered past Malta toward the Strait of Messina. In one summer they could only make a single trip with a full load from Alexandria to Puteoli or Ostia. The Roman emperors had the choice of employing many small ships or a few giant ships if the population of Rome was to be supplied with food.

Augustus decided in favor of the large freighters and started construction on the grain fleet, which was built in conjunction with Greek and Phoenician shipping firms in Alexandria, and traveled across the Mediterranean to Rome every summer on into the fourth century A.D.

Fortunately we have a very good description of one of these giant ships. One beautiful summer day in the second century, the rumor circulated in Athens that a giant ship such as had never been seen in the city had docked in Piraeus—now a quiet art and university center, outside the main traffic lanes. The Greek writer Lucian was among the curious individuals who hurried to the harbor. Lucian inspected the sailing vessel, which had been driven off course by a storm, and spoke with the captain and crew. What was told him, which he wrote down faithfully, was so fantastic, that even today some scholars view it as a sailor's yarn invented by the crew to make a fool of the writer.

According to Lucian, the Alexandrian wheat ship *Isis*, decorated with beautiful figures of that Egyptian goddess, was 180 feet long and had a beam of forty-five feet. Her hull was forty-four feet deep. Ship archaeologists have calculated from these figures a cargo capacity of 1,200 to 1,300 tons and a displacement of 2,000 tons. Not even the great sea powers in recent times—up to 1845— ever built a ship of this size. Yet the Jewish historian Josephus (A.D. 37–100) also writes of a ship that carried a large cargo in addition to six hundred passengers, and the story of Apostles tells us that the ship in which Paul was brought captive to Rome had 276 persons on board. And finally Pliny, a very observant man, who was a stickler for facts, wrote that the freighter that brought the obelisk to Rome which today stands before St. Peter's Cathedral, also had 1,300 tons of grain on board. But the obelisk alone weighs five hundred tons! Divers have as yet not found any wrecks of ships this size on the sea bottom, but maybe it is only a question of time before they do.

In most history books the age of antiquity ends with the migration of nations; only a few pages are devoted to the eastern Roman Empire. But there the great ancient traditions lived on, and into the high Middle Ages the West could only learn from Byzantium.

At sea, "Greek fire" gave the eastern Roman navy its superiority over the fleets of the attacking Arabs. The east Romans shot it in clay jugs from the decks of their galleys with catapults. If the jugs hit the attacking ships they would burst open, and a secret mixture invented by the Egyptian architect Callinicus flamed up and spattered in all directions. The galleys of the enemy became flaming torches, and their crews, more and more often pirates, jumped despairingly into the flame-covered sea in which the Greek fire continued to burn just as on land. The Byzantines invented rockets and even equipped their merchant ships with long tubes that shot long flames at the enemy—the first flame-throwers in history.

Ancient sea trade flourished for a few more centuries before the caliphs took over. We know little of these centuries, but since Peter Throckmorton's reports on the wrecks of Yassi Ada, divers and archaeologists have been learning about them from fragments brought up from the sea floor off the coast of Anatolia.

VI

A Submarine Journey
to the Roman Era

The gold coin glittered in the bright Mediterranean sun as if it had just left the mint. Diver Waldemar Illing handed it to George F. Bass, leader of the University of Pennsylvania expedition, who inspected it closely. It bore the profile of a young man in Caesarean clothing. A Latin inscription identified him as the Emperor Heraclius, ruler of the Byzantine Empire from A.D. 610 to 641. The coin confirmed the date of the Yassi Ada wreck, estimated by Gladys Davidson Weinberg, to whom George F. Bass had given ceramic samples. A scientist from the American School of Classical Studies in Athens, who is considered one of the best specialists in the area of ancient ceramics, she had dated the ship in the seventh century on the basis of the amphoras recovered. We know much more about the great age of Athens than we do about the development of the Western world in this epoch or about the development of the distinctive Byzantine culture out of its ancient heritage, Christianity, influences from migrating peoples, and the Orient. Just as the scarcity of written records causes difficulties in exploring early Western history, so did the Crusades and the centuries of Turkish wars, which to a large extent destroyed the Byzantine heritage. Furthermore, science was for a long time only interested in classical antiquity—the culture and history of the Greeks and the Romans. Only in the last few years have scientists concerned themselves with Byzantium and recognized its significance in world history. Thus, even a specialist like Gladys Davidson Weinberg could be mistaken, for the information found in standard charts and tables of Byzantine ceramics is less dependable than comparable information pertaining to the classical era. But Bass and his colleagues had intentionally chosen a wreck from the seventh century. They wanted to cast a little light into the darkness of this unexplored chapter of seafaring and world trade and find the "missing link"—a wreck that would fill the gap between ancient and medieval ships.

Their choice fell on a field of some thousand round amphoras—the wreck of a sailing vessel which, like so many others before and after, had grounded on the death reef of Yassi Ada and sunk in eighteen fathoms of water. The wreck was fortunately located—eighteen fathoms meant it lay below the destructive effects of the surf and currents that had left so little of the wreck at Cape Gelidonya and at the same time permitted comfortable work in frogman outfits. This last was especially important, for the team wanted to glean with military precision as much information from the site as possible and to develop new methods for archaeology underwater. Their goal was to re-create the ship from the finds—plank for plank, nail for nail, from keel to captain's cabin.

The winter months were spent in thorough preparation. Money had to be collected and a crew hired and equipped. Since the tremendous success at Cape Gelidonya, however, collecting money was not difficult. The National Geographic Society, the Catherwood Foundation, and many other foundations lent financial support to the University of Pennsylvania. In spring of 1961 the expedition set up its headquarters in an old stall in Bodrum. It was a fifteen-man team of archaeologists, art historians, architects, photographers, artists, students, a geologist, a technician, a doctor, and divers. Only a few of the participants on the expedition already knew how to dive. The others had to take a short, eight-day course near Yassi Ada. Bass preferred working with experts who couldn't dive than with archaeological laymen, in order to prevent the many mistakes previously made in underwater explorations. Captain Kemâl Aras and his sponge divers were engaged as "auxiliary troops." Soon the *Mandalinci* put out of the harbor of Bodrum with a flat eighty-ton freight barge in tow. With three anchors it was brought into position over the wreck, protected from the wind by the island of Yassi. But the flat island offered only minimal protection from the harsh northern *meltem* wind, and newcomers quickly learned that an underwater expedition was no bathing party on a sunny beach. In sweaters and windbreakers they had to exercise behind the machines of the barge in order to warm up after they had put in their second shift on the sea floor. Each diver was able to spend a total of forty-three minutes in two shifts per day underwater. At this rate four divers a day were able to perform only three full man-hours of work. This necessitated fast, precise work, for they had a tremendous job to do.

Sand and mud had partially buried the amphoras, and sea grass had grown over everything. The sea grass had to be pulled off with bare hands and the amphoras cleaned with wire brushes. Meanwhile other divers began setting up measuring instruments. George F. Bass and his assistant Frederick van Doorninck had made a thorough study of measuring methods employed so far in underwater excavations—the use of the grid square, the making of a photomosaic of the wreck *Le Titan*, and many other experiments.

None of these methods had led to really accurate results. Especially weak was the method of measuring differences in height, which is extremely important for the reconstruction of an antique ship from the remains of a wreck. A grid square permits only an exact measurement of the location of finds in a plane, and Bass did not wish to take soundings as had been suggested by Frédéric Dumas. This could have been destructive to valuable remains of the wreck and other finds. But Dumas came up with another solution. He devised a metal framework that could be put together like a lightweight scaffolding, grid square attached to grid square—not all in a single plane, but elevated according to the angle of the rise. This provides a three-dimensional system of coordinates.

Just as in archaeological excavations on land, the location of each find can be determined with millimeter accuracy. A dozen divers worked for two weeks on the bottom before the framework was fully in place over the wreck. Now the artists could begin measuring and charting the top layer. Of course their work was much more tedious than in previous underwater excavations. They not only had to locate each find in a plane, but also determine its exact height with a plumb and measuring stick. Meanwhile the divers situated two movable tripods above the first grids. Underwater cameras were attached to them, lenses down—so that the archaeologists were able to get exact photographs in spite of changing currents, for their cameras were solidly mounted. As soon as one grid square was photographed, the tripod was placed over the next. The divers began with the recovery. Bass deliberated whether he should have his crew work the rest of the summer and the following spring recovering a good thousand amphoras among which there would be little variation. This had always been standard procedure, but to Bass it seemed irrational. Once the amphoras have been inspected and entered on the chart, and their contents checked, scientists are interested only in samples of each kind to determine their age and source. Bass finally decided to save only a hundred selected amphoras and to have the others placed aside. There they could remain until some museum was interested in acquiring them—or forever. Bass was also dissatisfied with the recovery methods used so far. Why should time and money be wasted with a crane? Amateur divers on an amphora hunt had long since devised a simpler method. They took large balloons down with them, attached them to the amphoras, and filled them with compressed air from their breathing tanks. The balloons sped their cargo to the surface. From a platform on the barge assistants were then able to fish them out of the water. Fully laden with Byzantine amphoras, the *Mandalinci* putted each day to the expedition headquarters in Bodrum. A layer of sand had gathered under the top layer of amphoras. Two mud suckers were put to work. But the summer came to an end. The *meltem* whistled with increasing force across the flat rock island of Yassi and the unprotected barge that danced on the white-capped waves. They hated to leave the wreck

Vessels from the death reef of Yassi Ada

S. Köster

they had excavated with such labor and care to the winter storms and plundering amateur divers but they had no choice, for each day could mean the beginning of the autumn storms. So Bass had the wreck covered with the rubberized fabric of cut open air mattresses, weighted on the edges with rocks. This safety precaution, along with the strict Turkish laws against stealing antiques, guarded the ship from destruction until the next spring, when members of the expedition could again travel to Bodrum from all corners of Europe and the United States. A second summer of hard work awaited them, which was to be followed by a third and a fourth (1964). For layer after layer had to be removed, after which everything—really every crumb—was measured, charted, and photographed.

With growing impatience Bass and van Doorninck observed the slow progress. Archaeologists, divers, and photographers all discussed the problem without success—until one of them remembered a publication by Dimitri Rebikoff, a pioneer of underwater photography who had experimented with stereophotography underwater, producing unique and fascinating pictures. With a stereo camera it would also be possible to measure a wreck photographically, in Rebikoff's opinion. Bass listened attentively and realized that they could photograph the wreck the way a reconnaissance plane photographs a landscape. If it succeeded, it would mean the greatest step forward in underwater archaeological reserach in years.

Bass was right. The experiments which the team soon began led to research methods which today permit scholars to descend into the Roman era in a submarine.

Georgios's Ship: The Missing Link

But at first the difficulties seemed insurmountable. Stereophotography works as vision through human eyes does. Whereas a one-eyed camera does not see in three dimensions, man is able to see a single picture with two eyes at the same time but from slightly different angles, thus permitting him to determine distances. In the

An amphora is sent to the surface by balloon.

same way a stereocamera has two parallel lenses at a few centimeters from one another. The two slightly different pictures are united to a single, 3-D image in a stereoviewer. In air reconnaissance, such as with the famed U-2 airplanes, they are of course not satisfied with simply seeing the 3-D pictures. When they know the distance between camera and object, and in the case of airplanes, the plane's altitude, the focal length of the cameras and the distance between the lenses, they are able to measure the variations between the two pictures and with these figures and a simple optical law determine differences in height. Underwater stereocameras were not available on the market. But the archaeologists did not let themselves become discouraged. They used a trick.

An underwater camera was installed over the wreck, and after a picture was taken, the camera was simply moved a bit to the side. Of course a normal photograph taken underwater at a distance of three fathoms from the bottom shows nothing. Even clear water is as opaque at this distance as fog on land. But here Donald Rosencrantz, a physicist who had at one time done research for Eastman Kodak, was able to assist. He experimented for a while with various developing techniques. Then he hit upon the right one. Julian Whitlesey, a city planner with considerable experience in aerial land surveying who volunteered his services to the expedition, was able to begin with measurements and calculations. The experiment was a success! Layer after layer was photogrammetrically measured.

Now the work went faster. The bow was freed, then midships, finally the stern. Six iron anchors, each as tall as a man, lay in the bow. Not far away lay the seventh, on the bottom where it had fallen. This find was reminiscent of a story in the New Testament. In the description of the shipwreck of Paul on his journey to Rome (Acts 27: 28,29) it says: ". . . and when they had gone a little further, they sounded again, and found it fifteen fathoms. Then fearing lest we should have fallen upon the rocks, they cast four anchors out of the stern . . ." They wanted to throw more anchors from the bow. Operating with so many anchors is uncommon in medieval and modern seafaring. The anchor finds of Yassi Ada thus show that the author of the Acts of the Apostles was a faithful reporter and a sharp observer even in such incidental matters as the anchor technique of the seafarers. Even the sounding lead mentioned in Apostles—"they sounded"—was found. The first piece of gold came to light and more and more wood was freed of sand. But the iron nails had long since rusted away. Microorganisms had gnawed away planks and beams, the sand had worn them down in size, often to mere splinters and crumbled them so that they threatened to drift away with the next current as soon as they were cleared of sand. Would the men be able to do anything with these meager remains? Everyone doubted it, but van Doorninck, the team's reconstruction specialist, did not give up hope. He only insisted on precise measurement, even of the tiniest splinter. In order to prevent the currents from carrying off the fragments before they had been measured in position and entered on charts, the researchers improvised a device which was as simple as it was effective. In Bodrum they bought two thousand bicycle spokes, ground their ends to points, and nailed the wooden pieces down with them. Van Doorninck was soon able to demonstrate that this effort was not in vain. . . .

Meanwhile the excavation had reached the captain's cabin. Would it also prove to be a treasure chest like the cabin on the wreck by Cape Gelidonya? The archaeologists had great hopes, for it was in this part of the wreck that a diver had found the first piece of gold. And it wasn't long before another frogman surfaced triumphantly holding up another piece of gold. Sixteen gold coins and thirty-two copper ones lay in the cabin, and almost all of them bore the image of Emperor Heraclius. The ship's kitchen was also in the cabin. Divers found a brick hearth there, and, nearby, plates, cups, pitchers, pots, a copper kettle, and a stone mortar. The ship's water container stood directly behind the cabin. Some of the vessels were so badly broken that visitors to the site only shook their heads and laughed when they saw how the divers carefully numbered each fragment and stowed it away. But with a practiced hand Ann Bass, the wife of the expedition leader, reconstructed them into fine ceramics in the headquarters in Bodrum.

Two hand balances—one of them complete with silver inlaid

bronze weights ranging from one ounce to one pound—doubtless used in selling small quantities of wine from the amphoras. The sale of liquids by weight is still practiced in Turkey today.

Gradually the divers also learned things about individual persons in the ship's crew. "Georgios Presbyteros Naukleros" (George the Elder, Captain) was engraved in one of the captain's balances in Greek letters. The name "Johannes" was engraved into a lead seal, and a glass medallion bore the cross-shaped monogram of a certain Theodore. Captain Georgios was apparently a pious man who took the new teachings of Christianity seriously. Perhaps he even held religious services on board his ship. The divers not only found a bronze cross in the cabin, but an incense burner.

While some divers were working on the cabin, others raised and registered every conspicuous piece of stone. The material was taken to a small workshop in Bodrum which archaeology student Michael Katzev had set up. With a diamond-edged tool, he cut the pieces in half. It was an exciting moment each time the saw blade cut screaming into a stone. Sometimes it was only a clump of limestone and mollusk shells—but once in a while it was the fossil of an old iron object. More than 150 of these pieces had an interesting center. Rock-hard mineral sediments had deposited themselves around a tool or a nail while the object itself disintegrated into iron oxide. The mold formed in this way was filled by Katzev with a kind of synthetic rubber. When it had hardened he was able to pull out a hard rubber tool in the form of the rusted iron one: a double-bitted ax, a sickle, a pick, shovel, or even a nail. The ship was abundantly outfitted with tools and equipment for replenishing its supply of firewood or wood for making repairs any time it anchored in a protected cove.

The exploration proceeded like clockwork. Nobody considered the possibility of an accident, for everyone strictly obeyed the regulations regarding decompression procedures set up by biologist and diving instructor Larry Joline. For this reason they had no decompression chamber on the barge. But the laws of the deep are still a mystery. One day Joline himself got cramps. He and other divers took them for stomach cramps, for he had followed the decompression procedure strictly. But Captain Kemâl Aras shook his head. Joline was not the first victim of bends that he had seen. He had seen men collapse and die, and therefore insisted on immediate help.

The *Mandalinci* started out on the sixteen miles to Bodrum under full power. By the time they reached the harbor, Joline's legs were already paralyzed. Now his friends feared for his life. In Bodrum there was only a small portable decompression chamber. Joline was put into it, but his legs remained paralyzed. The small chamber couldn't reach a high enough pressure. Then Bass ran to the post office and notified the American consulate in Izmir. While a Volkswagen bus carried the chamber and the stricken man from Bodrum to Izmir, five hours away, an airplane was already landing there. Joline was scarcely in the plane when it started taxiing again. The pilot flew low over the sea, for the reduced air pressure at normal flying altitudes would only have made his condition worse. Joline lay thirty-eight hours in the large Turkish navy's high-pressure chamber in Istanbul. Then he was out of danger. The paralysis had disappeared, although the left leg was weakened for the rest of his life.

With increased safety precautions the men worked on. Now the divers brought up the wood of the wreck. The fragments were quickly put into water basins to prevent the 1,300-year-old rotten wood from shrinking. Ultimately the pieces were preserved in polyethylene glycol. This substance drives out the water, replaces it, and hardens. "So much trouble for a couple of lousy chunks of wood," muttered the divers, shaking their heads. But a few months later Frederick van Doorninck showed the astonished team the result of his evaluation work: he had succeeded in reconstructing the appearance of the Byzantine ship from bow to stern, from keel to captain's cabin.

And what is more, the wreck really was the "missing link" between medieval and ancient shipbuilding. The lower sections had been built along ancient lines: the outer layer was first built of joined planks, then the ribs were drawn in. But the upper portion of the hull was built in the medieval style which is still used today in the construction of wooden ships: first the ribs were placed, then covered with planks.

A Submarine for Science

While the team was at work on the wreck at Yassi Ada, Bass's thoughts were already on another ship—the sunken sailing vessel that had once carried the Demeter of Smyrna (Izmir). Bass knew that it lay in thirty to forty-five fathoms in the waters by Marmara, although he did not know just where, for the fisherman who had found the bronze statue had not noted the exact location of the find. Bass's hopes that still more treasure might rest in the deep along the coast of Anatolia were given new encouragement when, in 1962, an excited fisherman entered the expedition headquarters, laid a wrapped bundle on the table and began slowly to unwrap it. It was the original bronze of a Negro boy—a valuable piece from the Hellenistic era. The Turk had brought the statue up in his net from a depth of at least fifty fathoms—and with it a small Fortuna statuette.

But how could these treasure ships be found? Time and again the men discussed this problem—until one day someone made a "crazy" suggestion that they use a submarine with underwater cameras and floodlights. That way they could not only search vast areas of the sea bottom for sunken treasures of antiquity, but they could penetrate to depths too great for frogmen. They could also measure wrecks photogrammetrically while passing over them. The archaeologists and divers became enthusiastic, until they were struck by a sobering thought. Where would they ever get the enormous sums of money necessary? Would they be able to find contributors for such an "insane" project? And further: all the specialists they consulted considered the plan technically impossible. But Bass and his friends were not discouraged. The idea opened up fascinating prospects for underwater exploration. It had to succeed.

Then they found in Professor Harold Edgerton of the Massachusetts Institute of Technology a true expert who was infected with their enthusiasm, looked deeper into the project, and assisted them with plans and advice. The engineers at General Dynamics, builders of the American atomic submarine who had so far been engaged in building only military vessels, were also interested in the new and unusual project. And soon they had a detailed project study completed. In their judgment the plan did not present any special technical difficulties. At this point the National Geographic Society and the National Science Foundation declared themselves prepared to provide financial support to the University Museum of the University of Pennsylvania. The keel of the *Asherash*, as the research submarine was to be named, after a Phoenician goddess of the sea, was laid. On May 29, 1964, the submarine left the slip. It performed beautifully on its trial runs. The *Asherash* is fifteen feet long, weighs four and a half tons, and provides comfortable seating for its two-man crew. At ninety fathoms it reaches the diving depth of the average military submarine. Batteries weighing one ton provide power for the two side motors for ten hours. Its underwater speed is four knots. Six portholes provide the crew with a view of the sea floor, and strong floodlights provide illumination. About the same number of instruments and controls must be watched as in a large sub: speedometer, depth gauge, pressure gauge, indicator for oxygen and CO_2 content in the air, voltmeter, and gyrocompass. A breathing air regenerator supplies the occupants with fresh air, and radio keeps them in contact with the surface. But the most important equipment on the sub are the two modified FB-1 aerial cameras in waterproof housings mounted on the bow, five and a half feet apart, with their lenses directed straight down, much as they are in reconnaissance planes.

The co-pilot inside operates them by electrical remote control. In this connection the engineers in Groton had a particular inspiration. In order to permit the *Asherash* to take exact photographs of interesting details of a wreck they constructed the propellors and steering mechanism in such a way that the sub can hover over a site like a helicopter, go up, down, sideways, frontward and backward—and all with centimeter accuracy.

In the summer of 1964 this masterpiece was already transported to the Anatolian coast. After a few trial runs the Turkish archaeologist Yuksel Egdemir and his American colleague Donald Rosencrantz made two runs over the wreck of a late Roman ship lying not far from the death reef of Yassi Ada, in twenty-one to twenty-three fathoms. In each pass over the wreck co-pilot Donald Rosencrantz took a series of overlapping stereophotographs. The whole operation took less than an hour. Of course, at the International Training Center for Aerial Surveys another fifty-six hours' work with the same instruments used in evaluating aerial photographs was necessary to prepare and evaluate the films. But then they had an excellent measurement of the wreck which would have taken dozens of divers and archaeologists with conventional methods weeks or even months to acquire. Since then the *Asherash* has made dives into the sea off the Turkish Mediterranean coast every summer, looking for new wrecks, measuring and seeking the treasure ships from which the valuable bronzes had been recovered. It is tedious work, for the enormous areas to be covered are gigantic even for a submarine. But the archaeologists are convinced that they will be successful before too long.

Events along the other Mediterranean coasts meanwhile support the assertion of American archaeologists that man will be able to wrest secrets from the deep only with the most modern methods, for purely manual labor is too complicated and tedious for underwater research. A single site occupies a large team for years—and each year new sites are found and lost again when scientists are not able to beat souvenir hunters and antique dealers to them. Thus archaeologists and amateur divers serving science have been able to select only a few of the most promising wrecks for investigation; such as the Bronze Age ship of Béziers in southern France and the church wreck near Marzamemi on the eastern coast of Sicily.

Scientists chose the wreck off Béziers because it again promised to close a gap in ancient seafaring history—that between the oldest Graeco-Roman ship excavated to date and the ship off Cape Gelidonya. Consequently they were somewhat disappointed to find that nothing of the ship itself had withstood the centuries. However, the cargo repaid them for their labor and expenses. It consisted of 760 weapons, tools, and jewelry as well as more than half a ton of copper and bronze bars. The ship had sunk toward the end of the Bronze Age, in the eighth century B.C., when iron was known but was still so expensive that it was used exclusively for jewelry, surgical instruments, and for the weapons of the most respected warriors. Even so, the find casts some light on the extent of bronze trade in early antiquity, especially since a similar ship had already been found in 1923 near Huelva, Spain. The ship of Huelva had sunk in a river mouth with a cargo of bronze implements, among them swords, spears, arrowheads, brooches, and bronze scrap. The sinking must have occurred in the seventh century B.C.

In December 1963 a group of Spanish amateur divers were searching for fish in the coastal waters off Pinedo, near Valencia, when suddenly, at a depth of thirty feet they saw a foot sticking out of the sea grass. At first they thought it was a man who had drowned. But on investigation it turned out to be an antique bronze statue of a youth in a sitting position—a masterpiece obviously of the school of Praxiteles if not by the great artist himself.

A Sunken Church of the Early Christian Era

A discovery of the German underwater explorer Gerhard Kapitän on the ocean floor near eastern Sicily has led to exploring some of the history of early Christianity. Gerhard Kapitän built a small private station for archaeological research under water in Syracuse and has investigated, among other things, an ancient marble freight on the *secca* of Marzamemi. There he met a fisherman by the name of Alfonso Barone, who knows the sea floor along this coast like nobody else, since he usually spears octopi from his boat. With sharp eyes he searches the depths of Marzamemi up to three fathoms through a glass-bottom box, looking into cracks and holes for octopi, in order to spear them with his many-barbed spear.

One day this fisherman came to Gerhard Kapitän and told him of blocks, columns, and decorated slabs he had found while fishing on the *secca*. He added in a mysterious tone that his eldest son, who also dives occasionally, had seen a cross on one of the pieces. For a small reward, Barone was willing to tell him where he had made the find. The report sounded so promising that Gerhard Kapitän agreed. He promised to give the fisherman a gold watch if what he said was true and the find proved to be of value to science. While the man was hesitating, Kapitän's Italian colleague drew out a bundle of lire notes and placed them alongside the watch. Barone agreed. He invited the two men into his boat. Beyond the entrance to the harbor they proceeded north into the open sea. Kapitän knew that the water here was only a few meters deep. Barone might be right. When they had reached the Punta Bove Marino, the fisherman looked around for landmarks, finally shut the motor off, looked through the viewing box, rowed a little farther, and dropped anchor. Kapitän and Gargallo looked through the box. On the bottom below them they actually saw carved marble blocks.

A few minutes later the men slipped into the water with their diving equipment. The bottom here was rocky and about three fathoms deep. At one point it dropped off sharply into a large sink filled with sand and rubble. And in it, almost covered with rocks, lay many blocks, parts of slabs and columns.

There was no doubt. It was a freighter with construction pieces. After the divers had taken a few pictures the fisherman showed them a ditch in which a stone anchor was supposed to lie. Gerhard Kapitän and Pietro N. Gargallo dived again. Alfonso Barone's "stone anchor" was a large decorated block. Next to it lay the pieces of a second, similar piece. At the end of the ditch Gerhard Kapitän came across three pillars. And everywhere they saw decorated slabs. Judging by the style of the ornaments the pieces must have originated in late antiquity.

Both men recovered some parts and reconstructed them in Syracuse. A few days later Gerhard Kapitän consulted with Professor J. B. Ward-Perkins, the director of the British Archaeological Institute in Rome, showing him drawings and photographs. The professor, a specialist in ancient architecture, identified the material as green marble from Larissa in northern Greece. This

The wreck found near Marzamemi once carried tons of marble.

stone was especially popular in church construction in the early Christian era. And one of the pieces recovered from the sea was, in his opinion, definitely the stair lining of an *ambon*, the name given to the pulpit in the middle nave of a Byzantine basilica. After the Byzantine liturgy the faithful gathered on either side of the *ambon*. Men and women separate, the men on the right, the women on

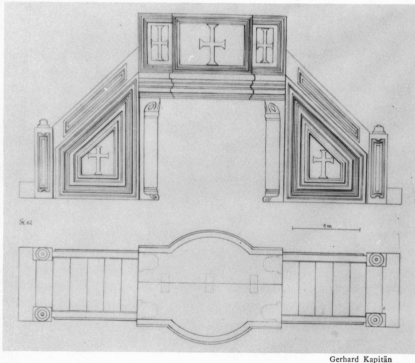

Gerhard Kapitän

Drawing of the ambon *of the Byzantine basilica found in the wreck near Marzamemi*

the left. Land finds of such Byzantine church outfitting is rare, for owing to numerous alterations and renovations it is almost impossible to distinguish the form and appearance of early Christian churches. But through comparisons with the Church of the Holy Kirikos on the Greek island of Delos and another early Christian church in Notium on the coast of Asia Minor, Gerhard Kapitän was able to determine that Professor Ward-Perkins had correctly identified the finds. There are similar pulpits in both basilicas. Kapi-tän also found a very similar slab built into St. Mark's Cathedral in Venice. Crusaders had brought this slab and many other building parts from St. Marco—and also the four famous bronze horses by the Greek sculptor Lysippos on the roof of the cathedral—to Ven-ice after plundering and destroying the Eastern empire in the fourth crusade in 1204. Was the ship by Marzamemi then one of the booty-laden Crusade ships? Additional diving work was to an-swer this question. The next year Gerhard Kapitän investigated the site further. He determined that on the *secca* of Marzamemi a complete early Christian church lay in pieces. Its recovery would bring to light for the first time one of these Byzantine churches free of all subsequent alterations and additions. He succeeded in in-teresting the American air travel pioneer E. A. Link in an expedi-tion. Link and his wife had become fascinated by underwater re-search during an expedition in Port Royal. And so, in 1962, Link headed for Syracuse in his research ship *Sea Diver*. The *Sea Diver* expedition soon recovered the major part of the freight. A clay bowl from the ship's dishes with the Christian figure of an orant, with right hand raised in blessing, on the bottom, was the sought-after proof of the origin and the age of the freight. In its shape and clay mixture, this bowl follows Roman tradition exactly. Thus the church must have been put aboard ship shortly after its completion in the fifth century A.D. As the exploration was continued in the fol-lowing years with the aid of the Council of Underwater Archaeol-ogy in San Francisco and Cologne amateur divers under the direc-tion of Gerhard Kapitän, additional clay finds further supported this theory.

More and more building parts were brought to the surface and gradually the scientists were successful in reconstructing the essen-tial parts of the Byzantine church. For the first time a church from the early-Christian period—the Justinian epoch—was available for study to the modern world.

The marble of the church had been cut by stonecutters in Con-

The Sea Diver, *owned by Edward Link, from which an expedition recovered most of the cargo of the wreck off Mahdia*

Fragment from the ambon, *found in wreck off Marzamemi*

stantinople in the fifth century—a few stonecutter's marks were found on some of the pieces. Then they had sent the complete church to a new Christian community in the western Mediterranean realm. In those days the peoples of the eastern Mediterranean area who had been Christianized earlier used to give material support in this manner to their new fellow Christians in the West.

VII

Sunken Cities

Anyone who opens an ancient sailing handbook reads name after name of places which are today unknown, thriving cities of thousands of years ago, with lively harbors along coasts that today are barren and deserted. The debris of the ages lies over most of them, and archaeologists have been working for a long time at digging their way down to them. But others have left scarcely a trace on land. Where are the walls of Epidauros and the tremendous harbors of Tyre and Sidon? Were they swallowed up by the sea, as is reported in legends of some of the cities?

The man in the dark robes of the Jesuit Order pulled his horse up short; then he gave him spurs and galloped up the hill. From there he gazed thoughtfully for a long time at the small village on the peninsula, over which an occasional sea breeze wafted.

The rider—the army priest and archaeologist Antoine Poidebard —was at the end of a long journey. For years he had followed early trade routes and studied them. His search for the silk route traveled by Indian and Chinese caravans thousands of years before Rome became a world power, and for a long time thereafter, had led him to the deserts of Syria. Desert sand covered the old trade route and made it indiscernible. But Poidebard did not give up. Instead, he borrowed airplanes from the French Levant Army—reconnaissance planes—and had them fly over "suspicious" areas.

And there it was! Where the naked eye could only discern monotonous sand, aerial photographs showed dark shadows. In this way Poidebard found the ancient route, the resting places, the fortresses of the Roman sentries, and the destroyed and forgotten villages along the trade route. For five years he retraced the route discovered by air, but on horseback, in order to verify the aerial photographs. Now the end of the trade route lay before him—this sleepy little fishing village, which still today bears its once significant name: Tyre.

According to the Greek historian Herodotus, immigrants from the mountains of Canaan had founded this city on three islands off the coast of modern Lebanon in 2550 B.C. The location was good, and later inhabitants, the Phoenicians, were skilled in shipbuilding and maritime trade. After the turn of the first millennium, Tyre surpassed all the Mediterranean cities in size and wealth. King Hiram of Tyre, as early as the tenth century B.C., managed to add fill to the land arms connecting the three islands, thereby uniting the islands. The walls and fortifications of the city were strengthened continually. Along with a giant fleet they made the island city into a nearly invincible bastion against which even the massive armies of the Babylonian King Nebuchadnezzar II (605–562 B.C.) fought thirteen years in vain.

Tyre did not owe its power and wealth to military victories. Its strength was the result of its skillful shipbuilders, daring seamen, and the enterprising spirit, experience, and good trade connections of its merchants. Tyre was the main crossroads of the large trade routes. From sunrise till sunset long caravans of heavily laden pack animals crossed uninterrupted over the ramp which connected the islands with the mainland; ships tied up at the large wharves, and others departed from the harbors and jetties of the city.

Father Poidebard looked back at the ancient road he had traveled and at the city and the sea. He recalled the words of the Jewish prophet Ezekiel who prophesied the fall of the proud city of Tyre and depicted the bustling, colorful life there with as much astonishment as condemnation.

". . . O thou that are situated at the entry of the sea . . . a merchant of the people for many isles . . . Thy borders are in the midst of the seas, thy builders have perfected thy beauty. They have made all thy ship boards of fir trees of Senir: they have taken cedars from Lebanon to make masts for thee . . . all the ships with their mariners were in thee to occupy thy merchandise. . . . Tarshish was thy merchant by reason of the multitude of all kind of riches; with silver, iron, tin, and lead, they traded in thy fairs . . . they traded the persons of men and vessels of brass in thy market. They of the house of Togarmah traded in thy fairs with horses and horsemen and mules. . . . Syria was thy merchant . . . they occupied in thy fairs with emeralds, purple, and broidered work, and fine linen, and coral, and agate." (Ezekiel 27: 2–16)

In his mind's eye Father Poidebard envisioned large ships from Greece, Italy, Egypt, from the Black Sea, from North Africa and Spain sailing heavily laden into the harbor, and other ships leaving for the same places. He saw the pack mules of the caravans from Palestine, Anatolia, and Mesopotamia, from Babylonia, India, and China, the camels of Arabia, and from the mysterious realm of the Queen of Sheba, when still more words from the Prophets occurred to him:

"Judah, and the land of Israel, they were thy merchants: they traded in thy market wheat of Minnith . . . and honey, and oil, and balm . . . wine of Helbon, and white wool . . . bright iron, cassia, and calamus. . . . Arabia, and all the princes of Kedar . . . merchants of Sheba, Asshur, and Chilmad . . . all sorts of things, in blue clothes, and broidered work, and in chests of rich apparel. The ships of Tarshish did sing of thee in thy market . . . Thy rowers have brought thee into great waters: the east wind hath broken thee in the midst of the seas." (Ezekiel 27: 17–25)

Even Alexander the Great had to besiege Tyre for seven months, employ the fleets of the conquered Greek cities and the Phoenician coast, and build a wide dike from the mainland to the island under constant fire from the catapults and marksmen, before he finally succeeded in breaking through the walls of Tyre with giant battering rams. But the city recovered even from this blow. In the Roman Empire it was one of the most important Mediterranean ports, and only gradually was the prophecy of Ezekiel fulfilled:

"Thy riches, and thy fairs, thy merchandise . . . and all thy men of war, that are in thee . . . shall fall in the midst of the seas in the day of thy ruin." (Ezekiel 27: 27)

Today hardly a single stone of the old Tyre is intact. Earthquakes destroyed part of its walls, the rest decayed or were destroyed in the wars between Byzantium and the Arabs, the Crusaders and the Turks. Later settlers used the remaining building stones in the erection of their own modest dwellings. Tyre has become a place "to dry fish nets," as the prophet had predicted. Only the large dike built by Alexander has withstood the passage of time. Mud and sand have collected on its square stones, widened it, and made Tyre a peninsula.

The rocky ground of Tyre hardly promised arachaeologists great discoveries—at best the sand dunes might be covering a few wall ruins from Roman times. But the rider on the high hill had another idea: the harbor—the unique harbor of the city! The Prophet Ezekiel, son of a priest and one of a people that understood nothing of seafaring, would not have let it go unmentioned had he come from seafaring stock. For the harbor facilities had been an architectural miracle. Probably Ezekiel had never seen Tyre, but only knew it from reports of others. Otherwise he surely would have mentioned the gigantic size of the harbor, its jetties, piers and docks, and the outer basins in which a forest of ships' masts jutted up over an area of several square miles. But even more admirable than the size of the Tyre harbor was its ingenious structural arrangement, through which the Phoenicians wrested a lasting harbor from an extremely unfavorable coastline, as builders of later ages were never able to duplicate.

How the Phoenicians were able to do this was still an unsolved mystery. Year after year storms rage over the flat coast of Lebanon. Storm waves, strong tides, the constant rolling surf and sea currents fill up every newly built harbor basin with sand and mud. Today many dredge boats are required to keep the important harbors of Palestine and Lebanon open. But the Phoenicians did not yet have dredges, and yet Tyre was a flourishing port for over a thousand years. Apparently, then, the harbor engineers of Tyre, Sidon and the other Phoenician ports must have had other means of keeping harbors free of sediments—with the aid of an ingenious system of jetties, moles, and breakwaters which deflected and redirected surf, waves and currents.

In vain Father Poidebard looked over the glittering water to see if he could not detect a shadow somewhere that might belong to sunken harbor structures. He spurred his horse and rode over Alexander's dike. He encircled the original island and compared what he saw with the few scanty descriptions of the ancient harbor. Connected to the remains of the small harbor basin within the fortifications, the Egyptian harbor to the south must have extended out into the sea. But nothing was to be seen. Only the restless dancing of the waves indicated a long stretch of reef in one place. Could the mighty harbor of Tyre have disappeared completely? The scholar remembered a travel description which was written toward the end of the seventeenth century and which mentioned a few harbor structures that could still be seen in Tyre.

Father Poidebard suddenly realized that sunken harbor structures would stand out distinctly on aerial photographs; currents carrying sand and mud would also be recognizable. Divers could be sent down to look for ancient remains.

He decided to take the next favorable opportunity to ask the French Syrian army—Syria and Lebanon were under French mandate in 1934—for their support in exploring the harbor of Tyre.

The Sea Reveals Sunken Cities

Fortunately, the French mandate officials were as eager to investigate the early harbor constructions of Phoenicia as Poidebard; their engineers, despite modern devices, were unable to do what the Phoenicians had done: namely, build harbors which did not fill up with sand.

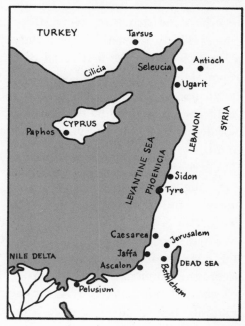

The Levantine Sea

Ships were able to use the harbors for a few years, and then they had to resort to dredges. The French mandate officials felt in need of some tips from the Phoenicians.

Admiral Rivet, commander of the French naval forces on the Levantine coast, agreed enthusiastically with Poidebard when he explained his exploration project to him. The air force also agreed to help by supplying Poidebard with the reconnaissance airplanes necessary for the aerial photography. When the French and Lebanese governmental officials had provided enough money, work could begin.

In 1934, one of the reconnaissance planes which Poidebard had borrowed from the air force warmed up for the first flight over Tyre. At an altitude from which the houses of Tyre looked like sandbox toys, the restless surface of the sea appeared quiet, and the sea around Tyre became a carpet design of confusing lines and forms. But upon closer inspection these lines and dark shadows took on meaning. Reefs, underwater cliffs, and deep places could be distinguished. Some places showed the direction of the currents, and in others the structures were strikingly rectangular and straight-edged. This was even clearer in the aerial photos. Poidebard sat for a long time over the first aerial pictures to come out of the darkroom. He was convinced that these gigantic, regular structures could not be natural formations cut from rock by the sea. They had to be harbor buildings! And he began to draw the original harbor design on a map of Tyre and its vicinity. Soon there were more, and the picture of the one-time harbor became clearer and clearer. The structures would have to be checked out more closely because they might prove to be simply a bizarre formation of the sea. That meant sending divers to the bottom. For this, Father Poidebard had already arranged for support from the navy, which supplied him with boats and helmet divers. The divers were to investigate the findings of the aerial photography and at the same time investigate the manner of construction of the buildings. But the archaeologist did not rely entirely on the navy divers. He knew how clumsily helmet divers moved around on the bottom of the sea, and he therefore engaged the services of one of the most experienced sponge divers in the area. Lebanese sponge divers did not use diving suits. Like their ancestors, the Murex divers of Phoenicia, who dived for purple snail, they went to the bottom clad only in loincloths. The man in Poidebard's team could dive six fathoms, and the air in his lungs lasted a full minute and a half working time at that depth.

He was always the first into the water. He was given the more promising places to investigate and to measure, and he led the heavily outfitted divers to their work places. They then did the heavy work. Not only did sand and mud cover parts of the sunken harbor facilities, but many of the clearly visible rock formations were hard to identify. Were they rocks or walls? The sea had gnawed away some of their surface, and some it had covered with a thick crust of sediments, algae, mussels, and sponges. The navy divers had to probe them with pickaxes, and it took many hours of underwater work before they could penetrate to the original rock. And then came the equally difficult job of measuring and drawing. Time and again the Lebanese diver had to untangle the air hoses of the navy divers, or even lead them back to the boat when they got lost in the labyrinth of reefs, cliffs, and rocks.

The exploration took three summers, and afterward Father Poidebard sat for a long time over the findings, which had to be evaluated. But the work paid off. In 1939 Father Antoine Poidebard was able to present the astonished specialists with a book containing the former harbor facilities of the proud city of Tyre. This map showed not only the remains of the north harbor of the city, but also the entire south harbor, the giant Egyptian harbor, with its moles, breakwaters, wharves, basins, and fortress towers. Just the location of the south harbor was reason enough for wonder. The builders of the old city had not at all capitulated to the

The harbor of Tyre

fact that there was no bay in the vicinity of their city suitable for a harbor. They also had not wasted much time trying to dig enough basins out of the land, but rather showed themselves to be real masters of the sea. Their eyes were on the chains of reef which encircled the island. Giant breakwaters were built on these reefs. A seeming confusion of other structures completed the work, so that a peaceful anchoring place of many square miles was wrested from the sea.

These structures stood up to the raging of the sea for more than a thousand years. Only when Tyre had fallen to a small, insignificant village and its great seafaring tradition was forgotten was the sea slowly able to conquer it. In a constant, century-long attack, the sea ate away the reef, and the large harbor structures slowly sank into the deep. But it could not destroy the mighty granite blocks of the moles. The large mole, which once shielded the south harbor from the open sea, still measures 750 yards. The blocks from which it was built weigh from ten to twelve tons each. In some places Poidebard was even able to photograph parts of the wall. For this he used the underwater camera which had shortly before been devised by the French underwater pioneer Yves le Pieur. The findings of the exploration at Tyre have given engineers of our time valuable ideas for future harbor construction along the coast of Palestine.

Discovery Sites on All Shores

Strictly speaking, Father Poidebard was not the first to think of searching under the sea for the remains of old buildings. He had three equally successful predecessors, the Italian engineer Giuseppe de Fazio, the Oxford archaeologist Robert Theodore Günther, and his French colleague Gaston Jondet. Already in the first half of the last century de Fazio took a boat and a select crew of sponge divers and followed the shore of the Bay of Naples. He found the sunken harbor structures of Puteoli (Pozzuoli) and the Roman fleet base of Misenum (Miseno).

In 1901 and 1903 Günther, a professor at the University of Oxford, continued the work of de Fazio. He had experienced local fishermen take him to the locations of sunken ruins in a rowboat, and studied and drew them through a glass-bottom box. Many Mediterranean fishermen use such boxes to find fish, which they can then reach with long spears. When the box is laid on the water, it opens the "silent world" to view as does a diver's mask. Through the glass, Günther was able to see many ruins of ancient villas, small pavilions, and columned temples which the sea had flooded over as the land sank.

In 1910 Gaston Jondet finally succeeded in discovering the ruins of the spectacular old harbor of Pharos near Alexandria. Minoan architects had cooperated with Pharaoh Sensuret in creating this harbor. The size of its harbor structures had even exceeded that of the harbor at Tyre. Its breakwaters alone measured almost a thousand yards in length. Yet this mighty structure doesn't seem to have held up very long. It probably decayed when the Minoan sea power declined and the Egyptians, as traditional "landlubbers," didn't know what to do about it. In the fourth century, anyway, when Alexander's troops marched into Egypt, the harbor had already disappeared. No one even knew any more where it had been; a new harbor was constructed on a much less favorable site near Alexandria. Jondet not only succeeded in rediscovering the harbor, but in 1915 he already had a precise map of the harbor of Pharos.

But the explorations of Giuseppe de Fazio, Günther, and Jondet were not given much attention. The time was not yet ripe for such discoveries. Most archaeologists were devoted exclusively to art archaeology, and the others had so many sites on land, over which the sands of the ages lay, that they couldn't start thinking of investigating the sea for sunken structures.

Thus it wasn't until the discoveries of Poidebard at Tyre that the attention of many scholars was drawn to the underwater world, and in the years to follow many of them followed suit by investigating underwater harbors and the streets of sunken cities.

One day in the early thirties remarkable rumors reached the ears of the Soviet archaeologist Professor Grinevich, and he finally tracked them down. The rumors said that fishermen in the Black

Sea had caught their nets on underwater remains of walls near the town of Sevastopol. Grinevich sent divers down to the place the fishermen had designated off the Crimean peninsula, and proved them right. The divers reported to the professor that they had seen towers, houses, and the ruins of many other structures down there. But Grinevich was still not completely convinced. He put on a diving suit, had the helmet fastened in place, and jumped into the water himself. A few minutes later he stood in the streets of the ancient Greek colonial city of Chersonisos (Kherson).

After the end of the Second World War, Father Poidebard led a second large expedition to the coast of Palestine. This time the goal was the harbor of Sidon, the second biggest Phoenician city. Meticulous exploration made it possible to penetrate further into the secrets of Phoenician harbor architecture. The expedition discovered an ingenious system of sluices cut into the rock reefs, which directed countercurrents to the sea currents carrying mud and sand.

Like Poidebard's explorations at Tyre, this expedition too would have been impossible without the aid of governmental agencies and the army. Without their cooperation and the divers, ships, and airplanes they supplied, the expedition would have cost sums of money in excess of the treasury of any archaeological institute.

And perhaps Poidebard's and Grinevich's work would have remained without a following and slowly been forgotten had not frogman diving gained rapidly in popularity in the postwar years. The diving mask, fins, and independent diving apparatus opened to the diver the silent world of sunken harbors and cities of antiquity. And soon the first divers began to search through the ruins.

Gradually more and more harbors and cities were discovered on the coast of the Mediterranean which had previously been known only by name from ancient writings and traditions: Fos-sûr-Mer, Caesarea, Chersonisos, Mochlos, Apollonia. . . . In the Black Sea, Russian and Georgian archaeologists have discovered the ruins of two sunken Greek cities on the bottom of the Bay of Sukhumi. They were once called Dioscurias and Sebastopolis, but until now they had only been known through legendary tradition.

Exploration at Fos-sûr-Mer was begun in 1948. For four years divers under the direction of the bold French archaeologist Dr. Beaucaire carried away layer after layer of mud and sand from the bottom at the mouth of the Rhône near Marseilles until they had reached the foundations of the Roman houses.

The exploration of the sunken harbor of Caesarea, modern Cherchel, on the Algerian coast was conducted by an enthusiastic loner, the French journalist Philippe Diolé. The location of Caesarea was known, for Cherchel is built on its foundations; but even so it posed mysteries to science. Its ancient harbor is supposed to have served as Rome's largest fleet base between Gibraltar and Carthage. But the local situation seems to stand in sharp contrast to the implications of the old writings. Cherchel has only a small anchoring place. The French scholar René Cagnat calculated that at best thirteen galleys could have found room there. Then Philippe Diolé dived to the bottom and found there the sunken facilities of a large harbor.

On their own, Pietro N. Gargallo and Gerhard Kapitän investigated the "small harbor" of Syracuse. With the aid of numerous finds dating from the sixth century B.C., up through the Byzantine era, Gerhard Kapitän was able to reconstruct the exact location and appearance of the harbor. From the time of Syracuse's peak importance down to the rise of Rome many stone anchors were lost on the harbor bottom, doubtless because of weak anchor ropes. So far no remains have been found of the ingenious constructions of Archimedes, who, during Rome's siege in 212 B.C. of Syracuse, put his technical and physical skills to work in defense of the freedom of his home city and built enormous war machines. But perhaps further searching will reveal remains of those machines, which seized enemy ships with huge grapplers and smashed them to pieces.

Finally, Apollonia was the goal of a well-equipped team from the University of Cambridge. In 1958 the British crossed a dusty stretch of desert and arrived at the miserable fishing village which today stands on the coast of the Libyan peninsula of Cyrenaica. The place has only a few houses. The poor live in ruins of ancient build-

A mine detector is used to explore the ancient harbor of Syracuse.

ings. The surrounding land is dry and unfertile—desert. When the archaeologists tell the Arabs that the best wheat once ripened to a golden brown here, the reaction is incredulous astonishment.

But the land was fertile when the Phoenicians founded the port of Apollonia and in the nearby hills the splendid city of Cyrene. The Cyrenaica was a few centuries later one of Rome's most fertile grain areas. Apollonia had several thousand inhabitants then, and every year countless grain freighters sailed from its port, heavily laden, in the direction of Puteoli and Ostia. But unlike other sites of fallen ancient cities, only a few ruins in Apollonia stand as reminders of its golden age. The others have sunk. Approximately half of the city with all its harbor buildings and fortifications lies on the bottom of the Mediterranean. Tedious work in 1959 and 1960 permitted the British to uncover the sunken parts of the city and to prepare an exact map of the ancient city and its two har-

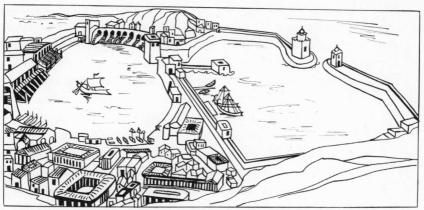

Reconstruction of Apollonia's harbors, based on the discoveries of the diving expeditions of 1958 and 1959

bors. The unfortunate city had experienced the same fate as many another ancient place: it sank as the result of a tremendous earthquake.

For thousands of years—until only a few centuries ago—people saw in such natural cataclysms the conscious actions of the gods in which sinful cities were punished. Many legends have thus originated, which are still told along the coasts.

Today geologists can give natural explanations for such catastrophes as the sinking of whole cities into the deep. The firmness of the ground under our feet can be misleading. Only a thin crust covers the probably molten center of the earth. This crust did not develop smoothly, but consists of a confused mass of broken clods, often covered with sedimentary rock and deposits from the mountains. When clods of earth shift in the deeper strata of the earth, the surface sways and shudders. Mountains rise, islands disappear. Some movements occur very slowly—then land sinks slowly into the sea or new land rises out of it. In this manner new islands arose from the sea in 1963. Other violent changes take place in sudden earth cataclysms with volcanic eruptions and earthquakes. The skin of the earth has a clearly distinguishable earthquake belt, which passes over the Mediterranean area and on to the far East;

a "thin" seam dotted with volcanoes. In addition there is a constant change in the climate of the earth. During times of increasing warmth the icecaps on the poles and alpine glaciers melt somewhat. The water from this melting enters the seas and raises their levels.

This "eustatic" ascent of the level of the sea has been measured precisely at many Mediterranean sites. At the southern point of Crete, the sea has climbed about eight feet since Minoan times—enough to submerge the Minoan tombs. Between the ages of Classical Greece (about 500 to 400 B.C.) and the Roman emperors, the Mediterranean along some coasts has risen from one-and-a-half to two feet. Since the days of the Roman Empire, the sea level has climbed another six feet. Many coastal regions have been drowned during the centuries and ancient towns, villages, castles, and harbors submerged. Yet great volcanic eruptions have often caused a reversal of the process—land has sunk below sea level.

Of course great cataclysms rarely occurred without destroying the buildings of the sinking city. And the sea completed the work of destruction. The search for sunken cities of the past is therefore very difficult, for not much is left of many of them. Divers and archaeologists in Greece sought in vain for the cities of Helice and Bura which sank into the Gulf of Corinth in an earthquake in 373 B.C. Ancient authors report that after the earthquake many people came to the Gulf of Corinth to view the ruins of the cities under the water when the sea was calm. Today thick mud covers the bottom, and exploratory efforts are further hampered by muddy water from two rivers which empty there. So far divers have only been able to find a few amphora fragments and the pieces of a silver Greek bowl.

The taking of test borings as it is done in searching for oil would lead to speedy success. But the certainty that more original works of art from the fourth century B.C., and from earlier times lie in Helice than have been found so far in all other sites causes archaeologists to hesitate. Borers could destroy precious finds. Scholars therefore are attaching their hopes to locating devices which work with sound waves. Such apparatus send out waves and register the kind of reflection through the ground layers which they have struck. These reflections vary according to the nature of the layer. Thus a diagram of reflections can provide information concerning the sea bottom. Elisha Linder of the Israeli Society for Underwater Archaeology and Olivier Leenhardt of the Museum for Oceanography in Monaco had great success experimenting with such devices in 1963 while exploring the Roman harbor of Caesarea in Israel. Archaeologists now hope that in a few years locating devices will have been improved enough to lead them to ancient Helice.

Port Royal, the notorious pirate city on Jamaica, was covered by the sea with a layer of mud a scant three hundred years after its sinking. On June 7, 1692, the city sank into the sea complete with inhabitants, freebooters, pirates, and lawless riffraff from all leading countries as the result of a mighty earthquake. When in 1956 the well-known American flight technician Edwin A. Link and his wife Marion went to Jamaica to search for the sunken city, they experienced a great disappointment: "To our surprise we found in the places where buildings once had stood, now only a flat mud bottom in about six fathoms of water. Not a mound or outline of an old city was to be seen." Under five feet of mud they finally found the first brick wall, encrusted with coral and hardly recognizable as a wall. But the Links did not let themselves be discouraged. In 1959 they returned to Port Royal with their eighty-foot *Sea Diver*, a boat especially outfitted for underwater research. With sonar, they prepared a diagram of the sunken city. Of great help was an old city map they had found in an archive. Now the divers began with sample excavations, and from the city fortress, a kitchen, and a ship-outfitting shop they brought up hundreds of finds of copper, brass, tin, iron, glass, and clay. But the most interesting find was a gold watch which had stopped at exactly the time when the earthquake began.

The Treasure of Attila

The story of Poidebard's discovery of the ancient harbor of Tyre was almost repeated in Italy, two decades later, when the

Italian archaeologist, Professor Fontani, traced an historic street. It was a street that once rang with death and destruction; Fontani was following the trail of Attila the Hun on his retreat from Northern Italy. At the beginning of the fifth century A.D., hordes of his riders swept down from the steppes of Asia, destroyed the kingdom of the Goths in South Russia, overran the Roman provinces on the Danube and the Rhine and penetrated into Gaul. After the battle at the "Katalaunische Felder" in A.D. 451, Attila advanced on Rome. But he did not destroy it. The bravery of the Pope, who opposed him alone without weapons, saved the city, although nobody knows why Attila changed his mind at their meeting and quickly withdrew his troops. The last fortress his riders held in Italy was Bibione. There is an old legend that he buried his treasure there before his warriors retreated and he died. But historians have not been able to find a trace of Bibione, and some of them have doubted its existence—until Professor Fontani realized that the street of Attila's retreat ended on the North shore of the Gulf of Venice in a shallow lagoon near the mouth of the River Tagliamente. When he studied the coastal region closely, he found strange stones in the masonry of the fishermen's cottages. The fishermen said they had found them in the lagoon. They had also found some coins. Fontani examined them; they were coined during the time that Attila was in Italy. This made him certain that the old fortress of the Hun lay at the bottom of the lagoon. Soon skindivers scoured the waters. They found neither gold nor silver, but the remainders of walls, towers, and halls, weapons, coins, tools, and urns that held the ashes of the warriors killed during the retreat. The news of the discovery of Bibione spread, and adventurers rushed to search for Attila's legendary treasure. Although the archaeologists were unhappy over the treasure-diggers' careless methods, they were overjoyed when amateur divers made a great discovery. Only one and a half miles away from the Lido of Venice, they came across the walls of Metamauco. The *Cronica Altinante*, written during the early Middle Ages, says of this forerunner of Rialto (now Venice) that it had large squares, rich palaces, and a grand Basilica. Once Metamauco was the flourishing center of commerce on the Adriatic Sea. When Attila invaded Italy, the inhabitants of Padua, led by their bishop, found shelter and safety in Metamauco, because it was well fortified and surrounded by the sea. During the eighth century, civil wars raged through the area, and many of the town's noblemen were murdered or exiled. One of the factions asked Pippin for help, but his men overwhelmed the town, killed most of the inhabitants, and set it on fire. Metamauco never recovered. Its site was not completely lost—but only the fishermen knew where it lay. They pulled in good catches from the town—antique art, which they sold to tourists. Fortunately, scientists learned about the site before the beautiful marble tombs of noblemen, bishops, merchants, and the ruins of palaces were completely sacked.

Epidauros—Mirage on the Sea Floor?

Once a sunken city has been discovered, experienced specialists must take over the work. For the explorations require just as much care as the excavation of ancient shipwrecks, and the observation of inexperienced divers on the bottom of the sea can be misleading. The sea is capable of confronting them with mirages. A good example of this is the controversial "discovery" of the walls of the sunken Illyrian Epidauros on the Dalmatian coast not far from Dubrovnik, the Ragusa of the Middle Ages.

Illyrian Epidauros was a daughter city of the Greek Epidauros, one of the many Greek colonies along the Mediterranean coast. Forty thousand people lived within its walls until the sea swallowed up a large part of the city. In the course of thousands of years, knowledge as to the exact whereabouts of the city has been lost. Even in our own time no one was concerned about it until one day the adventurers Ted Falcon-Barker and Hans van Praag met in a café on the island of Ibiza in the Spanish Balearic Islands.

Falcon-Barker owned a modest yacht built in 1927 and was secretary of a London underwater exploring club. He was cruising among the Balearics with vacationers who wanted to spend their time diving in the Mediterranean. The Dutchman Hans van Praag, a fifty-six-year-old one-time colonial officer, geologist, amateur archaeologist, and art dealer, who had already made a dozen expeditions into the interior of New Guinea, Celebes, and Borneo, told Falcon-Barker of a peculiar vacation experience. A few years before, while on vacation near Dubrovnik in Yugoslavia, an old fisherman rowed out to sea with him and showed him the walls of a sunken city below the crystal-clear water.

An expedition to solve the mystery of the sunken city was soon planned. Friends lent both of them money, and many English amateur divers and the Dutch archaeologist Dr. Arend Hubrecht offered to help the two men and Falcon-Barker's wife, Bel, with the exploration. While the expedition was being outfitted and the necessary equipment was being acquired, the scholars, enthusiastic at the thought of an expedition, sifted through all the archives at the Archaeological Institute in Belgrade. From old writings they learned that the city might be Epidauros. But since ancient times so many wars had passed over the land that the annals of Epidauros were unknown. It is assumed that the city was probably destroyed by Germanic tribes in the sixth century. But these tribes probably found only a part of the city remaining to plunder, for the rest had already disappeared into the sea.

Where Epidauros once flourished, the small town of Cavtat, the

Epidauros, now Cavtat, on the Yugoslavian coast

Ragusa Vecchia of the Middle Ages, now stands at the foot of hills covered with olive terraces and cypress groves. The *Pagan II*, the expedition ship, anchored in one of the two bays near Cavtat. And then it became apparent that even a whole city is not easily found on the sea floor. The divers searched for three hours before Hans van Praag came up waving excitedly. A buoy was thrown out and the engines of the *Pagan II* were stopped. A group went into the water. The strangely shaped hill which van Praag discovered loomed up rapidly before Falcon-Barker's eyes. He reached into the soft mud—and pulled his hand back with a start. They had found a dead horse! Now old Niko had to help, the man who had shown the walls to Hans van Praag years before. But where Niko led the expedition, only mounds and hills of mud could be seen. Were the walls underneath? Had they simply been freed of mud for only a short time by a storm?

Another fisherman remembered having seen walls shortly after a storm, which were taller than he was, and a street paved with flat stones.

The divers probed the mounds with iron rods and found that the mud was yards deep. But Falcon-Barker and his friends thought they could make out from the forms of the mounds that they covered houses, a road, and grain silos. They drew up an approximate map of the hills and mounds.

A large portion of the bottom was covered with a thick jungle of sea grass which blanketed everything with an impenetrable green. In spite of this the search for exposed portions of wall continued right along with the cartography work, and it was finally successful. Only a dozen yards from a pebble beach five walls extended straight into the deep water where they disappeared into a large hill of mud.

By the time the archaeologist Dr. Arend Hubrecht joined the expedition he was thrilled, for throughout the ship was stacked pottery that had been found by the divers near the walls and mounds—amphoras, jugs, clay bowls, vases, fragments, oil lamps, and tiles. But not everything that comes from the bottom encrusted and covered with coral is antique. With pained expressions the divers watched as Dr. Hubrecht heaved overboard one antique-looking item after another, muttering each time, "Chamber pot, eighteenth century," or "Hm, maybe ten or twenty years old." Yet, after careful sifting, 357 finds still remained at the end of the expedition which Yugoslavian archaeologists took to their institutes, among them rare Greek pieces such as had never been found in Dalmatia before.

Now they had to get a pump with which to remove the mud coat from the city. The Cavtat fire department gave them a helping hand, with an old, dilapidated, worn-out fire pump with a spitting, coughing gas engine, a relic from their tool shed. With it the divers were at least able to raise a corner of the mud blanket. Seconds after the diver began his work on the bottom, the water all around him took on a gray-black color. He had to feel his way forward like a blind man. Not until the next day was the water clear again, and then the efforts of the previous day could be evaluated. No more than three or four feet of wall had been cleared away to a depth of less than two feet. Ted Falcon-Barker figured that with a good team and even the best equipment it would take five years to free the entire sunken city from mud. But the four-month expedition was over. The divers had to be satisfied with having scratched into the mud hills in order to check them for walls and mark them on their map. The blank places on the map gradually filled with houses, city walls, a castle; aqueducts and a market place were also charted.

In front of one of the bays Falcon-Barker and one of his friends discovered an ancient shipwreck and an anchoring place. Deeper in the bay they found the remains of the harbor facilities. And everywhere there were pottery finds and coins which told of the flourishing sea trade of the one-time Epidauros. They found thirty-one amphoras in which trade goods had been brought to Epidauros in all periods and from all Mediterranean countries, and coins which had been minted many days' sea journey from Epidauros. A local legend gives the year A.D. 375 as the date of Epidauros' sinking. Yugoslavian archaeologists found in the writings of an unknown Italian monk a report of an earthquake that destroyed the city and a

Divers swim through the ruins of what may have been Epidauros

tidal wave that poured over it sometime after the death of the Emperor Julian the Apostate. Julian fell in a battle against the Persians in 363, and many scholars have no doubt that the local legend and the monk's writing provide a pretty accurate date for the demise of the city.

But many scientists harbor grave doubts regarding the entire findings of Falcon-Barker's expedition.

One glance at the photographs of the sunken walls of Epidauros sufficed for one well-known German underwater archaeologist to expose them as "falsifications" from the workshop of nature, to which, according to the scientists, Ted Falcon-Barker and his archaeologically inexperienced colleagues had fallen victim. The scholar cited discoveries of "sunken walls" near Syracuse and Portoferraio on the island of Elba that resembled those of Epidauros. Closer investigation had revealed that they were basalt rocks, layers of regular-shaped cyrstallized rock which protruded from the sea floor. A few Yugoslavian archaeologists shared the views of the German underwater explorer. To be sure, the academic battle over the walls of Epidauros has not yet been settled. And maybe the truth lies in the middle: a part of the walls are no more than natural basalt rock, the rest belongs to the ruins of the sunken city.

A strange coincidence gave the mother city of the Illyrian Epidauros, the famous Epidauros on the Peloponnesus, the same fate as her daughter city. A large part of the city sank to the sea bottom. Its ruins can be seen today in a few feet of water. Apparently the whole Peloponnesus has sunk a few feet in the course of the last two thousand years.

For an expert in Greek culture and history, Corinth holds many associations. Once it was one of the most cosmopolitan towns in Greece and a center for land and sea trade, not only for the Greeks but for the Mediterranean world. Cenchreae, too, was famous. Pausanias mentions the sanctuaries of Aphrodite, Asclepios, and the Egyptian goddess, Isis. The temple remembered because in *The Golden Ass* of Lucius Apuleius, the first picaresque novel, the hero resumes his human form in it after traveling through Greece as an ass. The apostle Paul set up some of the

Greek missions from Cenchreae. But present-day visitors to Corinth are usually disappointed; what they see is a typical provincial town. Very few relics of the ancient settlement and its castle remain. At Cenchreae, too, only a couple of ruins testify to its former glory. Nevertheless, Professor Robert L. Scranton chose it as a site for an expedition from the American School of Classical Studies at Athens sponsored by the University of Chicago and Indiana University. The first summer of the expedition was 1963. Scranton and his team had modest hopes. They thought the ruins might throw some light on ancient commerce and the development of religions during the Roman period, when Greek and Oriental cults flourished and a few young Christian communities existed. But the ruins held a great surprise. . . . After the general exploration of the area in the summer of 1963, Scranton concentrated on a strange church-like structure the following year. One part of it rose above sea level. Scranton's curiosity was casually aroused by a thickening of a wall in the structure. It proved to be the top of a flight of stairs that descended below sea level. A second floor lay beneath the waters, paved with beautiful mosaics. It was covered with debris. Skindivers reported that the debris included many pieces of wooden furniture, often elaborately carved. Then came the biggest surprise. In one corner the frogmen discovered some sheets of glass mosaic showing Nile scenery, in which egrets and ibises wandered through lotus and papyrus plants and a man rode on a crocodile. The divers were certain that they had uncovered the sacred temple of the goddess Isis. Professor Scranton was more cautious. But whether or not the site turned out to be a famous sanctuary, at least the team had unearthed fine glass mosaics of a type unknown until then. During the following two summers, 1965 and 1966, the team found that the room under the sea was a warehouse of glass mosaic panels. They were able to recover 108 panels and stow them in crates. Then they dammed the ruin and pumped out the water to salvage the fragile panels. Unfortunately, their restoration has been difficult, because the panels were clumped in masses, and has not yet been finished. To this date it is not certain that the mosaics were decorations for a temple to Isis. But everything points to the assumption. The panels may have been removed from the walls in the fourth century A.D. when the structure was remodeled and then stored below because Christianity had become the dominant religion. Perhaps the expedition will soon throw further light on the mysterious church under the sea.

Baia—a Sunken Pompeii

Nearly all rediscovered sunken cities have disappointed those who believe that every sunken city must resemble Pompeii in its state of preservation. One city has proved to be an exception in this: Baia (ancient Baiae).

Today Baia is a small, quiet town on the Bay of Pozzuoli in the large Gulf of Naples. Visitors stream into Naples, Capri, Amalfi, and Sorrento or come to see the ruins of Pompeii. Things were different when Puteoli still stood on the road markers along the way to Rome.

No modern city can be compared to the ancient Baiae. If we imagine the millionaires' villas of Hollywood, gambling casinos of Las Vegas, and Rome's Via Veneto all transplanted in Nice, and then add a part of the Montmartre, this combination would still lack the color which the many festivals of the Roman emperors gave the beach town of Baiae.

Following the examples of the emperors and senators, the "high society" of the Roman Empire devoted themselves to the healing effect of the thermal springs, luxury, and pleasure in this splendorous city. Ships from Greece, Asia Minor, and North Africa brought marble for the pompous villas of the rich Romans to Baiae. The richest among them lay on precious boards fashioned from giant Mauretian citrus trees and inlaid with ivory from central Africa while enjoying their gluttonous meals. These couchlike boards were purchased for the value of several dozen slaves.

The meals featured guinea hens from Numidia in North Africa, French fish sauce and roasted thrush, German honey, and oysters raised in the vicinity by a clever Roman. For months before they decorated the salons of Baiae, precious woods from the Far East and tapestries from Inner Asia were underway on the backs of camels and in the holds of freight ships.

Archaeologists found ruins of the city under thick layers of earth and debris, but a good part of the area of the one-time Baiae is covered today by the waters of the Tyrrhenian Sea. Time and again fishermen reported that they had seen the walls, columns, and streets of the sunken city rising from the sea floor on quiet, windless days.

Aerial view of Baia, showing ruins over large area

Mondadori

Diving into the Past

In 1930, finds made while dredging the harbor cast aside all doubts regarding the claims of the fishermen. Archaeologists sent helmet divers down to the bottom of the Bay of Baia. They actually did find buildings and streets, and brought up several marble statues from the ruins. The art works are parts of the decor with which the palaces and villas of ancient Baiae were trimmed.

Scholars suspected that Baiae was a Pompeii on the sea bottom. But the constantly muddy waters of the Gulf of Pozzuoli clouded the vision of the divers who were already hindered enough by their clumsy suits. The water was often so muddy that they could not see their hands in front of their faces.

The years passed and Baia was almost forgotten again, when in 1958 Raimondo Bucher, an explorer and diver from Naples, published a sensational pictorial report. Bucher had himself pulled over the remains of the city by a boat on a quiet day when the water was clear and the visibility good. He succeeded in getting some spectacular photographs.

When Professor Nino Lamboglia, head of the Centro Sperimentale di Archeologia Sottomarina in Albenga saw them and heard Raimondo Bucher's report, he decided on an expedition for the following year.

In September, 1959, the research ship *Daino* of the Underwater Research Center sailed into the Gulf of Pozzuoli. The cannons and machine guns had been demounted from the corvette, which does military service with the Italian navy during the winter months. In their place Professor Lamboglia had the necessary equipment for underwater exploration brought on board: air compressor, suction pumps, recovery baskets, and underwater vehicles. Professor Lamboglia's divers swam through an eerie, ghostlike world. The city extended for miles along the sea floor. Stretches of wall, columns, stairs, canals that carried the water from the thermal springs to the bathers, galleries, servants' quarters, marble steps that led to the sea—all came one after another into the view of the astounded divers. In the middle rose the altar of a temple.

The divers passed through the large hotels of the city. Here rich Romans used to take their vacations and young couples spent their honeymoons. Small cuttlefish had nested in the suites and spiny lobsters crouched in the nooks and crannies of the walls. Fish darted through the business streets with their once exclusive stores where important Romans led their elegantly dressed wives on shopping sprees. Once these stores held gems—beautifully carved jewels —from India, fine gold and silverwork, valuable swords from Spain, statuettes and expensive art works, carpets and furniture. The women bought rich perfumes from the Orient, silk from China, fine muslin, cotton and woolen fabrics, and strong German linen.

It is quiet now in these streets. The heavy cobblestones in the large Via Herculea are still as smooth and firmly in place as ever, and in places, as clean as if they had just been swept. Rows of light mud cover the costly mosaic and marble floors of many villas. But the motion of a fish or a slight rub of the hand is enough to uncover the splendid designs and colors. Some of the salons look as if a party

Ruins in the sunken city of Baia

Gerhard Kapitän

of Romans were just about to partake of a Lucullian meal. Small stages seem to be awaiting the appearance of beloved comedy troupes or a group of gaily clad Spanish dancers. For 150 years Baiae was the city of sin for the Roman Empire. Under Nero the ostentation and hedonism of the inhabitants of the city reached its peak, but the end was near. In August of A.D. 79, the earth began to quiver and shake. A huge cloud of smoke and fire hung over Vesuvius. It grew and rolled over the Bay of Naples as far as Capri. A heavy rain of stones and ashes fell to the ground. When the sun finally shone pale through the cloud again, Vesuvius had annihilated Pompeii, Herculaneum, and Stabiae. Baiae had been spared. But the land had risen. The sea had withdrawn and had given up a wide strip of land. The raised land later sank gradually, deeper and deeper, and took Baiae with it. The sea washed its streets clean and finally closed over its villas, hotels, and palaces.

In 1959, Professor Lamboglia with the help of his divers prepared an exact map of parts of the city, but excavation in the manner of Pompeii poses insurmountable difficulties. Ten thousand tons of mud would have to be removed—and the next storm could render the entire effort worthless. But maybe the sunken city will rise again—in hundreds of thousands of years. The land along the Gulf of Naples is in constant motion. The rising and falling sea level has left its marks in the columns of the Serapis Temple of Pozzuoli. Today they stand deep beneath the water. But more than three feet above the current sea level the marble has been damaged by stone borers. The columns were once underwater to this height. During an eruption of the now extinct volcano Monte Nuovo near Pozzuoli in the sixteenth century, the land rose again, but since the eighteenth century it has been sinking further into the deep. Whoever wants to see the sunken city must equip himself with diving mask, fins, and snorkel, take a fishing skiff in Pozzuoli or Baia—and have good luck and clear water.

The Mystery of the Sunken Island of "Atlantis"

"Beyond the columns of Hercules sank Atlantis in a bad day and

Corroded walls of Baia

a bad night." Thus wrote the Greek philosopher Plato some four hundred years B.C. Ever since, Plato's Atlantis report has occupied scholars and dreamers. In all parts of the world they have sought "sunken Atlantis," whose appearance, people, and fate were described in detail by Plato.

According to him, the king's island of the Atlanteans was a fertile plain in the sea, beyond an unusual island of red, white, and black rock protruding sharply from the sea and looking as if it had been cut off with a knife.

In the middle of the king's island, the mighty royal palace rose on a hill called Basileia, which was surrounded by stone walls. Next to it stood the temple of the supreme god of the Atlanteans. Plato continues: "[The Atlanteans covered] the entire temple . . . externally with silver, with the exception of the spires, which were covered with gold. Inside, the ceiling was decorated with gold, ivory, silver, and orichalc [amber?]. Everything else—walls, columns, and floors—was trimmed with orichalc. Golden statues were also erected . . ."

But one day awful natural catastrophes broke out over the earth. Terrible heat and drought burned many areas, huge fires laid waste to the parched land. Then earthquakes and tidal waves devastated the land. In a day and a night they destroyed the flourishing king's island of the empire of Atlantis. An impassable sea of mud covered the area where the island once stood, or so the Greek philosopher reported in his dialogues *Timaeus* and *Critias*.

The kings of Atlantis abandoned their devastated homeland and led their people on a violent campaign to bring all the countries of the Mediterranean under their rule. They subjugated the principalities of Greece, and only Athens, according to Plato, was able to maintain its freedom through heroic fighting. Finally the Atlanteans were conquered by the Egyptians.

It sounds fabulous, but Plato attested to the truth of the story often in his writings. "This report is no fairy tale, but completely historical in every respect." He cites the philosopher and legislator of Athens as his authority and source, Solon, who lived from 640-559 B.C. and once traveled to Egypt, according to Plato, to gather "information about earlier times." In the city of Sais on the Nile delta an old priest told Solon the story of Atlantis from old documents and inscriptions.

Soon after Plato wrote down his Atlantis report, the scholarly battle over the veracity of the text began. Ever since, the catchword "Atlantis" has had the ability to divide scholars into two bitterly opposed camps. The vast majority of scholars hold Plato's Atlantis to be a fiction invented by the philosopher for the clarification of his teachings.

But in every century there have been a number of serious scientists as well as laymen who have believed Plato's words, and have searched for the "sunken island" and the "Empire of Atlantis." Nearly thirty thousand books on Atlantis have appeared, and every few years an expedition sets out in some part of the world to find the "sunken island." Theories on Atlantis are each more fantastic than the other. Thus some seekers of Atlantis—"Atlantomaniacs" they are called by a few scholars—are seriously of the opinion that Atlantis lay in the vicinity of the Azores and sank there into a depth of 1,500 fathoms. But an investigation of the sea floor in the Azores area by the American oceanographer Eving shows that there hasn't been any dry land there in the last twenty million years.

A seventeenth-century map of the legendary Atlantis

In 1953 a book was published by an unknown outsider, Pastor Jürgen Spanuth from the north German village of Bordelum. Decades of study and research preceded the publication of his book.

Spanuth occupied himself with Plato's Atlantis report and Homer's *Odyssey*. He became convinced that Plato's Atlantis and Homer's Phaeacia, where the shipwrecked Odysseus was cast ashore were the same. Spanuth believes that he has found places in both texts which indicate that Atlantis lay in the North Sea area, east of Heligoland, and sank at the beginning of the Iron Age around 1200 B.C. Among other things the pastor cites in his book, *Atlantis—the Mystery Unravelled*, are the sailing directions which Odysseus received from the goddess Calypso on the island of

Ogygia, according to Spanuth the Azores island of São Miguel, for the voyage to Scheria, the land of the Phaeacians.

According to Spanuth's calculations, a seaman following these directions would have to sail through the English Channel and across the North Sea in the direction of Heligoland.

The pastor's thesis was still fragmentary, until from 1927 to 1936. The Oriental Institute of the University of Chicago excavated the temple of Pharaoh Ramses III who ruled over Egypt from 1198 to 1167 B.C. Among ten thousand square yards of murals and hieroglyphics was a report of a violent attack on Egypt by a seagoing people. The impressive pictures on the walls of the temple in Medinet Habu immortalize the pharaoh's victory over these intruders from the "islands in the great water circle" at the "ends of the world." He annihilated them in a great sea battle in the Nile delta. The captured North Sea warriors and kings were tried and their statements were also written on the walls of the temple. As the reason for their war campaign they gave severe catastrophes which had struck their homeland.

"Their (the Northerners') land is annihilated . . . torn loose and carried away in a storm . . . the capital of their cities . . . destroyed." The insurgence of the sea folk to Egypt is obviously a part of the second great Indo-European migration. The first had brought Indo-European tribes to India around 2000 B.C., and somewhat later led the Ionians and Acheans into Greece. Today scholars are of the opinion that the second migration in 1200 B.C. actually was precipitated by great catastrophes and worsening of the climate. The Dorians pushed into Greece at that time, conquered the Ionian and Achean castles, and destroyed the flourishing principalities of the Mycenaean rulers. Only the Acropolis in Athens was able to repel them. But not only Greece was conquered—the entire Orient was disrupted, Crete and Cyprus were occupied, and the mighty empire of the Hittites fell.

When Pastor Spanuth learned of the inscriptions found in the Medinet Habu, he was convinced. That was the keystone to his theory, the final, decisive proof. Hadn't Plato reported that Solon had heard the story in Egypt? Plato's Atlanteans, Homer's Phaeacians, and the North Sea warriors who attacked Egypt had been Bronze Age Germans who had lived in a powerful, flourishing empire extending over north Germany, Denmark, and southern Sweden. Their palace island Atlantis sank in a violent catastrophe, a combination of earthquake and tidal wave, east of Heligoland in the North Sea. For many years the pastor collected proofs of his assertion, excerpts from ancient works, legends, traditions, geological and archaeological clues. In his book he draws attention to the similarity between the arms of warriors depicted in the Medinet Habu and those found time and again in the area of the "Atlantean realm," and to many other things. But a large part of Spanuth's proof is strongly contested. His book triggered an impassioned scholarly controversy, and it has met with enthusiastic agreement and intense disagreement.

The one way for the pastor to prove his theory was to explore the sea floor east of Heligoland.

The Search for the Palace Island of Atlantis

Not only Plato's report, the *Odyssey,* and the inscriptions of Medinet Habu gave the pastor reason to believe that there had actually been a large island east of Heligoland a long time ago. The Marseilles merchant Pytheas, who undertook an exploratory journey into the North Sea area in 350 B.C., also reported an island Basileia, rich in amber, opposite Germania in the sea—a day's voyage from the mainland, as Pliny later added. Was Pytheas's Basileia the remainder of Plato's sunken island Atlantis after its desolation by the tidal wave? And is this Basileia identical with the holy island "Fositesland" of the Friesians, where the Christian missionaries Wolfram, Willibrord, and Liudger preached? On the other hand, Adam von Bremen (1075) equates Fositesland and Heligoland. Most scholars followed his example, and geoogists say that in the seventh and eighth centuries there could no longer have been any island east of Heligoland. Pastor Spanuth, on the other hand, cites an old Friesian tradition which contends that the last remains of this island which was later called "Uthland" and "Suderstrand," did not finally disappear until 1216. A map of Heligoland from 1570 indicates "Steinwirk east of Heligoland, where once seven churches stood. They may still be seen when the water is calm."

After completing his theoretical research, Pastor Spanuth got hold of a sea map—and at the place which Plato had designated as the island of Atlantis he found indicated a hill with many large rocks that protrude several yards above the otherwise flat sea bottom. Geologists took this area, marked "rocky bottom," for a moraine. But no one had investigated the rocky bottom. In the summer of 1952, a diving expedition set out. On July 31, the first

A map illustrating Pastor Spanuth's theory of Atlantis

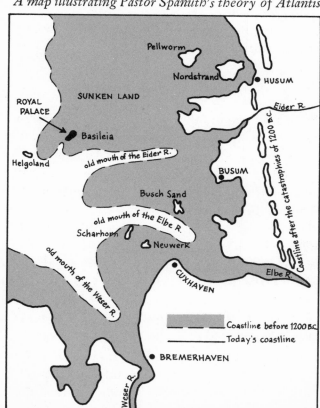

diver from the expedition ship descended to the rocky sea bottom. After only a few minutes he called into the telephone:

"Straight ahead of me I see a high wall made of stone. . . . At the base of the wall lie large stones. . . . I will attempt to climb the wall . . . it is at least six feet high, made of huge rocks. . . . Now I am on top of the wall . . . it runs completely regular from right to left. Now I see another wall running perfectly parallel to the one I'm standing on."

On the following days Pastor Spanuth had the walls measured. Each was thirty-six feet wide and six to seven feet high. The entire walled area was a half a nautical mile (930 yards) long and 250 to 300 yards wide.

After the work was finished, the diver stated his opinion that it was impossible that these walls, which were so symmetrical and run so parallel, could have come into existence naturally. He did not doubt that they were built by the hand of man.

But the scholars remained skeptical, for there are many creations of unusual forces of nature which every layman would take for works of man. Furthermore, an archaeologically inexperienced diver can easily be deceived under water.

Pastor Spanuth was not discouraged. In 1953 he undertook another expedition to the bottom of the sea. And this time divers succeeded in bringing up slabs of flint which really had been formed by human hands and tools. They lay next to one another on the bottom, all sharply rectangular in shape.

This was no proof, for the recovered slabs—of Danish flint—might be from sunken structures, but they might also be simply the remains of a boat laden with carefully stowed building materials that sank off Denmark.

In 1961 a third expedition ship was sent out to the rocky ground. This time the frogmen of the Siegen amateur diving club offered to help the pastor from Bordelum. Again they managed to recover flint slabs, but stormy seas rendered all other dives into the deep impossible.

In the next few years the answer may be found to whether the unusual rocky ground bears the ruins of the sunken city of Atlantis or an inhabited island of a later period. The suggestion has also been made that it could be debris deposits from Ice Age glaciers.

Right or wrong, Pastor Spanuth's theory should serve to direct our glance at prehistory and early history in countries north of the Alps. While Egypt was building its pyramids, while Agamemnon was ruling over golden Mycenae, the people in central and northern Europe were by no means living a primitive existence. Anyone who looks into a modern book on the prehistory of central Europe learns that cultures flourished north of the Alps that were scarcely inferior to some in the Mediterranean area. Of course, the prehistorians of the northern area have a difficult job. The Nordic peoples built with wood which decays fast, and the climate at these latitudes did its part to destroy many monuments. Fortunately, it is becoming apparent that the rivers and lakes, the North Sea and the Baltic are scarcely less richly filled treasure chests than the Mediterranean Sea.

There is some evidence to show that, even if Heligoland was the residence of a prehistoric king, it was not Atlantis. Many archaeologists believe that Egyptian records about the great flood of Atlantis are really an account of a disaster that struck the Minoan Empire of Crete in 1500 B.C. The disaster is one of the great mysteries of history. At the same time all the palaces of Crete, among them the famous palaces of Knossos, Phaistos, and Mallia, the splendid mansions of the island, and many towns and villages were destroyed. Did invaders conquer and sack Crete? In that case, why did the Minoans rebuild the palace of Knossos without fortifications? Sir Arthur Evans, the expert on Minoan culture, put forth the theory that the disaster was an earthquake, for every hundred years there are an average of two destructive earthquakes in the Knossos district. But Evans' theory had two weak points: other areas of Crete are not so susceptible to earthquakes, and an earthquake has never destroyed at one time any island in the Eastern Mediterranean as large as Crete. However, the Greek archaeologist Spyridon Marinatos has offered an explanation which might support Evans' theory: he associates the destruction of the

Minoan Empire with the volcanic eruption of Thera, which occurred in 1500 B.C. This eruption blew up a part of the Cycladic island of Thera and submerged a large area, leaving three tiny islands—Thera, Therasia, and Aspronisis—and a great abyss, originally more than eighteen hundred feet in depth, surely the most imposing caldera in the world. The Minoan settlements on Thera were first buried by enormous quantities of volcanic ash and pumice stone in a layer ninety feet thick and then many of them were submerged. We have no records about the disaster, but we can imagine what it was like if we compare the eruption of Krakatao in the Dutch-East Indies on August 26-27, 1883. A series of gigantic waves, more than 90 feet high and traveling at a speed of 120 miles per hour, destroyed towns and villages on the coasts of Java and Sumatra, at a distance of 40 to 80 miles from Krakatao. Some 36,000 people died. Now, Crete is only 66 miles south of Thera and the sea between them is much deeper than between Krakatao and Java, so the waves must have been considerably higher and more frequent. The palace of Knossos would have escaped the waters, because it was built on high ground, far from the sea. But all great volcanic eruptions are followed by a series of severe earthquakes, and the destruction and burning of Knossos were the gloomy epilogue to the disaster. The Minoan Empire could not recover from the blow. Not long afterward, the Achaeans invaded Crete, and the Achaean dynasty ascended to the throne of Knossos. The brilliant civilization of the Minoans was no more.

Many signs tend to support Marinatos' theory. In a number of ruins excavated on Crete, the floors were covered with volcanic ash and pumice stone. Some ruins show that the inhabitants barely had time to carry off their household goods. Archaeologists from the French School of Athens excavated houses on Thera that lay under thick layers of pumice stone. But the most significant discovery on Thera was made by an expedition under Marinatos in summer, 1967. His team excavated a palace, also buried by a thick layer of ash and pumice stone, whose walls were preserved to the height of the first floor. The work is only beginning, but the findings point to a little Minoan "Pompeii." On one site, where the archaeologists dug down to the ground floor, they found a kitchen with its crockery still in place. Archaeologists hope that the submerged parts of Thera will prove to be a treasury of Minoan art, which some day, when machines that allow divers to work at a depth of 300 feet are in standard use, will be recovered.

So far it has not been proved whether the fall of Thera and the destruction of the Minoan Empire suggested the Egyptian Atlantis records, mentioned by Plato. But it is not hard to imagine that many of the survivors fled from Crete and, in their search for a place to settle, invaded Egypt. The catastrophe may even have been identified with an older legend of Atlantis and been immortalized in the records of the Egyptian priest, who wrote about the land that "was drowned in one terrible day and one terrible night."

VIII

Diving Expeditions in Rivers and Lakes and the Baltic Sea

In the lakes of Switzerland, when the last of the resort guests take flight before the damp cold of autumn weather, the low temperature of the water also retards the growth of the lush underwater vegetation along the shore. Algae, creepers, and floating plankton disappear and the lake becomes clear and transparent.

At this time, a person who knows the area can row you out to certain places on the lake where countless black stumps rise up from the bottom.

These places are pole fields, locations where prehistoric villages of the Stone Age and Bronze Age once stood. In the flat shoreline waters of many alpine lakes in Germany, Austria, Switzerland, and even in northern Italy and Hungary, such pole fields are very common.

But if you are especially lucky at Lake Constance or some Swiss lake you will come across a group of frogmen who have anchored their boats and a work float over one of the prehistoric pole fields. They dive to the bottom, investigate the pole fields, discover new ones, take measurements, photograph, sketch, and recover precious finds. Clay food vessels, jugs, bowls, stone axes, lances, arrowheads, knives, and also wooden implements, cloth, and leather are removed from the mud and clay and brought to the surface in recovery baskets. The less common, later pole fields have a variety of bronze implements. The Lake Constance Underwater Exploration Club of Uberlingen alone has discovered numerous pole fields, remains of stilt villages of the earlier Stone Age, and six from the Bronze Age in their search along the bottom of the lake.

However, credit does not belong to the divers; the discovery actually began over a hundred years ago, in 1854, when the Swiss schoolteacher Aeppli in Obermeilen on Lake Zurich found implements from the early Stone Age, the Neolithic, among dark pole stumps. Aeppli took the finds to the Ferdinand Keller of the Antiquarian Society in Zurich. Keller suspected a connection between the black poles in the lake floor and the implements. He began investigations and brought up from the Swiss lakes secret after secret pertaining to the sunken pole-dweller cultures. His reports were well received. Now pole dwellings were found everywhere. With long wooden dredge scoops, fishermen pulled stone axes, implements of horn, and artfully formed clay vessels out of the shore waters by the basketful. But the eager amateurs caused more damage than good, for only through exact scientific methods and often with the help of specialists from other sciences, such as geology and botany, are archaeologists able to piece together a living picture of past cultures from remnants. When the pole dwellings were discovered, most of our contemporary methods of archaeological investigation were not yet known, so it is not surprising that at the beginning of the research on pole dwellings numerous mistakes were made. The science of prehistory is still young. At that time experts were just beginning to learn to recognize and interpret the few finds from prehistoric central Europe.

Only four years after Aeppli's discovery, a Swiss colonel named Friedrich Schwab rowed out over the flat spots of the Lake of Neuchâtel in search of pole dwellings. He studied the bottom carefully and now and then checked it with a tonglike device of his own invention. Near a prehistoric earthen wall by La Tène, a town on the east shore of the lake, he made a find. In only three feet of water lay bronze weapons, spearheads, and swords in profusion.

Their artistic forms aroused a great deal of interest. The colonel had discovered the La Tène culture—a thriving Celtic cultural epoch which was dominant from 400 B.C. to A.D. 50. The culture was named after La Tène, where most of the finds were made. Schwab then had a glass window built into the bottom of his rowboat and in calm weather spent three years investigating the prehistoric settlement. His finds were so numerous and fascinating that in 1862 the entire site was dammed off and drained. An abundance of valuables now increased his finds: pottery, weapons, fine work of bronze and gold, jewelry of coral and enamel. Precursors of this Celtic people must have reached into the area of the Scythians in southern Russia and even to the Orient, for many of the motifs of the art were taken from there and included in these artistic creations. Since then many sites on land and underwater in Lake Neuenburger have been discovered, and one of the most brilliant epochs of European prehistory has become revealed to us.

It is not surprising that people at first concluded that a mysterious pole-dwelling people had erected its villages over the water or lower Alpine lakes on countless poles toward the end of the third century B.C. Ferdinand Keller was the first to conclude from the countless remains of poles that the houses of the Stone Age people must have rested on poles standing in the water—similar to the present-day stilt dwellings along the coast of New Guinea. A few decades later this romantic notion was shown to be an error.

The discovery of the Stone Age pole dwellings was followed by the discovery of those of the Bronze Age that had been built along the shores of Alpine lakes toward the end of the Bronze Age, roughly between 1200 and 800 B.C. But the archaeologists were still dependent on finds which could be fished up from the surface, and what the early structures themselves looked like remained an unsolved mystery—until peat cutters came upon the first moor villages. In the peat of some moors such as the Federsee moor in upper Swabia, not only have the poles withstood the ages, but floors as well, and even walls and parts of roofs. In the moor at Federsee the world's oldest wheel was found. Its age is estimated at 25,000 years.

And now, with special thanks to the explorations of Professor

Hans Reinerth in Federsee, so much light has been cast upon the pole-dwelling cultures of the late Stone Age and Bronze Age that during 1938-1940 it was possible to erect two impressive pole villages in Unteruhldingen on Lake Constance. They are faithful copies of villages of past millennia, down to the last nail. Only one thing is incorrect. They rise over the water of the lake. These are called stilt dwellings. The pole dwellings of early central European history stood on dry ground.

Finds made in the moors gave Professor Reinerth his first serious doubts about stilt dwellings.

Finally, after 1940, the Stuttgart prehistory researcher and engineer Oskar Paret showed Keller's "stilt dwellings" to be in error with relative certainty.

Paret had occupied himself for many years with the technical aspects of pole dwellings, and came to the conclusion that for several technical reasons these lower Alpine pole villages found in lakes and moors could not have been built in the water. And to be sure, modern equipment had to be employed in the erection of the stilt villages at Unteruhldingen. Houses built on unimpregnated poles a few decades ago in Lake Atter, in Austria, were already victims of decay just a few years after their construction. The changing water level and the corresponding change in moisture and dryness of the poles made them extremely susceptible to rot. The pole dwellings of prehistoric times would have had a similar fate except for an insignificant few where resistant hardwood was used. The vast majority of prehistorians today share Paret's views.

But how did these prehistoric dwellings end up at the bottom of lakes? Severe variations in climate caused the level of the lakes to drop periodically for periods of several centuries. A wide strip of lake bottom was freed, and it dried up. It was quickly covered by grass. But this bog lime presented an especially favorable ground to build on, for it was hard only on the surface. A pole pounded into it would break quickly through the hard crust and one could then easily pound it down another two or three yards. On ordinary

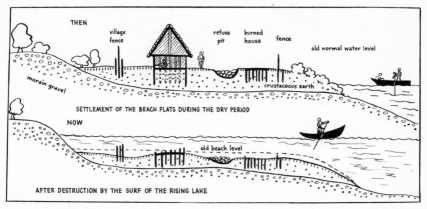

THEN

village
fence
refuse
pit
burned
house
fence

old normal water level

morain gravel

crustaceous earth

SETTLEMENT OF THE BEACH FLATS DURING THE DRY PERIOD

NOW

old beach level

AFTER DESTRUCTION BY THE SURF OF THE RISING LAKE

Origin of the pole fields in Swiss lakes, according to Paret

ground, the builders would laboriously have had to dig a post hole for every single pole.

The poles served as posts for the wooden houses. They held the walls and roofs. If a pole needed replacing, or if a house burned down, new poles were simply rammed into the ground alongside the old ones. When the water level of the lakes rose again, the fishermen, farmers, and hand workers of ancient times withdrew to higher ground. The surf of the lakes destroyed their houses, and all that remained was an accumulation of poles, which were enveloped in airtight, incrusted earth and kept for thousands of years. In lakes where sediment replaced the water and formed moors, the villages were much better preserved.

A stilt-dwelling culture would not fit into the picture of prehistoric times which prehistorians have meanwhile formulated. They have stated for a long time that such a culture never existed. The "stilt dwellers" belonged to the most diverse and widely distributed peoples and cultures, who by no means lived only on the edges of lakes. What would have motivated some tribes to live like swamp animals among the reeds while others lived a few miles farther inland on dry land?

These new insights do not detract from the value of the finds made in the moors and lakes. On the contrary, dry land has given up only a few, usually poorly preserved remnants of early cultures. But dry strips of shore land were settled for relatively short periods only twice in the course of millennia, and then washed over again by the waves. The farmer's plow and the builder's dredge did not have a chance to destroy the remains of the submerged villages. Soft mud, peat, and turf covered the cultural remains and protected them from weather and pressure, bacteria and tree roots. With land finds, scholars using even the most modern techniques are often unable to get more than a vague idea of a prehistoric culture. But the finds from lakes and moors produce a complete and colorful picture of these cultures. The excavator's shovel is the key to the moor villages. For collecting finds from lakes fishermen devised functional grappling devices. Soon scholars were no longer content with merely collecting finds. Only a systematic exploration of the entire pole fields and their culture layers could further the knowledge of prehistoric cultures.

Therefore, between 1928 and 1930, Professor Reinerth tried a new method of excavating at Lake Constance. There, in Sipplingen at Uberlingen Lake a pole village seemed to be very well preserved. Reinerth had a double-walled box of strong boards and iron poles built around the field which extended several yards down into the lake bottom. The space between the two walls was filled with clay. Throughout one night the pumps worked at removing the water from the box, and at dawn the first poles could be seen breaking through the surface. After a while the clay vessels and implements of the top culture layer were exposed. The box did not keep all the water out. It was soon filled with water again. Professor Reinerth had to have a third wall driven into the bottom before he could begin with the excavation.

He found a village with thousands of implements, many houses with spacious kitchens and bedrooms, woven walls and reed roofs, stone axes, jugs, bowls, plates, dishes, and wooden kitchen implements; everything was wonderfully preserved.

The quantity of finds from prehistoric settlements is surprising. One reason may be that there was no garbage removal in those

Heinz Finke

*Reconstruction of prehistoric stilt dwellings in Lake Constance
near Unteruhldingen*

times. Refuse was either dropped in middens near the houses or left about the houses—an elk bone gnawed clean, imperfect stone axes, torn fishnets, and broken pottery. Thus "culture layers" grew in the course of time.

Box excavation is today considered the best way to retrieve early artifacts from lakes, but it is so expensive that the example in Sipplingen has not been followed in Germany. Instead, frogmen search through Alpine lakes for pole fields. Under the direction of experienced archaeologists they investigate the discovered fields by the methods of underwater archaeology. Besides Lake Constance, good results have also been obtained in Switzerland, Austria, and France.

In Austria, frogmen are working primarily on the exploration of the "Mond Lake culture," a late Stone Age culture, which once was spread over wide areas of upper Austria and Salzburg. Thus far, frogmen have been able to recover numerous finds in good condition from the depths of Mond Lake, among them even dried apples, grain, and nuts from the food stores of these ancient people.

Many precious clay vessels withstood the millennia on the bottom of the lake intact, nestled in soft mud. Others, the scientists were able to restore from fragments—among them enormous provisions containers. When the investigations of a specialist in hydrology were made known, they supported Paret's contentions. A long time ago a landslide had closed off the lake's drainage, damming up the lake and raising its level by ten feet. But since the Stone Age village was only under seven and a half feet of water, the one-time settlement must have stood on solid ground. Therefore these were not genuine "stilt dwellings."

The bottoms of the Alpine lakes are just as much treasure chests of early times as is the ground of Italy and the sand of Egypt. In the Lake of Neuchâtel alone more than a thousand sites have been discovered. But the exploration of European prehistory is not as popular as classical archaeology and the exacavations of the high cultures of the Orient. Only a few scientists are dedicated to this field, and there is seldom sufficient money on hand to finance large projects. And so, in 1961, the amateur divers from the Underwater Sport Club of Neuchâtel began with their own means and under their own leadership to excavate Champeveyres. Following the precedent of expeditions in the Mediterranean they spanned the bottom with a grid square, photographed, measured, and finally dug deeper with a mud sucker. Their work not only delivered precious finds but showed the rise and fall of several settlements about three thousand years old that had been built on the site, destroyed, and rebuilt.

Thrilled by the amateur divers' success, the Swiss prehistorians formed a group with them, which rescues finds from prehistoric settlement sites that are threatened by construction work or shipping, and takes samplings with steel earth sounders from the individual locations. The divers drive the sounder into the bottom, and the scientists can tell by the succession of layers when the site was settled, when it was destroyed, and when it lay under water, for each of these events has left clues behind it in a layer—refuse, ashes, seed pods from trees, nuts, lake deposits, mussel shells. Frogmen have already recovered numerous valuables from Lake Zurich, and in many lakes unknown settlements have been discovered.

The Sunken Castle in Cambser Lake

If only a few of the legends of sunken castles and treasures in Germany's rivers and lakes prove to be true, rich finds from prehistory and early history and the Middle Ages are still awaiting discovery. And there are some good reasons for investigating legends. Among them is the discovery of the "sunken castle" in Cambser Lake near Schwerin in northern Germany, a water castle of the fourteenth century. Nothing was known about this kind of castle until it was found by the research historian Willy Bastian of Schwerin. Bastian made the discovery while studying ancient documents wherein it was reported that the princes in the fourteenth century, together with the powerful trade cities, had destroyed the castles of the Mecklenburg robber knights, made the noble-born thieves swear an oath of truce—obligating them to eternal peace —and forbade them to build new castle fortresses. The knights

Baugeschichtliches Archiv der Stadt Zu...

Zurich divers investigate a prehistoric settlement:
Above: A plastic net is used to mark off the area
Below: Foundations of stilt dwellings

Baugeschichtliches Archiv der Stadt Zu...

Stone Age vessels recovered from Lake Zurich

were permitted to build *Kemladen*—water castles—in the lakes of the Mecklenburg area. But from these fortresses they again pursued their activities as robbers, so their water castles were destroyed and the knights were sent to the gallows.

Following up the discoveries in the old documents, Bastian went from lake to lake and gathered legends of sunken castles from fishermen. But not a trace was to be seen of the castles themselves. Then in Zittow on Cambser Lake he ran into an old fisherman who remembered that his nets had once caught on some poles. The underwater explorer Gerhard Kapitän was consulted. He dived at the place the fisherman pointed out, near an alder grove some distance from the wide sedge belt of the lake, and there found the remains of an old robber-knight castle. It had been constructed on oak timbers. Almost a hundred of them still protruded from the vegetation-covered bottom.

In 1960, Gerhard Kapitän led an expedition to Cambser Lake and with thorough exploratory and research work slowly produced from the hundreds of small finds the story of the castle and the fate of its inhabitants. The remains of their robberies, pottery from the Rhine and a knife with a well-preserved leather handle bearing the coat of arms of a foreign family, probably that of a robbed merchant, lay with evidence of the measures of justice that followed. The castle was probably set afire and sank into the lake amid crackling of timbers and showers of sparks. Charred beams and stones were found among the dishes from the castle kitchen, with door hinges, crossbow darts, and weapons.

Doubtless Germany's rivers, too, are treasure chests, for they have long been the life arteries of central Europe. River boats have sunk in them over the centuries. Surely an occasional medieval merchant's wagon load of wares was tipped into a river at a difficult crossing point. Stragglers from the defeated armies were driven into rivers by the advancing enemy. Many treasures were hidden in rivers during uncertain times, and after the death of their owners were lost forever. One of the most precious finds from the era of Roman domination over southern Germany and the Rhine, the bronze statue of a boy, was found in the Rhine near Xanten. Also, many of the valuable swords, battle-axes, sickles, and other

Diver with a gun barrel found in the Rhine River

Unterwasserkrau

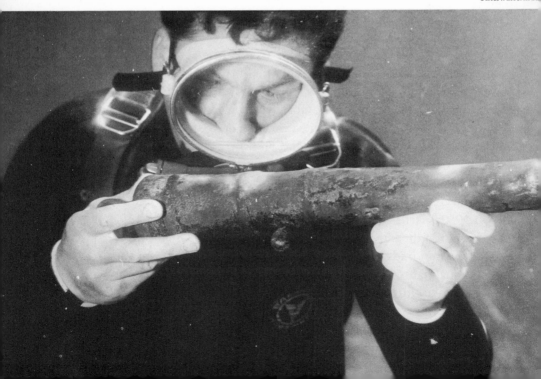

metal objects of the Bronze Age which lie in European museums have been pulled out of rivers: the Thames, the Rhine, the Saône, the Weser, the Danube, and the Seine.

Diving in rivers is not easy. Their surface currents threaten to sweep a diver against sharp rocks and into rapids, while the lower currents carry such cloudy water that the diver can scarcely see, and he must also beware of possible damage to his health from chemical and bacterial pollution. Also, in the course of time the original riverbeds have been covered by enormous deposits of mud and debris, and it is truly a matter of chance that a current reopens these layers of sediment.

A group of American amateur divers were not deterred by such difficulties. In 1960, while searching Lake Superior for shipwrecks, they chanced to have a conversation with amateur historian Dr. E. W. Davis, whose hobby was collecting information about the pioneer fur trade in Minnesota. When he encountered the divers, he suddenly thought of the rapids at Grand Portage. These rapids were of special significance in the time of the pioneers. From the seventeenth to the middle of the nineteenth century transport by large canoe from Montreal westward and back was the most important fur trade route of the north country. The fur traders were rugged men who paddled the three hundred miles from Montreal to Grand Portage for the fur-trading companies—men who now and then risked the trip through the rapids, instead of skirting them on land, to avoid the tedious job of pulling the boats and the hundred-pound packs. The risks were great; not only canoe and cargo were sometimes lost. A diary from the year 1800 records that at every rapid passed during a twenty-five-day journey a cross had been erected. At one place thirty crosses marked the casualties. Dr. Davis felt that the old fur trade routes ought to be followed underwater. The amateur divers agreed. A few weeks later found them at Horsetail Rapids, a once-dreaded passage where a person had to cling to rocks so as not to be carried downstream by the swift water and pounded against sharp cliffs. There they found ten copper and brass vessels in the river, such as are often described in invoices from the old fur-trade days. This success encouraged

227

Dr. Davis and his helpers to try further explorations along the American-Canadian border. They were supported by the Historical Society of Minnesota, the Royal Museum of Ontario, and other research organizations. The Basswood Rapids, forty miles from Horsetail Rapids, and among the most dreaded, was their next goal. Here they immediately found the loads of several canoes. One of them had carried thirty-five iron axes and twenty-four chisels and spears, and another carried about a thousand musket balls, bullet lead, knives, necklaces, thimbles, whetstones, and flints. Once the objects of such canoes have been dated—and this is done with the aid, among other things, of old records in which such accidents are recorded—it is then often possible to date historic sites such as old Indian settlements where similar objects have been unearthed. The study of early Indian cultures in North America involves just as many difficulties as the study of European prehistory and early history, for documentary records are often nonexistent and archaeological finds are rare.

The flooding of old settlement sites with artificial lakes is especially responsible for keeping archaeologists busy. The archaeologist Donald P. Jewell had to watch one interesting site after another along the California foothills flooded over as California's growing population created an ever-increasing need for reservoirs to supply drinking water. But since the California Indians varied widely in culture and language from one valley to the next, Jewell feared that "the flooding of just one large valley could conceivably bury the remains of a whole culture of thousands of years forever." All alone and with simple means, Jewell took up the fight for the preservation of old Indian cultures. With frogman equipment and a small float, he investigates the backwaters of California, registers remains of settlements, and recovers the finds.

Lord Cornwallis's Sunken Fleet and the Gunboat in the Yazoo River

Lake Champlain, Yazoo River, Lake George, York River —American historians, too, are able to point to more and more

sites of successful underwater projects. Most of the names of underwater sites belong to episodes of the Revolutionary War or the
Civil War. This makes the finds all the more valuable, for they illus-
trate written history, supplementing it where our knowledge is incomplete. An illustration of a well-known historical event was the
raising of the *Cairo*. This Northern gunboat was one of the first
armored warships in America and the first ship ever sunk by an
electrically detonated mine. The Confederates experimented with
submarines—the *Hunley*, one of the first submarines in the history
of naval conflict, sank the *Housatonic* in Charleston Harbor, South
Carolina, in 1864, and set out large jugs filled with powder and
connected to the bank with a copper wire. Near Vicksburg, Mis-
sissippi the *Cairo* ran into such a mine in 1862. The explosion ripped
a large hole in the ship's hull. From the diary of a cabin boy we
know how the ship went down: in spite of all attempts at pumping,
the water rose relentlessly in the ship. At the last minute, as the
water of the Yazoo River already covered the deck of the *Cairo*,
the 160-man crew was taken aboard another Northern ship.
Twelve minutes after the explosion only the stacks and the flag
mast, from which a flag still waved, could be seen above the surface
of the water. Salvage attempts were unsuccessful. The stacks and
flag mast broke off. The wreck lay only six feet underwater, but
owing to the muddy water, knowledge of its whereabouts was soon
lost.

The *Cairo* rested on the bottom of the Yazoo for almost a hundred years until finally E. A. Bearss, a historian with the National Park Service, took an interest in it and began to study maps
and documents from the time of the Civil War. In 1956 he set out
on the Yazoo with two of his colleagues in a small boat. An ordinary search in the muddy river would have taken months, but the
men had a clever idea. The *Cairo* was heavily armored—thus tons
of steel must lie in the river bed. What could be more logical than to
use a compass? And when they reached the vicinity of the
spot where the *Cairo* was supposed to lie, the needle of the compass swung to the side. Carefully the men rowed nearer. The
needle's deflection increased, then reached a maximum. When it was

180 degrees it could only be pointing at the lost ship. Bearss probed with an iron bar: he had found the *Cairo*.

Since Bearss and his friends didn't have enough money for an exploration they had to wait until 1959, when divers Ken Parks and James Hart offered their help. The two divers went to the bottom of the Yazoo and came up with numerous finds—objects that had been lying on the decks of the *Cairo* exactly where they had fallen almost a hundred years ago: knives, medicine bottles, an anvil, and the like. When in 1960 they used a floating crane, they were able to raise the ship's bridge—a structure of oak beams two feet thick and covered with two-inch steel armor. Now the officials too joined the activity. Navy divers, professional helmet divers, and an experienced salvage crew went to work. But at first they were unsuccessful. The trusses cut too deeply into the ship's sides, for the ironclad *Cairo* was too heavy for its hull of time-weakened planks. She had to be cut into three pieces and salvaged that way. But restorers at the new Vicksburg museum were successful in doing a neat reconstruction job. The historians were happy not only about the ship but about her contents. She contained thousands of finds, many of which provided clues to life aboard America's first armored ship.

The *Cairo* is not the first monument of American history to be found underwater. The first was the *Royal Savage*, which played an important role in the Revolutionary War . . . Lake Champlain, October, 1776.

The British were advancing with strong naval units. Their goal was to cut the colonies in two. On Lake Champlain Captain Benedict Arnold was preparing for battle. From his flagship *Royal Savage*, a seventy-ton schooner, he commanded a tiny armada of fifteen small gunboats. The battle lasted through the day. The severely damaged *Royal Savage* was beached on the island of Valcour where it was set afire by British troops. Her sister ship, the *Philadelphia*, held out throughout the day, but at twilight she too sank. Arnold then had the remainder of his ships set afire so that they could not fall into the hands of the enemy, and barricaded himself on land.

The British fleet won the battle, but was too weak to move on. The attempt to drive a wedge between the colonies failed.

The *Royal Savage* and her sister ship were sunk but not destroyed. When in 1932 Captain L. F. Hagglund, a department head for the salvage firm Merrit, Chapman & Scott set out in search of the wrecks, he found hull and equipment from the *Royal Savage* in three fathoms of water. In 1935 he dived in search of the *Philadelphia*, which he thought might be better preserved, since it received only a direct hit in the bow. And that is just how Hagglund found it. He was able to raise the hull with all cannons and five hundred objects of ship's outfitting and sailors' and soldiers' equipment.

Around the same time Cornwallis' fleet was found in the York River. It had sailed into Chesapeake Bay in the summer of 1781 in support of British land forces. But the French fleet under Count de Grasse followed in its wake and drove it up the river. The British fleet commander, Admiral Thomas Graves, was caught between French shore batteries which fired upon his flagship *Charon* and three transports, setting them ablaze, and the French warships which were pursuing him. Finally he sank his smaller vessels in the river as barricade against the pursuers. When the French were nevertheless on the verge of breaking through, he sent his last two frigates, the *Guadaloupe* and the *Fowey*, to the bottom.

In 1934, when the Mariner's Museum of Newport News, Virginia, and the Colonial National Historical Park started a cooperative exploration, they determined that the ships were too severely damaged for salvage. They were able to rescue an almost complete collection of weapons and equipment. But the state of preservation of some of the finds was disappointing: many of the iron guns and rifles fell apart in their hands.

Robert Bruce Inverarity, director of the Adirondack Museum, had better luck in raising three small warships in Lake George, New York. They were well preserved, and Inverarity was able to reconstruct from his finds the almost forgotten type of ship *bateaux*, which was important in the development of American shipping.

The *bateaux* of Lake George dated from the year 1750. This makes this type the oldest ever to be found in American inland waters. Only a few Indian canoes—excavated on land—are older.

A Major Harbor of the Viking Era

Conditions for preservation of sunken material are especially good in the Baltic Sea, which is so low in salinity that it almost constitutes a cross between inland water and the sea. Its coast has not yet been explored, but some significant sites have been located from the Viking era. Divers have found two Viking fleets, one of which was raised, and have explored the bottom of the harbor of Haithabu, an international harbor of the tenth century.

A thousand years have passed since Arabs, Jews, Franks of the Carolingian Empire, and Vikings met in the streets of Haithabu to trade all the precious things known to the world of the time. Along the Schlei River in Schleswig today only a few earthen walls and mounds remain of the metropolis that once stood there. In 1930 the prehistorian Professor Herbert Jankuhn began some extensive excavating in Haithabu. From his finds and the evaluation of discoveries which had already been made there before the First World War, a picture was slowly formed of life in this city from early history. "Metropolis" is not an exaggeration. In the tenth century, Haithabu was the size of Cologne, which at that time was one of the largest cities of Europe with its sixty acres of buildings. Haithabu was known in Spain and Greece; its name was spoken at the Bazaar in the Baghdad of Harun-al-Rashid.

Haithabu owed its importance to its unique location. Just as in early modern times, sailors of the early Middle Ages shied away from the dangerous voyage around Denmark and the trip through Skagerrak and Kattegat in order to pass from the North Sea to the Baltic and back. Instead they sailed the Eider and its tributary the Treene as far as Hollingstedt. Smaller ships even crossed the Rheider Au to the modern village of Gross-Rhede. There, a technical masterpiece for its time was built. Like the Diolkos at Corinth, it was a system of slide tracks and rollers on which the ships crossed

*Location
of the city
of Haithabu*

about five miles of land, ending at the Schlei. Slaves and oxen meanwhile carried the wares to Haithabu, where they were stacked, traded, and again stowed aboard ships.

The Viking settlement on the Schlei attracted almost all the northern trade. Priceless riches were sold and purchased in Haithabu, shiploads of amber, furs, honey, wax, wine from the Rhine and Moselle and Mediterranean countries, Friesian textiles and Chinese silk, iron swords and helmets, cattle, horses, and slaves. Payment was made in other trade goods, or with money which the Caliph of Baghdad had minted from Afghanistan silver. A breastplate of iron cost six oxen or twelve cows, a sword cost seven oxen. Endless columns of chained slaves marched through the city. Vikings had perhaps captured them on their numerous raiding voyages, or they were the booty of Nordic slave traders from the area of the Slavic tribes east of the Elbe. The men were used as servants on the large Viking estates or as galley slaves on the ships. The girls were sold to the harems of the Islamic world from Spain to Baghdad. Since the endless raids and petty wars of the time brought in a rich booty of human beings, slaves were cheaper than iron weapons. One mark of silver (400 grams) was paid for a woman slave—the value of a riding horse or two cows.

In 1939 the excavations in Haithabu were interrupted by the war. In 1950 the museum director of Schleswig, Professor K. Kersten, stood on the old walls of the city that had sunk a thousand years before, after King Henry I had conquered it in 934, and Hamburg and Lübeck under the protection of the Reich finally attracted the trade to themselves.

Professor Kersten noticed that Haithabu had an unusual location for a medieval city. Whereas cities of that time were generally built in the form of a circle, the Viking city was a semicircle which opened to the Noor. The Noor, a kind of fjord by which the sea was reached via the mouth of the Schlei, had been deeper in the Middle Ages than it is today, and had served as Haithabu's harbor. Professor Kersten had an idea. Maybe the fortification of Haithabu continued under the water in the form of harbor fortification and thereby completed the circle.

Kersten engaged a diver and asked him to help him explore the Noor. The two men dived into a harbor of the early Middle Ages. The palisades that once had stood on the fortress walls of Haithabu were evident under water. Still well preserved, the deeply driven pilings were stuck in the ground. Everywhere lay signs of the one-time harbor activity—millstones, implements, containers of horn, clay, and soapstone, and weapons. In 1953 the diving work was continued. In the muddy water, where for a depth of five feet total darkness prevails, the men found a Viking ship.

A thousand years ago it had burned and sunk with all its cargo at the entrance to the harbor. One of the Vikings who went down with the ship was found on the bottom of the Noor with battered skull. The ship, made of oak with ash ribs and planks caulked with beef tallow, was largely intact.

When Swedish scholars heard about the successful diving work done at Haithabu, they remembered reading that in the seventeenth century in Birka, where once the most powerful Viking city had stood, a great number of oaken beams were pulled from the water and sold to a carpenter. Surely the harbor of Birka also contains a few secrets for science.

Fleets on the Bottom of the Baltic Sea

Science owes much to Swedish amateur divers for the next significant discovery of the Viking age. In the summer of 1959 the divers found a sunken fleet in the Bay of Landfjarden, twenty miles south of Stockholm. Three ships are clearly visible in shallow water, and still more show through the mud farther out. It has not yet been determined whether they are Viking ships. But the find is reminiscent of a report in the Old Norse *Heimskringkla*. The historical writings of Snorri Sturleson (1178-1241) tell of a war that was waged by the Norwegian King, Olaf the Holy, in the year 1007 in the Baltic Sea: "In the fall, Olaf fought his first battle near Sotaskar in the Swedish Skerries. . . . He laid his ships between some reefs whereby the Vikings were able to launch severe attacks. But the closest ships [of the attacking Vikings] were pulled alongside by the Norwegians with grappling hooks and sunk. The Vikings fled and had lost many warriors."

A second fleet of Viking ships was found by Olaf Olsen, a custodian of the Danish National Museum in Copenhagen, while he was investigating the legend of the "Ship of Queen Margaret." The "ship of the queen" lay in the Roskilde Fjord on the northwest coast of the island of Zealand. The fjord fishermen knew its exact location, and an old legend tells how the famous Scandinavian Queen Margaret, who lived from 1363 to 1412 and ruled over Denmark, Norway, and Sweden, had it sunk in the fjord in order to cut off pirates who wanted to plunder the wealthy cathedral city of Roskilde. A few pieces of wood fished up from the wreck gave Olsen the suspicion that the ship was a few hundred years older.

The National Museum equipped a diving expedition which had been working under Olaf Olsen in Roskilde Fjord since 1957. The first thing the Danes found was nothing more than a fifty-yard-long pile of rocks covered with algae and mussels which cut off the passage in a depth of three to nine feet.

*Roskilde Fjord and
Gunderstrup*

But Olaf Olsen saw that it was not *one* ship, but a grand-scale barricade consisting of several ships. These, filled with rocks, had been sunk alongside and on top of one another.

Before raising one of the ships could be thought of, a tremendous underwater job awaited the divers. A work float, donated by a shipbuilding company, was tied at the site of the sinkings, and the men went to work with a fire hose, washing the ships clean of mud, stones, and mussels. Then rocks had to be removed. Five shiploads of them lay on the bottom, the largest pieces weighing three hundred pounds. The rocks had to be removed carefully, the heaviest with special tongs, for the wood of the ships, which had lain on the bottom for a thousand years, was soft and fragile. The ships were subjected to precise inspections and measurements, then sketched. Already the findings supported Olaf Olsen's suspicions: they were Viking ships, sent to the bottom in the fjord to protect the powerful capital city of Lejre, west of the modern Roskilde, from enemy attacks while the Vikings were off on a raiding foray.

A further finding of the museum custodian was of considerable interest to scientists: the five ships were merchant vessels. Merchant ships of the Vikings, called *knorr*, were known up to that time only

The recovery of the Viking ships from Roskilde Fjord

from writings. The famous Oseberg ship, found in 1899 near Oslo, which served as a tomb for a princess, had been built for speedy travel in and out of fjords and skerries and was hardly a seaworthy vessel. The Gokstad ship discovered near Oslo in 1910, although a

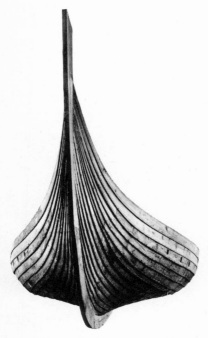

The Gokstad ship

Historisches Museum der Universität Oslo

fleet sailing ship, was surely not intended for long voyages on the high seas. The dragon boats were primarily designed as warships for sailing on the Baltic Sea, along coastlines, and on rivers. They were rarely used for battles on the open sea; the Viking ships lay too lightly on the waves for that. For merchant voyages and trips to Greenland and possibly Vinland (America), the Vikings had built wide ships with high sideboards, many sails, and a displacement of up to a hundred tons—the forerunners of the Hanseatic cogs.

The Vikings were by no means merely barbaric robbers in shaggy furs and horned helmets who just went on raids in their dragon ships. Besides the fact that they had acquired a high level of culture, wore trousers, vests and jackets, and elegant robes of beaver pelts and sable, they were also welcome merchants everywhere they appeared in their seaworthy *knorrs*. These ships make the stories of Vikings' trips to America easily credible.

Olaf Olsen soon had to realize that recovery of the ships by frogmen was impossible. Poor visibility at the bottom of the fjord and the strong currents ruined all attempts. There was only one alternative: to build a box around the wrecks similar to the one built in Sipplingen by Professor Reinerth. In the summer of 1962 the entire site was surrounded with waterproof walls of steel plate and

Weapons from the time of the Vikings

Historisches Museum der Universität Oslo

beams, then pumped out. And what came into view on the bottom of the box surpassed everyone's wildest dreams. There lay the wrecks of five well-preserved Viking ships. But not just any Viking ships—these were five different vessels which represented the Viking shipbuilder's art of the time. The ship barricade consisted of a light, a middle-sized, and a heavy merchant ship. In addition, a ferry and a converted warship lay in the channel. In fourteen weeks of work archaeologists recovered the sections of the eleventh-century vessels. They were placed in airtight plastic sacks and removed for preservation. Scientists want to reconstruct the preserved sections of the Viking ships and display them in a spacious hall in Roskilde.

At about the same time that the Danish frogmen were working on their ships in the Roskilde Fjord, their northern neighbors, the Swedes, succeeded in the most spectacular venture of archaeological underwater exploration to date—the discovery and recovery of the *Vasa*, the great flagship of King Gustaf Adolf (1594-1632).

IX

The Return of the Crown Ship

The story of the discovery of the *Vasa* begins in Dalarö, in the island world of the archipelago of Stockholm. In 1930, young Anders Franzen sat on the beach and dreamed of the ships that had sunk to the bottom with all hands when Sweden was a major power, taking their treasures to the depths of the sea. Anders Franzen's father, a historian in his spare time, had told the boy about such ships. Surely not all of them had rotted and disintegrated. The boy was convinced that they lay well preserved on the ocean floor.

The years passed, and Anders Franzen's youthful dreams received new impetus when he heard of an incident which had taken place in 1920.

On a summer day of that year the anchor of a fisherman, Erik Nordström, got stuck on the bottom near the island of Viksten in the skerries of Stockholm. The fisherman began to wonder, for at precisely that place he had already lost an anchor in much the same way.

As chance would have it, a salvage ship with several divers on board stood nearby, and the fisherman offered a bottle of cognac to the diver who would investigate the "suspicious spot." A bottle of cognac is just the reward for a man who has worked all day in the cold depths of the Baltic. One of the men wasted no time thinking about it. He jumped into the water and landed by the remains of a large, wooden ship. The Swedish government paid the finder $12,500—a goodly sum in those days—for the seven highly decorated bronze cannon he recovered from the wreck. The bronze ship's guns landed in the Stockholm Marine Historical Museum, where Anders Franzen stood fascinated before them.

But Anders Franzen's fantasies went beyond that. He not only wanted to fish cannon out of the deep; he wanted to bring one of the beautiful ships out of the water, on which almost three centuries ago Swedish sailors and seamen sailed off to the Thirty Years' War to fight for their country and the freedom of their religion.

When Anders Franzen grew older, he became a staff engineer in the Royal Swedish Navy and went on to occupy himself with development and testing of oils and fuels for modern ships.

His dreams of youth were still with him, and they preoccupied him all the more in 1939 while on a cruise along the west coast of Sweden, where he made a discovery of great consequence. At first he merely fished a few insignificant pieces of wood from the sea. The wood itself was solid and hard, though riddled with countless holes eaten into it by shipworms, the termites of the sea. A few years longer and the worms would have bored more and more holes in them until they resembled sponges and finally disintegrated.

Franzen was surprised, for he had never seen such wood in the Baltic Sea. Were there perhaps no shipworms on the east coast of Sweden? If that were the case then wrecks there must be able to survive centuries undisturbed and preserved on the sea floor.

The young engineer studied scientific works on shipworms and their distribution, and found he was right. The teredo loves salt water and avoids places where the salt content is less than 0.4 percent. However, the salinity of the Baltic Sea is normally lower than that.

Anders Franzen was now positive that some old ships were still lying intact on the bottom of the Baltic. He had little money, and he realized what such an operation would cost in time and money. He would need trained divers with expensive equipment, who would not risk adventure on the bottom of the sea except for high wages. The search wouldn't take mere days, but weeks or months. . . .

Verlagsarchiv

Gundestrup kettle found in ship wrecked on the coast of Denmark between 100 B.C. and A.D. 33

But it was destined to turn out otherwise. In the following years the Self-Contained Underwater Breathing Apparatus (scuba) was invented and frogman diving began. For Anders Franzen too it meant the key to the silent world. With fascination he read reports of the French pioneers of frogman diving, and as soon as he could he acquired his own compressed air breathing apparatus. A few of his friends soon joined him as "treasure hunters."

But the Baltic Sea is vast, and three frogmen who set blindly to work without real evidence to go on can spend decades on the bottom without turning up so much as a ship's nail. If the divers' efforts are to have a chance of success they must at least have a notion of where to look.

Franzen had to set to work like a regular treasure hunter, studying old manuscripts in dusty archives, checking through logs, sea charts, and even listening to seaman's yarns. From now on he spent every free minute studying the history of north European marine warfare; he searched through every archive in Stockholm. Many professional historians and specialists were already laughing at the young man who really thought he could find a century-old ship intact on the bottom of the sea and even raise it.

After a while Franzen finally had a list of fifty ships which had sunk along the east coast of Sweden. He chose twelve that seemed especially promising, among them the *Vasa*. With this list, he went to the specialists at the Marine Historical Museum. After they had listened to this enthusiastic young man for a while they began to take him seriously. To be sure, no one really believed that such an old ship could be raised intact, but it wouldn't hurt to look.

Together with the museum people Franzen chose the *Riksäpplet* for the first expedition. This ship had been lost by the Swedish navy in 1676. A storm in the Bay of Dalarö had torn the proud vessel loose from its anchors and driven it against a small rock island. The sharp rocks had pounded a hole in the oaken hull and the ship had sunk in eight fathoms, a depth in which frogmen can work comfortably. But when Franzen entered the water near the small skerry off Dalarö, not far from where he had dreamed of sunken ships as a boy, he found only a few planks and beams. Drifting ice and surf had smashed the ship to pieces, and the best part of the good oak from the ship had soon been salvaged by local inhabitants. But Franzen didn't let his disappointment get the better of him. He looked at the few planks he and his friends had pulled from the water and saw in them further proof of his theory: a few centuries on the bottom of the Baltic Sea can only blacken oak, but not destroy it.

He just had to find a ship that lay deep enough so that it was out of reach of surf and ice, but not too deep for the divers. He thought over the list of twelve ships: *Adler of Lübeck, Mars, Vasa,*

Schwan of Lübeck, Sastervik, Kronan. . . . Which of these promised a successful search?

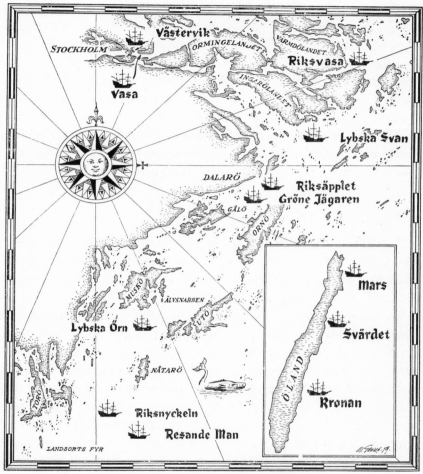

Sunken ships off the coast of Sweden

A lucky coincidence brought Franzen together with the famed historian Professor Nils Ahnlund. The old scholar listened long and attentively as Franzen told of his hopes, his hunt for sunken ships of the past, and the results. With the discovery of the wreck near the island of Viksten in 1920, Professor Ahnlund himself had studied old archives. He had determined that the divers had turned up the wreck of the *Ricksnyckeln*, which had run into a cliff near the island of Viksten and sunk in the dark of a September night in 1628 on the return voyage from Germany. While pursuing this research, the professor had rediscovered the remarkable, almost tragic story of the splendid ship *Vasa*, which, on August, 10, 1628, had met a similar fate. He encouraged Franzen to look for the *Vasa*.

Franzen went back to the archives. From the research of Professor Ahnlund and the results of Franzen's own archive studies, the whole story of this ill-fated ship of King Gustaf Adolf began to unfold, a story that justified Professor Ahnlund's hopes that the Stockholm Strom, a long sea arm, might be hiding a valuable segment of history of the time of the Thirty Years' War.

The Ill-fated Vasa

The Thirty Years' War had been devastating central Europe for seven years when, in 1625, Gustaf Adolf, ruler of Sweden from 1611 to 1632, called for Henrik Hybertsson, his Dutch master shipbuilder.

The king had been following the course of events on the mainland with concern. During the first seven years of the war there had been a single run of victories for the House of Habsburg, Bavaria, and their Catholic allies. Maximilian of Bavaria and his field commander Tilly had crushed rebellious Bohemia and defeated the troops of the "Union," the Protestant military alliance; Tilly had marched to Westphalia and had brought all of western Germany under the control of the Counter Reformation. Already the comet-like rise of Albrecht von Wallenstein had begun, the man whom the emperor in Vienna had made Duke of Friedland. With each day the serf army in Bohemia was augmented by another company. Gustaf Adolf saw a serious threat to his extensive plans for making the Baltic Sea into a *mare nostrum* for Sweden and for raising his empire to a major power. He was fearful of his throne and the Protestant faith, not only in the German realm but in Sweden as well. The king suspected correctly that Wallenstein, this military genius, would not stop at the shores of the Baltic after a victorious campaign through Germany, but would take Scandinavia as well for his emperor and the Catholic faith. For in those days it was true that *cuius regio, eius religio*—the faith of the ruler is the faith of the people.

Gustaf Adolf knew that the well-being of the Swedish kingdom depended on the might of his fleet. That is why he asked the Dutchman to build him four new warships, faster and stronger than any of all other maritime powers.

In the autumn of 1625 woodsmen entered the forests of Uppland and Sörmland and felled selected oaks for the royal shipyards. At Skeppsholmen, one of the many islands of Stockholm, the keels of the first three war galleys were laid. The carpenters built the ships under contract, and soon the first was ready to leave the stocks.

The showpiece, however, was to be the *Vasa*. The king himself praised the plans which Hybertsson showed him together with a small model of the three-master.

In 1627 the *Vasa* left the stocks, and in the spring of 1628 she was moored before the king's palace. There she was to be fitted with giant sails, take on cannon, ballast, ammunition, provisions, and a crew. Farmers and fishermen from all over the country poured into Stockholm to admire their king's mightiest ship. From a great distance they could already see her masts reaching to the sky, for the *Vasa* measured 180 feet from keel to mainmast, surpassing some church towers in height. Costly baroque carvings bedecked the 150-foot-long hull. The ship was decorated like an ostentatious baroque theater, and when the cannon ports were opened, ferocious golden lions' heads on a blood-red background terrified all who saw. The sight of the 1400-ton sailing ship alone would give the enemy a fright.

Some of the peasants from the nearby valleys of the Malär Lake area must also have viewed the ship with unpleasant feelings, for it was from among their number that the king's officials had gathered recruits for the navy. The duty on the king's ships was hard—even harder than in the field with the army. Sailors or marines who talked or misbehaved during one of the many long lectures were punished with fourteen days in irons. A man could be keelhauled for the slightest act of insubordination. Sailors and ordinary marines slept without straw or hay on the hard deck, and the food was usually meager and poor.

One highly decorated bronze gun after another was carried by the dock workers past the marveling observers and fastened to its wooden carriage.

The *Vasa* was outfitted like a fortress. Forty-eight heavy cannon protruded from the ports of its three decks. In addition there were smaller guns and six heavy howitzers. The ship sank down noticeably under the weight of its eighty tons of cannon and their heavy oaken carriages. In those days ships' guns consisted of heavy bronze barrels mounted on wooden carriages with four small wheels. At the command "Prepare to fire!" the cannoneers would open the cannon parts and shove the carriage up to the side of the ship. The muzzles now bristled threateningly from the ship's hull. The sharp kick of the guns drove them back from the ports and they would have rolled clear across the deck had they not been retained by strong ropes.

After the guns, the laborers carried the ammunition aboard and filled the powder and provision rooms. About three hundred marines and a hundred and forty sailors were to man the *Vasa*. About nine hundred cases of food and twelve hundred barrels of beer were considered in those days to be suitable provisions for that number of men for four months. On July 31, 1628, the *Vasa* was finally laden and the first sailors came on board.

Gustaf Adolf had awaited this day with growing impatience, for his worst fears were now being realized. While the Swedish king was fighting for the crown of Poland with his Catholic cousin Sigismund of Poland, Wallenstein had brought almost all of Germany under the control of the emperor. The emperor had given his field commander the title "General of the Oceanic and Baltic Seas" and commanded him to gain control over the Baltic Sea in order to break down the last Protestant resistance.

Wallenstein stood at the edge of the Baltic Sea and directed his troops against Stralsund so as to gain the key to the sea.

True, the "General of the Oceanic and Baltic Seas" still didn't command a single ship, but Gustaf Adolf knew Wallenstein, who was to become his chief opponent. The Duke of Friedland had in a matter of months also gathered the largest army on the continent out of thin air, and in a similarly short time would have a navy, for his messengers were already bargaining with the Hanseatic city of Lübeck over the positioning of ships. Lübeck was still reluctant to betray its fellow Lutherans. But it would not be able to stand firm long once Stralsund had fallen.

The Swedish king quickly sent as many auxiliary troops, guns, ammunition, and supplies as he could spare to Stralsund and gave his Baltic division the command: "Clear for action!" It was to defend Sweden until the king could end the war in Poland and intervene in Germany.

The maiden voyage of the *Vasa*, flagship of the Baltic fleet, was set for August 10.

The mighty ship was to head for Älvsnabben in the skerries of Stockholm where she was to lie ready under order of the king, "So that she might set sail at the time we wish for a destination which we will determine and announce there." But it turned out differently. The vesper bells at the cathedral had just died away as the sailors and marines boarded the ship. Many women and children came along. They were permitted to join the maiden voyage as far as the ship's station in the skerries.

August 10, 1628, was a warm, sunny Sunday and the cloudless blue sky over Stockholm gave even the muddy waters of Mälar Lake a bluish cast. Only to the south, over the peaks of the Södra Mountains, lay a patch of gray, like a storm announcing itself well in advance.

Thousands of shouting citizens of Stockholm lined the wharves as the *Vasa* left its moorings and slowly sailed down the Stockholm Ström through which Mälar Lake empties into the Baltic. Off Södermalm the *Vasa* fired a thundering salute which was answered by a thousand-voiced cry of jubilation from the wharves. The Swedish flag was flying from all masts. Captain Söfring Hansson ordered four sails set, a light breath of wind filled the half-reefed sails, and the ship glided smoothly to the Stockholm Ström.

But suddenly a strong gust of wind from the Södra Mountains filled the sails, and the ship lurched sharply to the side. Frightened men, women, and children clung to the railings, decks, and tackle and waited for the ship to right itself, but the wind persisted, pressing the *Vasa* hard to the lee into the water. The captain ordered the sails cut loose.

Ordnance Master Erik Jonnsson darted below deck and commanded his cannoneers to shift their cannons to the windward side in order to regain balance through their counterweight. But it was too late. Cascades of water poured through the lower cannon ports. The ship listed further, capsized, and sank rapidly in the Stockholm Ström. Gurgling waves closed over the blue and yellow flags, carrying sailors, officers, women, and children to the bottom. The breathless silence of those on the wharves gave way to screams of horror. The first rescue boats were sent out from the shore, but fifty persons had been swallowed by the deep.

Thus Stockholm's great day ended in mourning. Captain Söfring Hansson and the other rescued officers of the *Vasa* were arrested the same day. The directors of the ship's construction crew were also thrown into prison, except for the ship's designer, Henrik Hybertsson, who had died in 1627.

Parliament held a court-martial the following day to fix the blame for the catastrophe. Several scribes recorded the exact proceedings, as Anders Franzen discovered in the Stockholm Imperial Archive. The court wanted to know why the *Vasa* had sunk. Had cargo, ballast, and cannon not been properly secured? Did the ship carry insufficient ballast, and consequently rode too high and wobbly on the water?

The ship's officers were innocent; here the court had no doubts.

The master ship's carpenter, Hein Jacobsson, was called. The prosecutor asked him why he had built the ship so narrow and poorly that it had no depth to give it stability, as a result of which it tipped over. Master Jacobsson defended himself by maintaining he had strictly followed the plans of Henrik Hybertsson. But the man responsible for the plans was dead. The court called in his brother, Arent Hybertsson de Groot, who had worked with him on the plans. But even he could not be blamed, for the king himself had gone over the plans and approved them. The court finally had to close the case without naming a guilty party.

Today, most specialists are of the opinion that the ballast, cargo, and the heavy cannon of the *Vasa* were not properly distributed. As a result the center of gravity was too high, and the heavy ship, in spite of its heavy ballast, rode high and unstable on the water.

The Hunt for the Vasa

This was the story of the *Vasa* that Anders Franzen pieced together after years of study. He had to learn the old script in which the documents were written, and dig through all the available archives in Stockholm.

What he was really seeking he never found: a reference to the location of the sunken ship. The reports were contradictory even in approximations. But Franzen found something else: exciting old manuscripts that told of treasure hunters who had worked on the wreck of the *Vasa* centuries before. Maybe they would give the location.

The mourning bells of Stockholm were still ringing for the drowned of the *Vasa* when a young Englishman presented himself at the castle, asking to be allowed to raise the ship. His name was Jan Bulmer and he carried a letter that identified him as an "Engineer of His Majesty the King of England." Bulmer had witnessed the sinking from the shore and now hoped to make his fortune by successfully recovering the ship. By August 13, 1628, he received from Parliament permission to salvage. He was free to begin work. The deck of the *Vasa* lay some fifteen fathoms deep; only the very tip of the mainmast could be seen. As it sank, the ship had almost righted itself, although the angle of the protruding mast showed that the *Vasa* was still not on even keel. Bulmer hired divers who descended without breathing apparatus or diving suits and fastened ropes to the masts of the ship. The ropes were then taken to the shore where they were hitched to horses. The horses strained against their harnesses, and slowly the warship was righted. After that, Bulmer didn't know what to do. He gave up finally.

But his work was to be of benefit to Franzen and his helpers some two hundred years later. They found the *Vasa* in the same upright position in which Bulmer had left it.

In the fall of 1628 the navy had made an attempt. Chains and ropes with hooks on their ends were lowered and dragged over the *Vasa* until they caught in cannon ports or on the superstructure. But this was no way to raise a warship. The hooks broke and bent; the ropes and chains parted.

Finally in December, 1628, Admiral Klas Fleming reported to Parliament that the *Vasa* was "much heavier than I ever could have presumed." This same conclusion was reached by French, Dutch, German, and English soldiers of fortune who in the following decades tried again and again to raise the ship. They ripped up the decks and superstructures, left behind tons of anchors, grappling hooks, ropes, and chains on the ship and departed without success. Yet the wreck continued to attract adventurers. Besides the reward, there was rumor of a large chest of money aboard the galleon. But no one had even the slightest success, and the *Vasa* had begun to be forgotten when, in 1658, the Swedish former Colonel Albrekt von Treileben showed up in Stockholm. Von Treileben had come to know the German salvage specialist Andreas Peckell during a campaign in Poland. Peckell knew much about sunken ships and had considerable experience with salvaging.

Treileben had learned about diving on the continent and studied all kinds of devices with which they were experimenting in those days, such as the newly invented diving bell. With the plans of this invention in his pocket, Treileben won over Andreas Peckell to Operation *Vasa*, and in short order the two men applied for salvaging permits. The Parliament did not know what to make of their explanations of the diving bell, and the councilmen placed little trust in the strange apparatus. However, it wasn't their lives that were being risked, but Peckell's and von Treileben's. They got their permits. In October, 1663, they anchored over the *Vasa* with the diving bell built to their specifications and with various hooks and tongs. The two men were realistic enough to know that they could not raise the entire ship.

What they were after were the beautiful cannon on board the *Vasa*, for bronze cannon could be sold for gold. From the diving bell which was lowered over the decks of the *Vasa*, Peckell and Treileben and hired divers used sharp hooks to tear loose the deck planking in order to get at the valuable guns. After a long winter break they were able to raise the first cannon with strong ropes in April, 1664. The guns on the lower decks were pulled through the ports and up to the surface with a winch.

In three years' work the men netted more than fifty heavy cannon. The "treasure hunt" had paid off. Even today these guns would be worth $2,500 each for their metal alone.

News of Peckell's and Treileben's "treasure hunt" with a new-fangled instrument called a diving bell spread rapidly through Stockholm and round about. For months the men and their diving bell attracted curious people who shuddered each time they saw one of the divers disappear into the cold depths in the bell. What sort of device was it that let a man spend more than a quarter of an hour working on the sea bottom?

Among the visitors aboard the salvage ship was the Italian priest and world traveler Francesco Negri. He came to Stockholm in 1663, and in his book *Viaggio Settentrionale*, printed in Padua in 1700, after his death, he gave an exact description of the diving bell of Peckell and Treileben for his Italian readers. It wasn't hard for the educated and sharp-witted clergyman to explain the phenomenon.

At the Eleventh International Historian's Convention in Stockholm in 1960 a diving bell was constructed according to Negri's description. The commander of a navy salvage vessel, Captain Bo Cassels, got into the bell and descended to the *Vasa*, where he described his experience over a microphone for radio and television. Francesco Negri had already told how the diving bell worked. The diver stood on a strong platform which hung by chains from a heavy lead bell. The bell extended below his knees. As the bell was lowered into the Stockholm Ström, the water rose up the diver's leather-clad legs up to his hips, then at greater depth up to his chest. His head, however, was still in the air which the water pressure compressed in the upper part of the bell.

Negri had recognized that ". . . the water cannot entirely fill the bell, which can be observed simply by submerging an inverted water glass in a liquid." One had to be careful only that the bell did not tip while submerged, for if it did, the air would rise in great bubbles to the surface. For this reason the inventors had their bell made of lead and also weighted the platform with lead. Its own weight and the hanging lead weights pulled the bell straight down into the water. Of course the salvage work was tedious and required a great deal of skill.

The divers could not leave the bell and had to try to pry boards loose with hooks, and to snare cannon with rope loops. When Captain Bo Cassels returned to the surface in the old-style bell he was filled with admiration for Peckell, von Treileben, and their divers. How they were able to get those heavy cannon to land using such a bell was beyond his comprehension. In 1666, after the cannon had been salvaged, further diving activities gave little promise. Von Treileben equipped himself for an expedition to the West Indies where he wanted to search for the silver treasure of sunken Spanish vessels. The *Vasa*, meanwhile, now robbed of its masts and superstructure, sank from the memories of men into oblivion, and the mud of the Stockholm Ström buried its mighty oaken hull deeper and deeper. Eventually it was no longer known where the sunken crown ship lay.

In 1953, Anders Franzen returned the documents with the last chapters of the story of the ill-fated ship to the Swedish Imperial Archive. He now knew the names of the men who had built the ship and sailed it on its maiden voyage, and he also knew all about the many adventurers who had wanted to make their fortune from the old wreck, but he still didn't know where the *Vasa* lay. It was somewhere in the Stockholm Ström—"toward Lustholmen,

Blochusudden, near Danuiken," were the nearest indications obtainable from an old manuscript.

These directions were much too vague. The young engineer would have had to employ a whole company of frogmen for a successful search, for in the muddy waters of the Stockholm Ström a diver can hardly see his hand in front of his face. A diver would have to stumble headlong into the time-blackened hulk before he found it.

During the summer of 1954, Franzen decided to look again. Soon the Stockholm harbor and dock workers were laughing at the man who was exploring every inch of the bottom of the sea with cables, hooks, and plumb lines from the stern of a rented boat, and was finding nothing but dead cats, rusty bedsteads, old bicycles, iron stoves, Christmas trees, and similar refuse.

The summer passed, and the next as well. Still no sign of the *Vasa*. Anders Franzen explored the area with sonar. He invented his own sounder, a rocket-shaped steel instrument that dug into the sea floor, bringing up samples of the bottom when it was retrieved. With it Franzen tested the waters by Stadsgårdskajen. He had discovered a sea chart from the eighteenth century. Someone had drawn an "X" at the spot which he suspected was the site of *Vasa*: Stadsgårdskajen. But there, too, not a sign of the sunken ship was to be found. Thus the second summer passed without success.

When autumn came, Anders Franzen returned to the archives, no longer hopeful. The ice along the shores of the Baltic Sea was already beginning to break when Franzen came across a letter from the Swedish Parliament dated August 12, 1628. It contained the official report of Parliament to the king concerning the *Vasa* mishap. At that time the king had been on a campaign in Poland. Franzen read: "And on that fateful Sunday which was the tenth of this month, the *Vasa* set sail. But it happened that she got no further than Beckholmsudden, where she sank to the bottom with cannon and all else, and lies in eighteen fathoms. The reason for the misfortune . . ."

Beckholmsudden! It was there that the sonar had indicated a large hill! The reason he had not investigated this hill more closely was that engineers had told him it was nothing more than blasting debris from the construction of a drydock which had been cut into the rock of a small island some years before.

Beckholmsudden!

In August, 1956, Anders Franzen let his heavy steel sounder drop into the deep. Five fathoms . . . ten . . . fifteen . . . it hit bottom, bored itself into solid ground. Quickly Franzen pulled it back up, tore the sample from the tube: wood! Black oak! He needed more samples. It might be only an old rowboat, or even just a board. He rowed several feet farther and took another sample—and again he brought oak back to the surface. He continued sounding and recovered more samples of wood. Without doubt a wooden object about 150 feet long and several yards wide lay on the bottom. It had to be the *Vasa*.

Found—but Not Recovered

Now experienced divers would be needed to explore and to raise the *Vasa*. At first others didn't agree with Franzen. He had no idea where he would get the money for a diving ship and experienced helmet divers. For inexperienced amateur divers in frogman equipment it would be too dangerous an undertaking to penetrate the uncertain depths of the muddy Stockholm Ström.

Franzen finally went to the commander of the Stockholm diving school of the Swedish navy, told him about his search, his discovery and his hopes, and suggested to the officer that he conduct his next diving practice at the site. The commander agreed, and the young divers were pleased with the change in monotonous training which the venture promised.

Soon a diving boat was putting out into the Stockholm Ström, filled with experienced helmet divers and strong young frogmen.

The first man to make the descent was the head diver Edvin Fälting, a man with nerves of steel and invaluable experience from more than ten thousand diving hours. Franzen was able to follow his descent over the telephone which connected Fälting's helmet with the ship.

Fälting reported after only a few minutes that he was standing up to his chest in mud and could see nothing. Should he come back up?

"I don't care," grumbled Anders Franzen crossly. "Come on back up." Nothing, then! The young engineer's face betrayed his profound disappointment when, suddenly, he heard an astonished exclamation: "Wait a minute! I just ran into something solid . . . it feels like a wooden wall! It's a big ship, no doubt about it! Now I'm climbing up the wall . . . there are some rectangular openings . . . they must be cannon ports . . ."

"Here is a second row of cannon ports!" came Fälting's voice over the telephone a few seconds later.

Now there was no more doubt. The *Vasa* had been found.

The diver climbed slowly onto the deck that hadn't borne a human foot for more than two hundred years, and made his way among the welter of wood, salvage equipment, and anchors. Anders Franzen figured out what the recovery of the ship would cost. Besides divers, he would also need a crane ship, a few thousand yards of steel cable, some truckloads of wood for sealing the ship's hull. . . . And after raising the wreck, it would have to be taken to drydock immediately. The restoration would require years of work by laborers and experts. An engineer's income could meet only a minute fraction of the enormous expenses such an undertaking would entail. It probably would cost not hundreds of thousands, but millions.

Now newspapers, radio, and television were spreading the news of Anders Franzen and his discovery, and the young engineer received assistance. While the navy divers inspected the *Vasa* more closely, a committee convened, under the head of the navy yard commander, Edward Clason, to investigate the technical and financial possibilities of raising the sunken ship. The Neptune Salvage company offered to raise the *Vasa* without charge and the navy continued to put its divers and diving ships at the disposal of the operation.

Scholars, too, were in favor of the recovery plans. They hoped that with the sunken ship a piece of living history from Sweden's great past would rise from the brown depths of the Stockholm Ström. The operation would cost millions, but they felt this was a once-in-a-lifetime opportunity. For until the discovery of the V*asa* our knowledge of the ships and seafaring activity of the Middle Ages and the period of the Thirty Years' War was incomplete. There was a wide gap between the ships of the Viking period and modern times. The Viking ships from Norwegian princes' graves were pulled to land before the turn of the present millennia. The last preserved ship before the recovery of the *Vasa* was Admiral Nelson's *Victory*.

From the deck of the *Victory*, Nelson directed the battle of Trafalgar in 1805 where he destroyed the French fleet, thus saving England from Napoleon. The *Victory* is kept in the harbor of Portsmouth as a national monument, but it is more than a hundred years younger than the *Vasa*.

Not even plans for ships of the period prior to the eighteenth century have been preserved, for the master shipbuilders of that time worked exclusively from simple sketches which were not saved. Shipbuilding secrets were mostly passed on by word of mouth. Journeymen learned them from the masters, and when they became masters themselves, they in turn passed them on to their journeymen. Yet shipbuilding techniques and designs often changed rapidly, and old techniques were soon forgotten.

From spring of 1957 on, the *Vasa* committee tried to collect money. At the decisive meeting many suggestions had been made. Anders Franzen had brought along samples of wood from the ship's hull and a scientific affidavit as to its state of preservation and strength.

The committee's job was not an easy one: it was to work out a plan for a totally new kind of venture. After all, the *Vasa* was 150 feet long and weighed 700 tons even under water, as the expert Sam Svensson had calculated from the measurements of the navy divers and statistics on the ship gleaned from the archives.

Many imaginative suggestions lay on the discussion table. One inventor thought the ship's hull should be filled with ping-pong balls until the upward force exerted by the air-filled balls carried the ship to the surface. Another plan suggested pumping refrigerant into the ship's interior. The water would then turn to ice. Since ice is lighter than water, the *Vasa* would rise like a giant iceberg. But all these plans were too risky. The members of the committee were in agreement with Franzen that a precious find like the *Vasa* should not be subjected to experimental methods.

There was only one thing left—the standard method for raising a ship. This meant raising the hull in a network of steel cables attached to a pontoon on either side of the ship. But would the aged timbers hold up under the pressure of the cables? Wouldn't the cables just slice right through the planks? What if the hull collapsed like an eggshell from the pressure on the lateral walls during the raising? The committee had serious doubts.

For that reason Anders Franzen brought along an affidavit testifying that the wood of the *Vasa* still retained sixty per cent of its original strength. The sample passed from hand to hand was tested and bent. The committee decided to take a chance.

Now all that Franzen needed was money, and the venture could begin. To be sure, officials and the government still were doubtful of success and were not too generous with their donations. Nevertheless the Wallenberg Fund donated 27,000 Swedish crowns, and the Swedish King Gustaf Adolf VI, industries, and private citizens supplied additional thousands for the *Vasa* treasury.

That was only a drop in the bucket compared to the overall cost of the project, but it was enough to start work on.

A huge job awaited the navy divers. They couldn't simply run their cables under the keel of the *Vasa*, for in the course of the centuries the heavy ship had sunk several yards deep into the clay. Also, a thick layer of mud covered the hull. They would have to drive shafts into the ground along the sides of the *Vasa* and dig tunnels under the keel.

For this purpose Franzen had a mud sucker and a large water hose brought aboard the salvage vessel.

With these the divers descended into the deep—a deep that grew more dangerous for them each day.

The suction hose cut through the light mud like new-fallen snow.

Again and again the shafts caved in, at one point burying one of the divers on the bottom for a while.

Then the suction hose hit solid clay. Now the divers had to crawl into the tunnel on their bellies, holding the suction hose between their legs while the sharp stream of water from the hose bored into the clay. Above them lay tons of stones in the ship's hold. Would the old ship's planks hold? Would the ballast, which once was supposed to give the galleon depth and stability, break through? This would have meant death for the diver. Planks and stones would have squeezed off his air hose and squashed him in his tunnel under the mighty ship.

But the *Vasa*'s planks held, and the work proceeded. They had scarcely begun using the suction hose when the *Vasa* began to reveal its treasures. Sculptors of the seventeenth century had decorated the entire ship with valuable statues. Franzen's divers found some in the mud and also came across a number of baroque sculptures. The huge, ferocious lion figurehead, which was supposed to strike fear in the hearts of the enemy, was revealed in the

*Figurehead of snarling lion
from the* Vasa's *prow*

Kanzlit

mud. When the mud had been washed from its mane, the figure's gold finish shone in the sunlight.

Following the lion, more figures turned up—Greek gods and mythological figures carved by baroque artists from oak, pine, and linden. The shipbuilders of the Thirty Years' War had fastened the sculptures to the ship with iron bolts, which had rusted through so that the figures had fallen to the bottom. There they lay, surrounded in protective mud: the Greek god Nereus who had fifty daughters and was able to predict the future; the frightening lion masks of the port covers for the cannon ports; shields with coats of arms from the royal house of Vasa; and not far away, dragons, knights, a mermaid, Hercules with the bound hell-hound Cerberus that he had conquered, and King David holding a lyre.

A man kept constant vigil at the exhaust hose of the suction pump, and time and again he fished new lesser treasures from the deep. Art-history professors showed avid interest, examined the finds, and concluded that the divers had turned up a wealth of beautiful baroque art.

Specialists from the National Marine Museum took possession of the sculptures so as to preserve them as quickly as possible. Shrinkage, splits, and checks in the old, water-logged wood would have destroyed their beauty. The finds were put in baths of ethylene polyglycol, a waxlike kind of alcohol. Polyglycol dissolves in water, penetrates slowly into the water-logged wood, drives the water out, and strengthens the cell walls. With a protective coating against fungus and insect damage, the art works of the *Vasa* were preserved for centuries to come.

The restorers at the museum had their hands full. The divers continued to uncover more objects. Sometimes they didn't feel quite right about it. Divers, like seamen, are superstitious. There was the "Old Man" whom the experienced, gray-haired men feared and had taught the younger ones to fear. The Old Man was the ghost of a drowned seaman who lived in the wreck, or the spirit of the deep, the god of the sea who lived on in superstitious belief. He inhabited the deep, sometimes taking a find from a diver and carrying it off. It was the current from Lake Malär, which emptied into the sea, that carried off the finds, but the divers believed in *den gamle*, who became very angry when his booty was taken from him. One of the men finally got the idea of appeasing him with small offerings. And so each diving day was begun with shiny twenty-five-ore pieces tossed into the water.

Den Gamle *Gives Up His Booty*

In August, 1959, the Neptune Salvage Company's fleet arrived at the *Vasa*. The auxiliary ships towed the pontoons *Oden* and *Frigg*, two huge steel double canisters. Salvage Captain Axel Hedberg ordered the pontoons positioned above the *Vasa* so that they flanked her. The cables disappeared into the water and the divers had to pull them through six tunnels dug under the keel of the *Vasa*. At Captain Hedberg's command "Flood!" the workers opened the ports on the pontoons. Water rushed into their chambers and they sank until small waves were almost washing over their decks. "Ports shut! Winches on!" The crew of the recovery vessel closed the ports and slowly winched up the cables that held the *Vasa* as if in a net.

On August 20, Captain Hedberg had the pumps switched on. Clattering and thumping, they forced the water out of the pontoons. The *Oden* and the *Frigg* rose out of the water. They were supposed to raise the *Vasa* with them. Would the ship hold up under the strain?

Diver Sven Olaf Nyberg went down to observe the *Vasa*. With tense faces the rest of the recovery crew awaited his report. Then Nyberg called over the telephone: "A foot and a half! The *Vasa* rose a foot and a half. Everything is O.K." The pumping was resumed. "She's going smooth as a sleepwalker." Now the pontoons floated on the water, pumped empty—and the *Vasa* hung in its steel net, released undamaged from her three-hundred-year-old grave. But she still hadn't been raised. She now hung just above the sea floor. Only one stage had been completed, one of eighteen stages which were to follow in the days ahead.

Two tugs pushed the pontoons in the direction of Kastellholmen, onto gradually sloping bottom, until the keel of the warship touched the soft mud. Again Captain Hedberg gave the command to flood. The pontoons sank, and the cables between the *Vasa* and the recovery ships were shortened.

Captain Hedberg and his men fought their way into shallower water.

Day after day passed with lifting, moving forward, and lowering until, twenty-seven days later, on September 16, 1959, Hedberg was able to record in the log: "The *Vasa* has reached Kastellholmen. . . . She now lies forty-five feet below the surface . . . the mast stumps almost stick out of the water . . ."

Gustaf Adolf's ill-fated flagship had to spend the winter waiting at the foot of the old fortress of Kastellholmen until enough money had been collected for the actual raising.

But now Anders Franzen received a royal assistant. Crown Prince Bertil of Sweden took over the chairmanship of the *Vasa* committee, made successful pleas for donations, and convinced the frugal officials and the government that the pending final recovery stage of the *Vasa* deserved support.

The Neptune Company had fourteen hydraulic lifters placed on the inner sides of the pontoons *Oden* and *Frigg*. They were to pull up the cables until the deck of the *Vasa* broke through the surface. Under water the ship weighed about seven hundred tons; the lifts could handle that. But objects weigh more above water, for the buoyancy is absent. The committee decided to have the wreck pumped out as much as possible during the raising so that it might float to some extent on its own.

The divers had to go down again, this time with boards, beams, and carpenter tools. About ten thousand rusted nails and rotten dowels had to be replaced. The otherwise quiet underwater world echoed with hammering as the men boarded up the cannon ports and the damaged stern. This work lasted until 1961.

On April 14, 1961, the Neptune Salvage armada gathered for a second time at the *Vasa*. Navy divers attached inflatable rubber pontoons to the exceptionally heavy stern of the warship, to give it additional buoyancy.

On April 24th, everything was ready. The lifts went to work. Slowly, very slowly, the outline of the *Vasa* grew more and more distinct. Then the first masts and beams broke through the murky water. Like ghosts from another age the two "vassals," figures carved into wooden posts next to the mainmast, hung over the dark water. Now the pumps, too, were put into action. They emptied 7,500 gallons a minute out of the hull, and inch by inch the sunken ship rose from the bottom, slowly, as if against its will. But there was no going back for the *Vasa*—the sea had been robbed of its spoils. By May 4th the ship was riding so high that it could be towed to Beckholmen and into the dock. The water still stood at the upper battery deck. But in a few days the pump had emptied the last of the water from the hull, and while dock workers continued to bolster the sides, water poured out until the *Vasa* lay high and dry on the 170-foot concrete pontoon over which she had been maneuvered. An army of workers now crowded around the wreck, set up a system of hoses which kept a constant spray of water directed at the ship and on its decks, and covered all exposed parts with plastic to keep them from drying out. Preservation experts followed just behind them and replaced the water with polyglycol.

While the pumps were working, Anders Franzen and scientists under the direction of Per Lundström entered the accessible rooms in the ship. They pushed farther and farther into the mighty ship's interior, dug through the mud, and uncovered a piece of seaman's life and fate from the Thirty Years' War. Everything lay just as it had fallen three hundred years ago: sea chests, pieces of money, weapons, cooking implements, leather boots, ship's carpenter's tools, beer mugs, and powder kegs. One of the men held up a chunk of odd-looking substance, scratched at it, smelled—butter! Rancid, of course. In all, the hull of the *Vasa* contained some ten thousand objects, including some four thousand coins.

Among the cannon carriages the men found the remains of the unfortunate victims. Twelve skeletons of drowned sailors had been buried in the mud. Still partly clad in outer garments and boots, they presented a somewhat hideous sight which the scientists had to

Erik R. Eriksson

The Vasa at dock

endure. Such finds provided information about the clothing of common sailors of the time. The archaeologist Cederlund describes one of the skeletons, a man of thirty to thirty-five, in the following way: "The man's clothing and equipment were well preserved. He was dressed in a knit vest of thick wool and knit wool trousers which showed folds above the hips and were apparently fastened below the knees. Over the vest he wore a long-sleeved jacket with short, pleated coattails. Under the vest he wore a linen shirt. A pair of sandals and sewn linen stockings completed his dress. A sheath and a knife with a bone handle, as well as a leather money bag, were fastened to his belt. A few coins were in his trousers pockets. Altogether he had about twenty öre in copper money."

In the meantime the *Vasa* committee had a sixty-foot-high aluminum housing built over the ship to protect the fragile wood from the weather. In the interior of the ship specialists are at work pre-

Wasa-Foto

Money recovered from the Vasa

serving the hull with countless injections of polyglycol. Visitors to Stockholm are able to follow their work by means of a television circuit. The *Vasa* committee also wants to restore the damaged stern, the aftercastle, and the entire upper deck of the once splendid galleon. Dozens of specialists will be busy at work for several years before visitors to the Swedish capital are permitted to walk across the blackened oak planks of the *Vasa* and below to its century-old lower deck. About a dozen of the carved decorations are still missing from the ship, particularly from the splendid aftercastle. Divers are still busy sifting through the mud of the harbor in the hope of finding them.

The raising of the royal ship *Vasa* is probably the greatest accomplishment of underwater archaeology to date.

X

Exploring Ancient Cults and Cultures

"In times of drought the Mayans threw living human beings into this well. . . . They also threw in many other things, such as jewels . . ." says the Franciscan monk and Bishop of Merida, Diego de Landa, of the Spanish capital of Yucatán, in his book *Relación de las Cosas de Yucatán*. His story of the Mayans, a mysterious people conquered by the Spanish conquistadors, appeared three hundred years ago. The explorer Ponciano Salazar recalled these words in the summer of 1960 as he and his expedition neared the sacrificial grounds described by de Landa: the well of Chichén Itzá. The dusty path wound its way through corn fields under a blazing sun, passed through the ruins of temples, step pyramids, and palaces of the one-time beautiful Mayan city and then disappeared again into a strip of jungle where it ended abruptly.

The men climbed up on the rubble of a small temple and stood before the sacrificial site. Vertical rock walls dropped a couple of stories straight down to a pool of approximately 180 feet in diameter. The men looked silently at the dark water. It was here, according to de Landa's report, that Mayan priests had thrown young maidens into the well over a period of centuries as sacrifices to the rain god Chac.

Some of the men shuddered at the thought of diving into the depths of this well. All were seasoned explorers and frogmen and went willingly to work. Cranes had to be built at the edge of the well to take the divers and equipment into the deep. Then a rectangular pontoon was lowered to serve as a work platform. A rowboat and large float for the mud sucker followed. The men toiled for days, Mexican amateurs and navy divers, explorers from Mexico and the United States, along with Indians, descendants of the Maya people.

Then came the decisive moment. The mud sucker was ready. At the bottom of the dark water, two divers pushed its trunk into the mud. The motor started. A dirty gray fountain spewed forth from the upper end of the suction hose, carrying chunks of rock, pieces of wood, decomposed leaves, and the like from the surrounding jungle that had been carried into the well by wind and rain. And suddenly a small, bright chunk.

"Copal!" someone cried out.

Expedition leader Ponciano Salazar withdrew the fragment out of the mud and checked it. It was copal, a resinous substance from various tropical trees which the Mayans burned as incense. Now he was sure it was a good site.

More than fifty years ago Diego de Landa's book was rediscovered in a Madrid archive. But the scholars took the Spaniard for a fantastic dreamer who had made up the story of the sacrificial well. No one doubted that human sacrifices were common in the Indian cultures of Central America; one Spanish chronicler reported that on one day in the capital city of the Aztec realm some twenty thousand persons were slain at the pyramid altars. But all the writings of the Spaniards mention only step pyramids and temples as sacrificial sites. Except for Diego de Landa's work, none of the books known up to the turn of the century spoke of sacrificial wells.

However, Edward Herbert Thompson, the United States consul, explorer, and adventurer, believed the Franciscan. In 1885 he journeyed to Chichén Itzá. He spent only a short time around the magnificent buildings of the one-time religious center of the "New Empire" of the Mayans, and hurried to the well. The exploration of its depths was a challenge that could only be met with good technical equipment. Thompson turned to other things and searched through Yucatán for signs of the Mayan culture buried beneath jungle and debris. But the sacrificial well would not release its hold on him. He returned in 1904, after friends had lent him money for the necessary equipment. He began to dredge, at first without success. The dredge brought up nothing but mud and trash. After many days it coughed up two bright chunks. Thompson held them in the fire and they gave off a sweet, aromatic odor. He had found copal, proving that it was a sacrificial spot. Gold jewelry, jade, clay vessels, a wooden aspergillum, rattles, cloth, weapons, and tools followed, until eventually the dredge brought to light the first maiden's skeleton. Later, Thompson went to the bottom with a Greek sponge diver. More and more finds were brought to the surface: figurines, gold jewelry, female skeletons. But Thompson paid for his courage with an attack of the bends that left him with severe paralysis and injury to his eardrums. He was an invalid for the rest of his life.

Thompson at first had no followers, for the actual value of the gold found was minimal, and the many adventurers who searched for sunken treasure in the following decades were simply looking for gold. They went after sunken Spanish treasure ships and pirate ships laden with riches. Not much of the ships themselves withstood the passage of time, but many a chest of gold was recovered from their cargoes.

Mexican divers continued Thompson's work in 1925, but without real success. The well at Chichén Itzá again lay quiet and inaccessible in the jungle of Yucatán until Thompson's conviction that he had not been able to raise most of the treasures moved the National Archaeological and Historical Institute of Mexico to form an expedition. The discovery of the first piece of copal was an indication that more finds would follow. Soon the hose spewed out more copal, then the first clay fragments. Finally one of the frogmen came up happily waving a clay bowl in the air. Salazar had just taken it out of his hands when the diver Norman Scott gave a joyful shout as he pulled a curiously formed statuette out of the mud, a rubber idol. One of the archaeologists examined it and verified that it might well be the oldest rubber statue in the world.

Each day brought new surprises. The divers uncovered a wooden figure that must have been created by an artist from the mysterious Toltec tribe. The Mayans were primarily a trading people, and the divers repeatedly found valuable items from other high cultures of Central America, important evidence for research in cultural exchange in pre-Columbian America. "Pre-Columbian" is the scholarly term for the culture of Central and South America that flourished before the arrival of the Spaniards and Portuguese. Most of them are virtually unexplored so far; in the cases of some of them not even their ages are known.

Finally the divers found the first skull—the remains of a girl of about eighteen, doubtless a sacrificial victim. A diver brought it up from the deep, and some of the men who watched silently could visualize the eerie scene that probably took place here some centuries ago: a festive procession made its way to the well, drums and horns in the lead. Painted blue, the sacrificial color, the blindfolded girl was led by colorfully decorated priests. For the last time she heard the admonition to ask the rain god for rain for her people's fields. The blindfold was removed, she saw the murky depths below her, and dropped into the abyss. This uncanny rite was repeated for centuries at the well of Chichén Itzá, until the Spaniards arrived during the sixteenth century and converted the Mayan survivors to Christianity.

In 1961 the United States and Mexican expedition returned to Mexico City with four thousand finds. Yet only a fraction of the well's contents have been raised. The whole well is to be drained and explored dry.

Chichén Itzá is not the only place in Latin America where frogmen have revealed underwater secrets of the past. Just 120 miles from Chichén Itzá are the ruins of the unique city of Dziblichaltun.

Archaeologists have been excavating this city since the 1940's, but they still haven't uncovered much of it, for Dzibilchaltun's ruins cover an area of at least twenty square miles. The whole city of Chichén Itzá could easily be fitted into a part of this city; even the early imperial city of Rome could have found room here. Also unique for the New World is the age of Dzibilchaltun. When Chichén Itzá was founded shortly before A.D. 1000, Dzibilchaltun had already been standing two or three thousand years. Many peoples inhabited this city, the last of them the Mayans, who immigrated into Yucatán in the seventh century. In the center of Dzibilchaltun there is a well similar to the one in Chichén Itzá. Following Thompson's example, American explorers investigated it in 1958. After a few months' work they recovered no fewer than thirty thousand finds. Although indications of human offerings were absent—the remains of two skeletons seem rather to point to accidental drownings—the large quantity of finds suggests that all were sacrificial offerings. Perhaps the well cult of Chichén Itzá was spread in a somewhat less gruesome form throughout the Yucatán Peninsula.

The wells of Yucatán are vertical-walled holes in limestone—sink holes, as they are known to those who have visited Yugoslavia's Dalmatian coast. Rainfall and clear seepage from the surrounding limestone fills them and renders them inexhaustible sources of water even when drought affects the few springs and streams on Yucatán. No wonder the Indians believed these sources of life-giving water to be the seat of the rain god and the gateway to the realm of the gods and the dead. This implies that perhaps all of Yucatán's cisterns were sacrificial wells. Should future explorations verify this suspicion, archaeologists will be kept busy in the years to come. Although scholars will probably not complete the excavation of sunken cities in Central America in our century, sacrificial wells permit rapid recovery of numerous finds which provide a quick survey of the cultures of the peoples who once made offerings there.

Yucatán was already highly civilized when the Mayans migrated. They came from cities that equaled Chichén Itzá in size and splendor. Overnight the entire population abandoned these cities and towns, which lay for the most part in the mountainous regions southwest of the Yucatán peninsula and in the modern country of Guatemala, and headed for Yucatán. It is not known what mo-

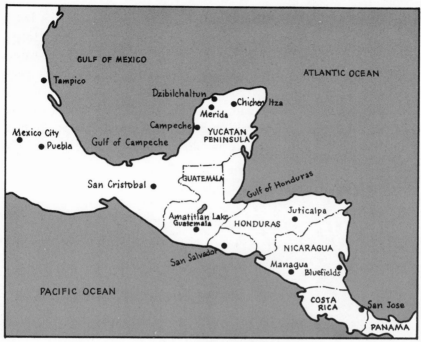

Sites where Mayan treasures have been found

tivated this mass migration. Many scholars suppose it was depleted soil and famine.

In the volcanic highland of Guatemala, the area of the old Mayan realm, lies Lake Amatitlan. Since 1955 Guatemalan frogmen have been swimming through its waters under the direction of scholars. The shallow shoreline waters are rich in finds from the period when the level of the lake was lower and a wide strip that is now underwater was dry land and settled. At greater depths countless precious Mayan sacrificial offerings are found.

During exploration under the direction of Stephan de Borhegyi, director of the Milwaukee Public Museum, divers found many beautifully preserved incense containers, often shaped like statues of Mayan gods. One cult vessel still contained mercury, cinnabar, graphite, and jade earrings. Another contained parts of a girl's skull. Many containers had been placed on the edge of the bank in order to placate the volcano Pacaya which towered high over the lake. The lava flow had then carried them into the lake. Altogether frogmen have discovered nine votive sites which were almost all at one time in the vicinity of hot springs, which the Mayans must certainly have worshipped.

A throwback to the Mayan custom of sacrificing at this spot is certainly evident in a rite still practiced at Lake Amatitlan today. Each year on May 3; religious people from all over the district go

A Mayan container found in Lake Amatitlan

Stephen F. de Borhegyi

274

on a pilgrimage to the shore, pray in the church of San Juan, and, in a festive procession, carry a wooden statue of a saint to a boat adorned with flowers. Then the people sail to the spot where, according to an old legend, a stone carved idol was thrown furtively in the water and the Christian patron saint of the district rose up out of the waves, amid terrible thundering. Praying and singing, the pilgrims toss flowers and fruit into the sea where the stone-carved idol sank.

Chichén Itzá, Dzibilchaltun, and Amatitlan are but three of the most important exploration sites of underwater archaeology outside of the Mediterranean area and central and northern Europe. Many more places might be named, such as Lake Chapala, Mexico, in Central America, Lake Guija between Guatemala and El Salvador, and Lake Ixpaco in Guatemala. Finally many lakes of South America are still unexplored. These, especially in the old Inca realm and in the Andes, are connected with ancient tales and legends, which probably contain an element of truth.

In Russia and its provinces ancient cultures arose simultaneously with Near Eastern and Mediterranean cultures. As early as the nineteenth century graves and ruins were known to be in Lake Issyk Kul in the Kirgiz Republic, Soviet Central Asia. Remains of oriental settlements were discovered in the Caspian Sea near Derbent and Baku. And a few years ago, when engineers began to divert the waters of the Armenian mountain lake Sewan in order to irrigate the dry Ararat plateau, they revealed a sunken city from the eleventh century B.C. A future work on underwater archaeology will doubtless contain chapters on the finds made in Soviet rivers and lakes and along the Soviet coastlines. It will certainly also disclose important sites in Asia and Africa, where frogmen will begin to explore new depths.

The story of the American architect Kip Wagner will also go down in the annals of underwater exploration. He found the Spanish silver fleet that sank in 1715 off the coast of Florida, not far from Cape Kennedy. Not only romantics are fascinated by the man for whom the dream of all treasure hunters was fulfilled— sunken galleons filled with legendary silver pieces of eight mentioned in all pirate stories, gold doubloons, gold vessels, jewels, and precious stones. Wagner is certainly the most successful treasure hunter since William Phips, later governor of Massachusetts, who recovered a million dollars in silver and gold from a Spanish galleon in 1687. Kip Wagner has also already recovered treasures whose value exceeds a million dollars. He and his team are on the trail of additional treasures whose value might be ten, twenty, or more million dollars. His diving projects are observed with equal fascination by scientists from the Smithsonian Institution and other research organizations with which the team works. They not only lead to sunken gold and silver treasures, but also reveal facts of American and European history.

The future of underwater archaeology has already begun. In December, 1962, off the California island of Santa Catalina, an expedition ship rode at anchor. An experiment of great significance was in the making. The young Swiss mathematics teacher and sport diver Hannes Keller planned to break his own world record in deep diving of 222 meters, by diving 300 meters in his frogman outfit where he would anchor a starred banner and the Swiss flag on the sea bottom. Because of technical flaws in the equipment, the venture ended with two deaths. Keller's diving companion, Peter Small, and an assistant died in the deep. But Keller was able to break his world record, and viewed his attempt as basically successful. This apparently senseless experiment may someday be listed alongside Cousteau's experiments with the aqualung in the 1940's along the Riviera as a major event in the history of diving.

At Santa Catalina and already in 1961 at Lake Maggiore, a new mixture of breathing gases was tried which should someday open depths of over one hundred meters to frogmen. Theoretically, such depths have been accessible for some time, but a diver breathing ordinary compressed air would then have to take many hours for his ascent to avoid death from the bends. Furthermore, he is threatened by the sort of intoxication that overcomes divers at those depths. For these reasons divers and marine specialists have long been working on the development of a gas mixture instead of nitrogen to accompany oxygen. Keller mixed oxygen with helium and some other rare gases. At Lake Maggiore he needed only forty-five minutes for the ascent from 222 meters. He believes his mixture has also conquered deep-water intoxication. Perhaps it won't be long before Keller's invention is further tested and refined and trained frogmen will reach depths of a hundred meters and more. Then archaeology will have the key to the great treasure chests of the seas and lakes of the world that so far have been inaccessible.

Meanwhile other research teams are working on the development of underwater houses. Without having to surface every day and thereby subjecting themselves to strenuous pressure changes, the divers would live in these houses for days at a time—eating and sleeping there. They would have whole days at their disposal for exploration of the sea floor. At night they could simply return to their houses, under the same pressure as the surrounding water. The men would surface only when the underwater project was completed. They would observe special decompression procedures, with many long waiting periods. Jacques-Yves Cousteau first experimented with some underwater houses in the Red Sea, where men lived a month at six fathoms while two of their party lived a week in another house eight fathoms deeper. After this successful experiment, Cousteau had some men live in a house fifty fathoms off the Côte d'Azur. Meanwhile he is working on projects for lowering houses ninety and more fathoms. Edwin A. Link and the United States Navy are experimenting with similar projects. Link constructed an inflatable rubber house in which Belgian diver Robert Stenuit, with Jon Lindbergh, the son of Charles A. Lindbergh, lived for two days in 1964 off the Bahamas at a depth of sixty-five fathoms. United States Navy divers spent eleven days in a steel capsule in thirty fathoms, thereby preparing the ground for the experiment of astronaut Scott Carpenter, who in 1965 spent a month at thirty fathoms.

In the near future archaeologists will have their "headquarters" in a house on the sea floor and be able to direct excavations in which divers will do their work under floodlights. The University of

Pennsylvania has devised a unique scheme for underwater arch-aeological research. Its first point—the construction of a research submarine—has already met with success. Now the scientists wish to concentrate on developing search methods, experimenting with underwater metal detectors, such as proton magnetometers, sonar devices, and underwater television cameras. In the future, submarines will be equipped with manipulators. Remote-controlled grapplers and suction pumps should obviate the need of divers for these jobs.

The work of archaeologists and divers on the ocean floor prom-ises to be most exciting during the coming decades, for man has only begun to conquer the vast depths of the oceans and lakes which hold the sunken treasures of the past.

Selected Bibliography

Bass, G. F., "Underwater Archaeology: Key to History's Warehouse." *National Geographic Magazine*, Vol. 124, p. 138, 1963.

—— Archaeology Under Water. London, Thames & Hudson, 1966.

—— "The *Asherash:* A Submarine for Archaeology." *American Journal of Archaeology*, Vol. 18, p. 7, 1965.

Borhegyi, S. de, "From the Depths of Lake Amatitlan." *Illustrated London News*, Vol. 233, No. 6214, p. 70, 1958.

Casson, L., *The Ancient Mariners*. New York, Macmillan, 1959.

Cousteau, J.-Y., "Fishermen Discover a 2,200 Year-Old Greek Ship." *National Geographic Magazine*, Vol. 105, p. 1, 1954.

—— *The Living Sea*. London, Hamish Hamilton, 1963.

Dugan, J., *Man Under the Sea*. New York, Harper, 1956.

Dumas, F., *Deep-Water Archaeology*. London, Routledge & K. Paul, 1962.

Falcon-Barker, T., *1,600 Years Under the Sea*. London, F. Muller, 1960.

Flemming, N. C., "Underwater Adventure in Apollonia." *National Geographic Magazine*, Vol. 31, p. 497, 1959.

—— "Apollonia Revisited." *National Geographic Magazine*, Vol. 33, p. 52, 1961.

Franzen, A., *The Warship* Vasa: *Deep Diving and Marine Archaeology in Stockholm*. Stockholm, Norstedt & Bonnier, 1961.

Selected Bibliography

———— "Ghost From the Depths: The Warship *Vasa.*" *National Geographic Magazine,* Vol. 121, p. 42, 1960.

Frost, H., *Under the Mediterranean.* London, Routledge & K. Paul, 1963.

Hurtado, E. D., and B. Littlehales, "Into the Well of Sacrifice." *National Geographic Magazine,* Vol. 120, p. 540, 1961.

Keller, F., *The Lake Dwellings of Switzerland and Other Parts of Europe.* London, Longmans, Green, & Co., 1866.

Link, M. C., "Exploring the Drowned City of Port Royal." *National Geographic Magazine,* Vol. 117, p. 151, 1960.

Marden, L. "Up From the Well of Time." *National Geographic Magazine,* Vol. 115, p. 110, 1959.

Ohrelius, B., Vasa, *The King's Ship.* Philadelphia, Chilton, 1962.

Olson, S., "Relics From the Rapids." *National Geographic Magazine,* Vol. 124, p. 39, 1963.

Pachulia, V., "Soviet Archaeology: The Search for Lost Dioscuria in the Eastern Black Sea." *Illustrated London News,* Vol. 244, p. 644, 1964.

Peterson, M., *History Under the Sea: A Handbook for Underwater Exploration.* Washington, D.C., Smithsonian Institution, 1965.

Plat Taylor, J. du, *Marine Archaeology: Development During Sixty Years in the Mediterranean.* London, Hutchinson, 1965.

Price, D. J. de S., "An Ancient Greek Computer." *Scientific American,* Vol. 200, p. 60, 1959.

Silverberg, R., *Sunken History: The Story of Underwater Archaeology.* Philadelphia, Chilton, 1963.

Throckmorton, P., "Thirty-Three Centuries Under the Sea." *National Geographic Magazine,* Vol. 117, p. 682, 1962.

———— "Oldest Known Shipwreck Yields Bronze Age Cargo." *National Geographic Magazine,* Vol. 127, p. 1, 1965.

Wheeler, R. C., "History Below the Rapids." *Minnesota History,* Vol. 38, p. 24, 1962.

Widding, L., *The Vasa Venture.* Stockholm, Gebers, 1961.

Index

Index

Index